AF686596

Children and Armed Conflict

Children and Armed Conflict

By

Chaditsa Poulatova

CAMBRIDGE SCHOLARS

PUBLISHING

Children and Armed Conflict,
by Chaditsa Poulatova

This book first published 2013

Cambridge Scholars Publishing

12 Back Chapman Street, Newcastle upon Tyne, NE6 2XX, UK

British Library Cataloguing in Publication Data
A catalogue record for this book is available from the British Library

Copyright © 2013 by Chaditsa Poulatova

All rights for this book reserved. No part of this book may be reproduced, stored in a retrieval system, or transmitted, in any form or by any means, electronic, mechanical, photocopying, recording or otherwise, without the prior permission of the copyright owner.

ISBN (10): 1-4438-4212-5, ISBN (13): 978-1-4438-4212-9

Dedicated to my late grandparents
Zilfikar Agous and Zilfikar-Alious Dade and my children Peter and Nekija

CONTENTS

LIST OF TABLES

ACKNOWLEDGEMENTS

First and foremost I would like to thank Peter N. Jones for his expert supervision, support and friendship. I am also grateful to Dr Kyle Grayson for his valuable expertise and advice.

I would like to thank a very special man in my life Peter Houlis who never doubted my ability to see this book to its conclusion,

For their unconditional support and for always being there, my parents deserve more thanks than I can express.

Finally to my late grandfather who helped make me the person I am and I hope he is as proud of me as I am of him.

ABSTRACT

The book examines international efforts to protect children from the effects of war and armed conflict through the Convention on the Rights of the Child (CRC), especially article 38, and the Convention's Optional Protocol on the involvement of Children in Armed Conflict (OPAC). It charts the evolution of the Convention and the place it occupies in the broader efforts of the UN to provide for human rights. The principal focus of the book is on the machinery the UN has established for implementing the CRC and OPAC, particularly the Committee on the Rights of the Child and the processes the Committee uses to monitor states' compliance with the CRC and OPAC. Detailed examination is made of the extent to which States Parties to the CRC and OPAC submit the initial and periodic reports by the stipulated deadlines, and of how far reports provide the information required by the Committee. The way the Committee deals with the information it receives is also examined. These investigations expose major shortcomings in the monitoring process. The book therefore concludes by examining possible ways in which compliance with the CRC and OPAC might be secured more effectively.

CHAPTER ONE

INTRODUCTION

"The question of children and armed conflict is an integral part of the United Nations' core responsibilities for the maintenance of international peace and security, for the advancement of human rights and for sustainable human development."
—Secretary-General Kofi Annan in a speech to the Security Council, 26 July 2000

1.1 Children and Armed Conflict

War and armed conflict have been enduring features of the human condition. For as long as they existed, their victims have included children as well as adults. That is as true of war and armed conflict in the modern age as it has been of previous ages. Indeed, in some respects children are more directly affected by military conflicts nowadays than they have been in the past. During and after conflicts, children remain exposed to the dangers of landmines and millions of pieces of unexploded ordnance – bombs, shells and grenades that fail to denote on impact.

Many of the wars of the previous century continue to the present day, and leave indelible marks on the lives of millions of children. Civilian deaths have far exceeded those of armed combatants. Due to the role that international politics and commercial interests play in initiating, supporting and maintaining these conflicts, we are all in some ways, like it or not, woven into the complex net of complicity and accountability surrounding them. Thus we cannot ignore this ongoing assault on the lives of children.

Armed conflicts affect the development of children from before birth into young adulthood in a myriad of ways, the effects accumulating in interminable civil wars as children grow, and diverting them from normal life pathways in the culture and societies in which they live. The consequences of these childhood experiences will continue to reverberate throughout their lives. Armed conflict also continually violates and undermines the rights of children as they are enunciated in the Convention on the Rights of the Child (CRC)[1] and in its Optional Protocol on the Involvement of Children in Armed Conflicts (OPAC).[2]

Children are specifically targeted to create terror and subdue local populations. They are forcibly recruited as "volunteers" in their thousands to fight adult wars. There is overwhelming evidence from recent armed conflicts that children are not only the incidental victims of crossfire and so called "collateral damage", but also that they are specifically sought out and killed, maimed and abused by warring parties. Youths with guns, rather than defending local communities, are often used to terrorise them. In January 1999, the Ugandan army executed five teenage boys between the ages of 14 and 17 who were suspected of being rebel soldiers.[3] When not actively engaged in combat, children are often used to man checkpoints. Adult soldiers tend to stand several metres further back at times of an attack so that, if bullets start flying, the children will be the first victims. And in any conflict where even a few children are involved as soldiers, all children, civilian or combatant, come under suspicion. A military sweep in Congo-Brazzaville killed all rebels who had attained the 'age of bearing arms'.[4]

Child soldiers are often depicted as victims and casualties of war, and they are indeed exploited, torn from their families, and deprived of their education, and forced into battle. But children are also assailants. Child soldiers are cheap and efficient weapons in asymmetric warfare. Accounts from the field tell of child soldiers who are virtually free to recruit, cheap to feed, and quick to follow orders. They readily learn how to employ brutal tactics. The Revolutionary United Front (RUF), a rebel group operating in Sierra Leone from 1991 to 2002, for example, was notorious for raping and mutilating the civilian population. It was often coerced children, frequently drunk or high on drugs, who perpetrated the acts. The Liberation Tigers of Tamil Eelam, fighting for independence from Sri

---

[1] Convention on the Rights of the Child. Adopted and opened for signature, ratification and accession by General Assembly Resolution 44/25 in November 1989. Entry into force 2 September 1990, in accordance with article 49.

[2] Optional Protocol to the Convention on the Rights of the Child on the Involvement of children in armed conflict. (OPAC). Adopted and opened for signature, ratification and accession by the General Assembly resolution A/RES/54/263 of 25 May 2000. entered into force on 12 February 2002.

[3] Alex Obote-Odora, 'Legal Problems with Protection of Children in Armed Conflict' *Murdoch University Electronic Journal of Law* 6 (1999). (http://www.murdoch.edu.au/elaw/issues/v6n2/obote-odora62_text.html#t34, 15 August 2008).

[4] Ibid.

Lanka, relied on children for their suicide bombing missions during their decades-long campaign. At times, they found that children could much more easily penetrate targets than their adult counterparts.[5] Trained and educated in the ways of guerrilla war, many child combatants grow up in a world where brutality is the norm. In Algeria, many of the killers are young boys under the age of 17.[6] In one incident, it was reported that some boys, who looked to be around 12 years old, decapitated a 15-year-old girl and played 'catch' with her head.[7] The result is a violent gift that keeps on giving – today's Taliban leaders reputedly cut their teeth in the field as child soldiers fighting the Soviets. In addition to inducing psychological trauma, a violent childhood reduces healthy educational opportunities, leaving militancy the only viable career path in later years.[8]

Child soldiers also pose unique challenges to professional armies. They are lethal combatants, but they are also victims who have often been forced to fight. For professional soldiers, hesitation out of sympathy may prove fatal. Furthermore, encounters with child soldiers can greatly demoralize professional fighters. [9]

The following examples are just a sample of the roles child soldiers have played in recent conflicts, and in some instances continue to play.

Sri Lanka:[10] The Sri Lankan government estimated that at least 60% of LTTE fighters were under 18.[11] The average age of children at the time of recruitment into the LTTE was 15[12], though some recruits were as

---

[5] Ibid.

[6] Ibid.

[7] Ibid.

[8] Simon Reich and Scott Gates, 'Think again: child soldiers' Foreign Policy May 2009 (http://www.foreignpolicy.com/story/cms.php?story_id=4944, 10 June 2009).

[9] Eben Kaplan, 'Child Soldiers Around the World' Council on Foreign Relations (http://www.cfr.org/publication/9331/, 12 January 2009).

[10] Charu Lata Hogg "Child Recruitment In South Asian Conflicts: A Comparative Analysis of Sri Lanka, Nepal and Bangladesh" (Coalition to Stop the Use of Child Soldiers: Chatman House, 2006): 9. (http://www.reliefweb.int/rw/lib.nsf/db900sid/PANA-794KLM/$file/chatham-nov2006.pdf?openelement , 15 January 2008).

[11] UN Doc. CRC/C/70/Add.17, 2002: Second Periodic Report of Sri Lanka to the UN Committee on the Rights of the Child: para.170.

[12] UNICEF, 'Action Plan for Children Affected By War, Progress Report January – June 2004' (http://www.unicef.org/videoaudio/PDFs/plan_progress_june04.pdf , 15 February 2008).

young as nine.[13] The UN Children's Fund (UNICEF) estimated that at least 1,440 children remained in the LTTE as of 30 April 2006. Of these, 859 children were under age at the time of recruitment.[14] Children were reportedly used from frontal assaults in major battles during the Eelam Wars.[15] Estimates of LTTE cadres killed in combat suggest that during the height of the Eelam Wars, at least 40% of the fighting force consisted of children aged between nine and 18. The nucleus of the 'Baby Brigade' was first formed in early 1984 and deployed heavily during the IPKF intervention.[16] The Sirasu Puli ('Leopard Brigade'), one of LTTE's fiercest fighting forces, was composed entirely of children.[17]

Uganda: As many as 25,000 children have been abducted by the Lords Resistance Army (LRA) for use as child soldiers, sex slaves and porters since the conflict began in 1986. 7,500 are girls, with 1,000 having conceived children during captivity. An unknown number have been killed.[18] Currently an estimated 30,000 Ugandan children – "night commuters" – walk quietly through the darkness every night, fleeing their homes on the look out for a relatively safe place to sleep in an urban area or in the centre of larger Internally Displaced Persons (IDP) camps – only to return back home in the morning and repeat the trip all over again as night falls.[19]

According to Article 1 of the Convention on the Rights of the Child, a child "is every human being below the age of 18 years unless, under the law applicable to the child, majority is attained earlier." Also, it is worth mentioning that there is no precise definition of the term 'child' in the

---

[13] Amnesty International, 'Children in South Asia – securing their rights' AI Index ASA 04/001/1998, 22 April 1998. (http://www-secure.amnesty.org/en/library/asset/ASA04/001/1998/en/d6b07591-e827-11dd-9deb-2b812946e43c/asa040011998en.pdf , 18 February 2008).

[14] Under-age Recruitment as of 30 April 2006, monthly statistics provided by UNICEF see UNICEF, 'Action Plan for Children Affected By War, Progress Report January – June 2004'.

[15] Rachel Brett and Margaret McCallin, Children: The Invisible Soldiers (Stockholm: Radda Barnen [Swedish Save the Children], 1996).

[16] UN Doc. CRC/C/70/Add.17, 2002, paras.170-1.

[17] N. Manoharan, 'Child Soldiers III: 'Baby Brigades' of the LTTE', Article No. 1184, 21 October 2003, Institute of Peace and Conflict Studies (IPCS: (http://www.ipcs.org/article_details.php?articleNo=1184 , 6 June 2009).

[18] Amnesty International, 'UGANDA: Child "night commuters" fear abduction' AI Index: AFR 59/016/2005, 18 November 2005 (http://asiapacific.amnesty.org/library/Index/ENGAFR590162005?open&of=ENG-UGA , 15 June 2008).

[19] Ibid.

laws of war (humanitarian law) whether customary international law or treaty law.[20]

An imprecise definition of the term 'child' is found in Additional Protocols I & II of 1977 to the four 1949 Geneva Conventions. Article 77 (2) of the Additional Protocol I discourages, but does not prohibit, recruitment of young persons who have not attained the age of fifteen.[21] Article 77 (3) acknowledges, though grudgingly, that children who take a direct part in hostilities may be taken as prisoners of war.[22] Thus, Additional Protocol I tacitly recognises that children will continue to take part in armed conflict. This is a weak prohibition of child participation in armed conflict as none of the above mentioned Protocols actually prohibit the use of child soldiers.[23]

Unfortunately, a 'child soldier' has received no agreed definition. According to the Cape Town Principles, a child soldier is "any person under 18 years of age who is part of any kind of regular or irregular armed force or armed group in any capacity, including but not limited to cooks, porters, messengers, and those accompanying such groups, other than purely as family members. It does not, therefore, only refer to a child who is carrying or has carried arms."[24] Meanwhile, the United Nations Children Fund (UNICEF) defines a child soldier as "any child—boy or girl—under eighteen years of age, who is part of any kind of regular or irregular armed force or armed group in any capacity." This age limit on an international scale is relatively new – as the Cape Town Principles have no international

---

[20] Obote-Odora, 'Legal Problems with Protection of Children in Armed Conflict', 30.

[21] Article 77 (2) of the Additional Protocol I of 1977 states: "The Parties to the conflict shall take all feasible measures in order that children who have not attained the age of fifteen do not take a direct part in hostilities and, in particular, they shall refrain from recruiting them into their armed forces. In recruiting among those persons who have attained the age of fifteen but have not attained the age of eighteen years, the Parties to the conflict shall endeavour to give priority to those who are oldest".

[22] Article 77 (3) of the Additional Protocol I of 1977 provides: "If, in exceptional cases, despite the provision of [Article 77 (2)], children who have not attained the age of fifteen years take direct part in hostilities and fall into the power of an adverse Party, [Prisoners of War] they shall continue to benefit from the special protection accorded by this Article, whether or not they are prisoners of war".

[23] Obote-Odora, 'Legal Problems with Protection of Children in Armed Conflict'.

[24] Cape Town, South Africa, 27-30 April 1997: The Cape Town Principles and Best Practices: Adopted at the Symposium on the Prevention of Recruitment of Children into the Armed Forces and on Demobilisation and Social Reintegration of Child Soldiers in Africa (http://www.unicef.org/emerg/files/Cape_Town_Principles(1).pdf, 15 May 2009).

application – established in 2002 by the Optional Protocol to the Convention on the Rights of the Child. Prior to 2002, the 1949 Geneva Conventions and the 1977 Additional Protocols set fifteen as the minimum age for participation in armed conflict. While some debate exists over varying cultural standards of maturity, nearly 80 percent of conflicts involving child soldiers include combatants below the age of fifteen, with some as young as seven or eight.[25]

Here are some facts illustrative of how children are affected by armed conflicts in the contemporary world:

- *As of mid-2004, up to 100,000 children—some as young as nine—were actively involved in armed conflict in Africa.*[26]
- *80 per cent of children aged 8 to 13 in Sierra Leone had suffered the death of a parent, sibling or close relative; 74 per cent had seen somebody being killed or injured with machetes; 68 per cent had seen somebody being burned to death or tortured; and nearly 10 per cent of girls had been gang-raped.*[27]
- *66 per cent of children in Angola had seen people murdered, and 67 per cent had seen people beaten or tortured.* [28]
- *55 per cent of children in Sarajevo, Bosnia and Herzegovina had been shot at, and 66 per cent had been in a situation where they expected to die.* [29]

Children are drawn into armed conflict by both push and pull factors. Push factors include negatives that children escape by joining an armed group. Abuse suffered in the family is a push factor – the child might join an armed group to escape an abusive situation. They may also seek to escape boredom, physical insecurity, extreme poverty, and the humiliation associated with personal or family victimization and shame. These push factors are only partial causes, since most children who have difficult family situations or live in abject poverty do not become child soldiers.

Equally or more compelling are the pull factors, which are the positive rewards or incentives for joining armed groups. Analysts have tended to underestimate the importance of pull factors, probably because the emphasis of much child-soldiering literature has been on protecting

---

[25] Kaplan, 'Child Soldiers Around the World'.
[26] Hogg "Child Recruitment In South Asian Conflicts: A Comparative Analysis of Sri Lanka, Nepal and Bangladesh".
[27] 'What is Child Soldier? Plan: (https://www.planusa.org/contentmgr/showdetails.php/id/2147 , 15 October 2008).
[28] Ibid.
[29] Ibid.

children from exploitation. Although most analysts view child soldiering as a heinous form of exploitation, children who join armed groups often see soldiering in different terms. Many view it as entering an opportunity space in which they can obtain things they could not obtain otherwise – including a family, power, revenge, wealth, education, and a commitment to a cause. To understand the lure of these incentives, one has to imagine the attraction felt by a child who comes from a very poor family and who has always felt powerless but who now carries a gun and is feared and respected by many.[30]

No situational influence has greater potency than the family. The profound importance of the family in children's recruitment is most visible in the case of separated children, who are no longer under the care of their parents or primary caretakers.[31] Separation typically occurs when a village is attacked; in the chaos of people's desperate flight, young children become separated from their parents and are ripped away from their primary supports. Some children's parents are killed, leaving the orphans with little means of protection and in a perilous situation. Separated children are at increased risk of nearly every form of exploitation, whether it involves trafficking, sexual violence, or child soldiering.

Not uncommonly, a separated child who encounters an armed group joins because the armed group provides for the child the only hope of food, medical support, or protection from further attack. For example, in Nepal, joining a rebel group brings an enhanced sense of group identity and collective activity among children and confers some privileges by way of free food in households in villages.[32]

A Philippine boy who had joined an opposition group at age 14 recounted:

> I was 14 when I joined the NPA (New People's Army). I was out of school then. My grandfather and grandmother sent me to school but I did not take my studies seriously. I had a friend who joined the movement. I thought that my life was meaningless because I had no parents to look after me. I

---

[30] Michael G. Wessells, Child Soldiers: From Violence to Protection (Cambridge, London: Harvard University Press, 2006): 46-7.

[31] Rachel Brett and Irma Specht, Young Soldiers: Why they choose to fight (London: Lynne Rienner, 2004).

[32] Hogg "Child Recruitment In South Asian Conflicts: A Comparative Analysis of Sri Lanka, Nepal and Bangladesh", 23bb.

went along with (my friend) because I thought what the heck my life is meaningless anyway.[33]

Child soldiers often include very young children, as young as seven in some situations, as well as older children and teenagers. The upper age of eighteen, as defined in the Cape Town Principles, corresponds to the threshold between childhood and adulthood defined in the Convention on the Rights of the Child. Children may be forced to join armed groups through forced conscription or abduction, though many join 'voluntarily' for their own protection and survival. The term 'voluntary' should be used cautiously when discussing child soldiers, as joining is often the only option available to children and their action is rarely 'voluntary' in any genuine sense.[34] Some of the methods used during this 'voluntary' enrolment are in fact as simple and brutal as those that were used to fill the ranks of the Janissaries. Armed to the teeth, insurgents supporting a particular ideology or warlord descend on a community. They plunder, pillage, rape and disappear back from where they came with a supply of new recruits destined to become soldiers by menace, threat or other means of coercion [35]

Children are recruited and used by armed groups around the world – both government and opposition – for a variety of reasons. It is generally easier to abduct, subjugate, and manipulate children than adults. Children are more impressionable and vulnerable to indoctrination. They can learn skills and tasks quickly, and they can be fast and agile on a battlefield. They are more willing than adults to take risks. Children are seen as more loyal and less threatening to adult leadership. It is easier for children to slip through enemy lines unnoticed, making them effective spies and bomb carriers. Children are typically viewed as cheap and expendable labour; they require less food and no payment. In addition, using child soldiers can present a moral dilemma to an army's enemies: should they kill children?[36]

---

[33] Wessells, Child Soldiers: From Violence to protection, 47 and UNICEF, 'Action Plan for Children Affected By War, Progress Report January – June 2004', 30.

[34] Mark Lorey, 'Child Soldiers: Care & Protection of Children in Emergencies: A Field Guide', *Save the Children* (http://www.savethechildren.org/publications/technical-resources/emergencies-protection/ChildSoldiersFieldGuide.pdf, 10 June 2009).

[35] 'Child Soldiers and Small Weapons of Mass Destruction' (http://www.achart.ca/publications/child_soldiers.html , 15 June 2007).

[36] Lorey, 'Child Soldiers: Care & Protection of Children in Emergencies: A Field Guide', Save the Children "Child Soldiers: Care & Protection of Children in Emergencies: A Field Guide" Mark Lorey', 3-4.

In Chad a senior officer in the Chadian National Army (ANT) stated that: “Child soldiers are ideal because they do not complain, they do not expect to be paid, and if you tell them to kill, they kill”.[37]

The extraordinary increase in the number of child soldiers since the cold war is closely related to the equally large number of small arms flooding the world market, advertised as 'cheaper than dirt' on the internet. The statistics are staggering. According to the Small Arms Survey of 2002 by the Graduate Institute of International Studies, Geneva:

- In 2002, 639m small arms were in circulation world wide; that is one for every 10 people on the planet.
- Forty per cent (255m) of these are in the hands of military formations; the remaining sixty per cent (384m) are held by civilians.
- The estimated annual sale of global small arms was $21 billion.
- Britain, France and the U. S. A. earned more from the sale of small arms than they provided in aid to the third world.
- Deaths from small arms were 500,000 a year. Of these, 300,000 were slain in armed conflict, 200,000 in domestic disputes. That is nearly one death a minute.
- In 2002, an estimated 16 billion rounds of ammunition were manufactured.[38]

The proliferation of small arms[39], such as handguns, light machine guns, revolvers and rifles has contributed significantly to the use of child soldiers. The widespread availability of these weapons is an important factor that enables children to participate as combatants in armed conflict. Small arms are lightweight, they therefore undo the disadvantage of children’s lack of strength. Firearms and guns are also cheap and easy to use. This problem is aggravated by the uncontrolled trade in small arms, with some 640 million small arms and light weapons in circulation around the world, according to a 2003 briefing paper by the Human Security Network.[40] Weapons availability can intensify and prolong violence and

---

[37] Coalition to Stop the Use of Child Soldiers, ‘Voices of Child Soldiers’ (http://www.childsoldiersglobalreport.org/content/voices-child-soldiers, 15 April 2009).

[38] ‘Child Soldiers and Small Weapons of Mass Destruction’.

[39] Small firearms include revolvers, self-loading pistols, muzzleloaders, sub-machine guns, light machine guns, assault rifles and carbines. Light weapons are larger weapons and include heavy machine guns, hand-held under-barrel and mounted grenade launchers.

[40] Centre for Humanitarian Dialogue, ‘Briefing Paper, Small Arms and Human Security: A snapshot of the humanitarian Impacts’ November 2003.

undermine the rule of law. According to the Small Arms Survey 2002, "Where there is an abundance of small arms in today's wars, there are armed children: where suicide bombers in Sri Lanka, soldiers in Myanmar, guerrillas in Colombia, or militia in Sierra Leone".[41]

The easy availability of small, low-cost weapons enables the arming of factions, creating a context ripe for armed conflict. Children can easily learn to operate these weapons, and many take pride in their skill. A 14-year-old boy from Sierra Leone said:

> I knew everything about my rifle – how to take it down, clean it, assemble it, load it. [I could do this] really fast! I could repair it, too. I was the fastest in my company…The commander had me train new soldiers. I liked the training…they looked up to me, and I taught them how to be good with the gun.[42]

While small-arms misuse may disproportionately affect the most vulnerable groups – women, children, the displaced – men are almost always the buyers, owners and users of guns. In conflict, women and children constitute the majority of combat deaths. The 2004 Small Arms Survey Yearbook observed that armed violence is "an overwhelmingly male phenomenon".[43]

Generally speaking, small arms are weapons designed for personal use, while light weapons are designed for use by several persons serving as a crew. Small arms are attractive tools of violence for several reasons. They are widely available, low in cost, extremely lethal, simple to use, durable, highly portable, easily concealed, and possess legitimate military, police, and civilian uses (so are present in virtually every society). These weapons are also relatively light in weight, and so can be used even by children.[44]

(http://www.hdcentre.org/files/RXbriefing.pdf, 15 March 2007) and ISN "Child Soldiers: The Use of Child Soldiers".

[41] International Relations and Security Network, 'Child Soldiers: The Use of Child Soldiers': 2. (http://www.isn.ethz.ch/isn/content/download/8067/80345/file/01%20Use%20of%20Children.pdf., 15 May 2009).

[42] Wessells, Child Soldiers: From Violence to protection, 19.

[43] "In-Depth: Guns out of Control: the continuing threat of small arms" May 2006 (http://www.irinnews.org/pdf/in-depth/Small-Arms-IRIN-In-Depth.pdf, 15 May 2008).

[44] Undule Mwakasungura, 'Firearms Proliferation: a real threat to Malawi's economy' (http://www.chrr.org.mw/press%20releases/April%202008/Small%20Arms%20Proliferation%20article.doc., 15 July 2009).

The origins of the small arms build-up lie in competition during the Cold War and struggles against colonialism and apartheid. More recently, as internal wars have become the predominant form of armed conflict, the influx of new weapons remains a preoccupation. But it is the illicit redistribution and flows of existing stocks from older conflicts which currently raise the greatest concern. Over time, the increased availability of unregulated and uncontrolled light weapons changes social values, making societies and individuals more, not less, insecure and violent. In many countries, such uncontrollable movements of small arms have occurred because peace settlements did not provide for the collection and destruction of surplus weapons. Accumulated weapons stocks became tradable commodities and circulated freely, contributing to continuing violence after the end of war.[45]

Child Soldiers include girls as well as boys. By the year 2000, when the war in Angola was winding down, it became apparent that thousands of girls had been soldiers in the Angolan war. In fact, many UNITA soldiers had two or more girls who had been abducted to serve as workers and sex slaves.[46] The girls had been invisible to analysts in part because the recruiters had wanted to hide their exploitation of girls. Also, the girls themselves had kept secret their lives as soldiers in order to avoid being stigmatised.[47]

For girls, recruitment may lead to sex slavery. In Uganda, for instance, young girls that had been abducted by rebel forces were commonly divided up and allocated to soldiers to serve as their 'wives'. A case-study from Hondura, prepared for the Machel report, illustrates one child's experience of joining armed groups:

[45] Virginia Gamba, 'Small Arms Foster Social Turmoil: Illegal Trafficking Disrupts African Communities, Spreads Crime' (http://www.un.org/ecosocdev/gen info/afrec/subjindx/121weaps.htm, 10 January 2008).

[46] Coalition to Stop the Use of Child Soldiers, 'CHILD SOLDIERS USE 2003: A Briefing for the 4th UN Security Council Open Debate on Children and Armed Conflict, Angola' (http://www.child-soldiers.org/document/get?id=690., 16 January 2008).

[47] Wessells, Child Soldiers: From Violence to protection, 85.

> At the age of 13, I joined the student movement. I had a dream to contribute to make things change, so that children would not be hungry… later I joined the armed struggle. I had all the inexperience and fears of a little girl. I found out that girls were obliged to have sexual relations 'to alleviate the sadness of the combatants'. And who alleviated our sadness after going with someone we hardly knew? At my young age I experienced abortion…In spite of my commitment, they abused me, they trampled my human dignity. And above all, they did not understand that I was a child and that I had rights.[48]

Although it is impossible to calculate accurately the number of children involved in armed forces and groups, it is clear that there are many tens of thousands of child soldiers. Child soldiers exist in all regions of the world and, almost inevitably, wherever there is armed conflict.[49]

The number of governments that used children in armed conflict has declined in recent years only marginally – down from 10 in the period 2001-2004 to nine in 2004-2007.[50]

The vast majority of child soldiers are to be found in the ranks of non-state armed groups. Dozens of armed groups in at least 24 countries have recruited under-18s and many have used them in hostilities.[51] Although Africa is the continent most commonly associated with the use of child soldiers, Table 1 shows that they are used throughout many other parts of the world.

So for example, in Latin America up to 14,000 children are estimated to be involved with armed political groups and army-backed paramilitaries in Colombia, while in Europe under-18s are believed to be involved in Turkey and a range of armed groups in the Chechen Republic of the Russian Federation, although the numbers are impossible to establish given the lack of information available.[52]

---

[48] 'Impact of Armed Conflict on Children: Children at both ends of the gun' UNICEF (http://www.unicef.org/graca/kidsoldi.htm , 15 December 2008).

[49] 'Child Soldiers : Global report 2008 "Facts and Figures on Child Soldiers"' Coalition to Stop the Use of Child Soldiers (www.childsoldiersglobalreport.org/content/facts-and-figures-child-soldiers, 10 January 2009).

[50] Ibid.

[51] Ibid.

[52] 'Frequently Asked Questions' *Coalition to Stop the Use of Child Soldiers* (http://www.child-soldiers.org/childsoldiers/questions-and-answers, 11 January 2008).

Table 1.1 Countries that have child soldiers fighting in current and recent conflicts[53]

Africa	Asia	Middle East	Latin America	Europe
Algeria (p/o)	Afghanistan (g/p/o)	Iran (g/o)	Colombia (p/o)	Russian Federation (o)
Angola (g/o)	India (p/o)	Iraq (g/o)	Mexico (p/o)	Turkey (o)
Burundi (g/o)	Indonesia (p/o)	Israel/Palestine (g/o)	Peru (o)	Yugoslavia (p/o)
Chad (g)	Myanmar (g/o)	Lebanon (o)		
Congo-Brazzaville (g/o)	Nepal (o)			
Congo-Kinshasa (g/o)	Pakistan (o)			
Eritrea (g/o)	Philippines (o)			
Ethiopia (g)	Solomon Islands (o)			
Liberia (g/o)	Sri Lanka (o)			
Rwanda(g/o)	East Timor (p/o)			
Sierra Leone (g/p/o)	Tajikistan (o)			
Somalia (g/p/o)	Papua New Guinea (o)			
Sudan (g/p/o)	Uzbekistan (o)			
Uganda (g/o)				

g=government p=paramilitaries o=armed opposition groups

The issue of child soldiers, nevertheless, arises not only for states characterised by civil conflicts, but for all states, including the most stable liberal democracies. All states, except the small number that have no army, have to confront the question of the age at which they should recruit soldiers. Several already impose an age-limit of 18, but many do not, including many 'Western' liberal democracies. Sixty-three countries permit the voluntary recruitment of under-18s by their armed forces. In Australia, New-Zealand and the United Kingdom calls to raise the

[53] Lorey, 'Child Soldiers: Care & Protection of Children in Emergencies: A Field Guide'.

minimum recruitment age to 18 have been resisted on the grounds of manpower requirements. In the USA, following a dramatic number of under-18s joining the military, and general requirement bonuses, increased enlistment bonuses were introduced and educational standards for recruitment lowered. Elsewhere, safeguards to ensure that minimum recruitment ages were respected were undermined by inadequate measures to determine the age of recruits. In countries such as Bangladesh, Botswana, Ethiopia, Guatemala, Guinea, India, Kenya and Zambia, the risk of inadvertent underage recruitment was created by low birth registration levels. In Paraguay, lack of birth registration facilitated forced conscription of children as young as twelve years old. In countries such as Afghanistan and Yemen, inadequate verification procedures to determine the age of new recruits meant that under-age soldiers were likely to be serving in security forces.[54]

1.2 International Action for the Protection of Children

As long as there are wars and other forms of armed conflict, children will be amongst their victims. Even so, just as the international community has adopted rules designed to curb some of the worst excesses of war, so it has taken steps to try to provide some protection for children against the consequences of war and armed conflict. The earliest measures were adopted in the 1920s and thereafter greater protection for the rights of children was provided through developments in human rights law and international humanitarian law. The most comprehensive provision for children's rights now in existence is the UN's Convention on the Rights of the Child (CRC), the drafting of which began in 1979. The Convention was finally adopted in 1989. All but two states have ratified it: Somalia[55] and USA[56].

The CRC recognises rights relating to very many aspects of children's lives, including education, health, forming his or her own views and freedom of expression. It also recognises rights of children relating to their involvement in armed conflict. The most relevant article of the CRC in this respect is article 38, which includes rights limiting the recruitment of

---

[54] 'Child Soldiers: Global report 2008 "Facts and Figures on Child Soldiers".

[55] Somalia is currently unable to proceed to ratification as it has no recognised government.

[56] The United States examines and scrutinises all treaties before ratification. In particular when the laws of several U.S. states are authorising execution of persons between the ages of 16 and 18 at the time of commission of the crime has been a major barrier to the USA's ratification of the Convention.

children into armies and armed groups. Articles 22 and 39 are also relevant. Article 22 applies to all children that have been affected by war or conflict and seek a refugee status, while Article 39 looks at the physical and psychological recovery of a child victim of armed conflict amongst other cruel, inhuman and degrading treatment.

While the CRC was a major advance in the international protection afforded to children, many of those who were party to the Convention thought it should have been more ambitious in its provision for war and armed conflict. Hence, in 1993 the first moves were made to draft a new document, which eventually became the Optional Protocol on the Involvement of Children in War and Armed Conflict (OPAC), adopted in 2002. The Optional Protocol goes a good deal further than the CRC in the protection it provides for children, including raising the minimum age for recruitment into the military from 15 to 18 years of age. At the time of writing, 110 states have ratified OPAC.

A major feature of the CRC and its Optional Protocols is the machinery that was established to monitor State Parties' compliance with the Convention and its Protocols. The task of monitoring compliance falls to the Committee on the Rights of the Child. States Parties to the Convention are under an obligation to report to the Committee at regular intervals and the Committee assesses their compliance with the CRC and its Protocols and makes recommendations to them.

The primary purpose of this thesis is to examine how well the CRC's machinery works. Clearly, states' pledging themselves to respect children's rights is worthless if they do not honour their pledge. The machinery established to monitor compliance with the CRC represents a significant effort by the UN to ensure that states honour the treaty obligations they have undertaken. The powers of the Committee in relation to States Parties are modest, in part because states are willing to go only so far in subjecting themselves to the authority of an external body. Nevertheless, it still matters whether the processes the UN has established for monitoring states' compliance actually achieves what they are designed to achieve.

The thesis focuses on the rights of children in relation to war and armed conflict for a number of reasons. First, the CRC is a very wide-ranging document and it would be impossible, within the scope of a single PhD thesis, to examine how its implementation machinery worked in relation to all of the rights set out in the Convention. Secondly, the rights relating to war and armed conflict are especially urgent. They concern life and death issues. The failure of states to comply with and to uphold these rights has much more dire consequences for children than their failure with respect to some other rights in the CRC. Thirdly, some of the rights in the CRC are stated in very general and imprecise terms and that often makes it difficult to judge whether a state has honoured them. The provisions in article 38 and in OPAC are rather more precise and that makes it easier for states to know what their obligations are and for others to judge how fully they are meeting their obligations. Finally, a focus upon children's rights in relation to war and armed conflict takes in OPAC as well as the CRC. This has two advantages. OPAC is a rather more detailed, precise and demanding document than article 38 of the CRC and therefore enables a more rigorous testing of states' compliance and of the Committee's monitoring of their compliance. Secondly, because OPAC is an optional addition to the CRC, one might expect a higher level of compliance from those states who have opted to be signatories to the Protocol. Thus, focusing on the case of war and armed conflict enables us to examine the working of the CRC's machinery in relation to two different parts of the Convention.

Chapter 2 explains the evolution of human rights from natural rights and, in particular, how during the 20th century the language of human rights replaced that of natural rights and the role that UN played in that development. Since the UN consists of states, this chapter also looks at the factors that affect states' willingness to commit and comply with the various human rights treaties that now exist. The analysis of these factors makes use of Beth Simmons' typology of states. Finally this chapter looks at the development of the role of NGOs over the years and the extent to which they have influenced the various human rights committees.

Chapter 3 examines how international recognition and provision for children's rights developed during the twentieth century. The story is a long one, beginning in 1922 with the International Convention for the Suppression of Traffic in Women and Children and 1924 with the League of Nation's Declaration of the Rights of the Child. Once the UN was established and human rights became internationally recognised, provision for the rights of the child was a natural consequence of the UN's developing provision for human rights, though one that took some decades to emerge. However, provision for children's rights, especially in armed conflict, also developed through international humanitarian law. The CRC and its Optional Protocols can be seen as the culmination and coming together of uneven processes of development in human rights law and humanitarian law. However, things have not stood still since the establishment of the CRC and the Chapter catalogues several important developments that have taken place since 1989.

Chapter 4 moves from general provision for children's rights to specific provision for those rights in war and armed conflict. The article in the CRC that provides most directly for children in war and armed conflict is article 38. The Chapter analyses the content of the article and examines quite what it does and does not prohibit, along with the debates and disputes that surrounded the drafting of the article. The Chapter also explains the origins of OPAC and why many states thought that its provisions were a necessary supplement to the CRC. Finally, the Chapter examines the machinery the UN has established to monitor states' compliance with the CRC and OPAC. It examines the constitution, membership and powers the Committee on the Rights of the Child, the obligations of States Parties in respect of the Committee, and how the machinery established to monitor compliance with the CRC and OPAC compares with that established for other Human Rights Treaties.

States Parties that are signatories to the CRC have an obligation to submit an initial report to the Committee on the Rights of the Child two years after they have signed the Convention. The report should indicate the ways in which and the extent to which that State Party complies with the CRC. Thereafter the State Party is obliged to submit further 'periodic' reports every five years. Signatories to OPAC have similar reporting obligations. Chapter 5 examines States Parties' performance in submitting these reports. It provides data on how many states submit their reports by the required deadlines and, for those that fail to meet the deadlines (which includes the great majority), data on how late their reports are. The data reveals a large degree of variation in states' performance. The Chapter goes on to examine how far variations in performance correlate with geographical differences and with differences in types of regime and in the income levels of states.

Chapter 6 turns to the actual content of States Parties' reports. The Committee on the Rights of the Child provides guidelines for the content of States Parties' reports, including for article 38 of the CRC and for OPAC. These guidelines are reasonably specific and provide criteria against which the adequacy of States Parties' reporting can be judged. Chapter 6 examines how far states report on article 38 in their reports on the CRC and, of those that do report, how adequately they follow the Committee's guidelines. Once again, the data reveals a large degree of variation in the performance of States Parties and, as in Chapter 5, an analysis is provided of how far variations in reporting correlate with geographical differences and with differences in types of regime and in the income levels of states. Chapter 6 also examines the use the Committee makes, in relation to article 38, of its 'Lists of Issues', through which it requests additional information from states, and its 'Concluding Observations'.

Chapter 7 conducts a similar evaluation of states' reporting in relation to OPAC. Since reporting on OPAC has to be much more detailed than on article 38, a three-point scale is used to grade the quality of states' reporting on the provisions of OPAC. This Chapter, like Chapter 6, reveals a high degree of variation in the adequacy of states' reports. It also examines how far the Committee has used its Lists of Issues and its Concluding Observations to comment on, and to seek remedies for, shortcomings in states' reports.

The machinery for implementing the CRC is unique amongst the UN's Human Rights Committees in making provision for NGOs to submit reports as part of the formal monitoring process. Chapter 8 examines how far NGOs have taken advantage of the opportunity to submit reports to the Committee and how far their reports have dealt with issues relating to Article 38 and OPAC. It also examines the quality of information provided by NGOs on the issue of child soldiers and the impact that information seems to have had upon the Committee.

Chapters 5, 6 and 7 provide evidence of extensive failings and shortcomings in the existing process for monitoring and implementing the CRC and OPAC. Chapter 8 shows that, while NGOs have made positive contributions to the monitoring process, their contributions have been too sporadic to correct the failings and shortcomings of the process. That evidence inevitably raises the question of how the existing process might be reformed so that it functions more satisfactorily. The CRC and OPAC are part of a larger set of Human Rights treaties, all of which have similar machinery for monitoring and assessing States Parties' compliance with their treaty obligations. The UN authorities have expressed dissatisfaction at the way in which much of this machinery works and have commissioned several reports on how the performance of Human Rights Treaty Bodies might be improved.

Chapter 9 examines the reform proposals in those reports that are most relevant to the concerns of this thesis and assesses which of several proposed changes are likely to result in significant improvements. However, the Chapter makes this assessment in light of the political realities of the current world and of the limited powers the UN can wield over its member-states. These realities limit the means the UN might use to police the conduct of its own members.

1.3 A Note on Methodology

The UN has a number of Conventions concerning human rights. For each of these, it has an administrative apparatus designed to monitor and promote states' compliance with the Convention. The principal aim of this thesis is to examine the functioning and the efficiency of that administrative machinery in relation to the CRC. The CRC is a long document covering many rights and, within a single thesis, it would not be possible to examine the effectiveness of its machinery in relation to all of those rights in any depth. I therefore focus this study on one category of right: the rights of the child in relation to war and armed conflict.

As previously indicated, one reason for choosing that category of right as the focus for this study is that children's rights in relation to war and armed conflict are especially urgent. But, a major methodological reason for focusing on article 38 – the principal article in the CRC governing war and armed conflict – is that it is formulated more precisely than many other rights in the CRC and that facilitates assessment of states' compliance with the article.

In addition, focusing on war and armed conflict enables OPAC to be a part of this study. A major merit of including OPAC is that it is a reasonably detailed and precise document and, in addition, the Committee has set out detailed and precise guidelines for states' reporting on the Protocol. So OPAC provides a good instrument for assessing states' compliance with their reporting obligations.

My research makes extensive use of the reports submitted by States Parties' for the CRC and OPAC. The period covered by my research runs from the introduction of the CRC in 1989 and of OPAC in 2000 up to the 44th session of the Committee, which was held in 2007. States' reports submitted during that period include their initial reports and their second and third periodic reports for the CRC. Of those states that have ratified the CRC, the great majority (95%) had submitted their initial reports during the period. The large majority (85%) should also have submitted their second periodic reports during the period, although a little more than half (54%) had actually submitted their reports. Because third periodic reports have more recent deadlines, only 43% of states were due to submit these reports during the period and only 11% actually submitted them. So the bulk of this study focuses on the initial reports and the second periodic reports.

This study also includes the 28 states' reports submitted for OPAC. Because OPAC did not become effective before 2002, only 28 of the 110 states who are signatories to the Protocol submitted reports during the period studied. Nevertheless, this is a large enough sample to assess how well states have been fulfilling their reporting obligations in relation to OPAC.

The availability of all of these reports on-line has enabled me to make comprehensive assessments of the regularity with which states have submitted their reports and of how adequately they have reported. The Committee on the Rights of the Child has set out guidelines for states' reports on the CRC and OPAC. These guidelines provide the criteria by which I assess the content of states' reports, so the criteria I use are those that laid down by the Committee for the reporting process, rather than criteria I have devised myself. I do, however, use my own grading scale of A, B, C or N to indicate how adequately states' reports have complied with the guidelines. 'A' indicates that a report contains all the information required by the Committee's guidelines, apart from trivial or insignificant omissions; 'B' indicates that a report has omissions that are minor but significant rather than trivial; 'C' includes reports that have major omissions, including failure to provide any of the information required by the Committee; 'N' is used to indicate that a particular article or guideline is not applicable to a State Party. Assigning reports to each of these grades is a relatively straightforward process; only rarely does a report seem to straddle two grades.

Given the large variations in states' performances in the reporting process, I conduct statistical analysis of the data I compile to discover how the performances of states correlate with their geographical region, income level, and type of regime. These correlations suggest that these factors have some bearing on differences in states' performances, but the usual hazards of inferring causal relationships from correlations need to be borne in mind. I conduct statistical analyses of these correlations in relation to the regularity with which states have submitted their reports on the CRC and the adequacy of their reporting on Article 38. I do not conduct similar analyses in relation to OPAC since only roughly a quarter of the signatories to OPAC have submitted their reports and those that have submitted are not a representative sample of the full set of signatories; they include a disproportionate number of European states.

The Committee's Lists of Issues, States Parties' responses to those Lists, and the Committee's Concluding Observations are also available on-line. These are vital parts of the monitoring process and their analysis forms an important part of this research.

As stated in Article 45(a) of the CRC, NGOs are formally entitled to participate in the monitoring process. I therefore examine their role in the process. Their reports to the Committee are available on-line. I focus on

NGO reports as they relate to Article 38 and OPAC and I give particular attention to The Coalition to Stop the Use of Child Soldiers, since that NGO is concerned specifically with children's rights in war and armed conflict. I also make an effort, by examining the Committee's Concluding Observations, to detect how far intervention by NGOs has influenced the Committee's response to states.

In examining possibilities for reforming the reporting process, I take account of how the failings I uncover compare with the findings of other researchers who have examined the workings of the UN's other Human Rights Committees. I also consider reform proposals for the Human Rights Committee system as a whole, since the failings I identify seem to be common across the system as a whole rather than unique to the CRC. Any reform instituted by the UN is likely to be reform of the system generally rather than of individual Conventions and their monitoring systems.

Finally, I acknowledge that this research is limited to the workings of the reporting process and does not attempt to assess the wider impact of the CRC and OPAC. The point of article 38 and OPAC is to improve the lot of children affected by war and armed conflict. Ideally therefore, research on this subject would attempt to assess the impact of both 'on the ground' rather than only through the reporting process. However, this research does not attempt that larger project for two reasons. First, it is very difficult to get reliable data on the actual use of child soldiers, particularly since child soldiers are often used by non-state militias; nor was fieldwork to gather this sort of data practicable. Secondly, even if there were reliable data, it would be extremely difficult to assess whether variations in the use of child soldiers had anything to do with the CRC and OPAC. Had use increased since the introduction of the Convention and the Protocol, that would not necessarily signal their failure – use might have been even greater in their absence. Equally, had use decreased since their introduction, it would be difficult to establish whether and to what extent that decrease could be attributed to the CRC and OPAC. Rather than grapple with such imponderables, this research focuses on those parts of the UN's efforts that are more accessible and where judgements of success and failure can be made more confidently.

CHAPTER TWO

THE EVOLUTION OF RIGHTS

2.1 Introduction

The UN's Convention on the Rights of the Child is part of its larger endeavour to establish, uphold and develop the idea of human rights. This chapter will explore the background to the CRC in the general idea of human rights which itself developed historically from the older idea of natural rights. It will also examine the UN's efforts to establish human rights as international norms, beginning with its Universal Declaration of Human Rights (UDHR) adopted in 1948. The UDHR provided a foundation from which the UN has gone on to establish far more detailed Human Rights Covenants and Conventions, of which the CRC is one. We shall also examine the behaviour of states and the activities of NGOs in relation to human rights.

2.2 From Natural Rights to Human Rights

Some scholars treat 'natural rights' and 'human rights' as different labels for the same kind of rights[1] and there is much common ground between these two ideas. It is nevertheless useful to distinguish between the two sorts of rights for historical purposes, particularly since the different historical contexts in which the two sorts of right have been asserted have meant that they have been associated with different background theories and with different conceptions of the rights human individuals have. John Locke is the most celebrated exponent of natural rights and we shall use his thought to examine the idea of natural rights.[2]

---

[1] Peter Jones, *Rights* (Basingstoke: Macmillam, 1994): 72.

[2] Other advocates, such as Thomas Hobbes, presented different understandings of natural rights, but Locke's understanding better represents the orthodox view and consequently it is his understanding that will be the principal focus here. See Jones, Rights, 72.

Natural rights were conceived as part of the natural order of the world. They were not created by rulers or by any other human being; rather they were rights given by God. What God had given to his human creation, no-one was entitled to take away; they were integral to what it was to be a natural human being. [3] Natural rights were rights conferred upon individuals by God's laws of nature. Locke regarded natural rights as rights that gave individuals control over themselves. They were rights of self-ownership: 'everyman has a property in his own person' (II.27)[4]. These rights entitled each individual to conduct his own life in his own way provided only that, in doing so, he did not trespass on the rights of others. While he thought of natural rights as self-ownership rights, he did not think that all natural rights were property rights in the ordinary sense. For example, the right of the innocent to remain physically unmolested was a right that they always had[5]; it was not a right that individuals acquired through any particular event. Nonetheless, it is true to say that the moral relationship among human beings was changed to a significant extent by Locke into a relationship among "owners" of rights.[6]

Locke used the familiar devise of a state of nature to portray man's natural moral condition, including his possession of natural rights. In the state of nature individuals also possessed the executive power of the law of nature, which entitled them to uphold natural rights against those who would violate them.[7] A state of nature would have obvious disadvantages for mankind, particularly since it would be a condition in which every individual was judge in his own case (II, para.13). Since the law of nature was unwritten, people driven by their passions or their self interest would misinterpret or misapply it and would not be easily persuaded of their error (II, para.136).[8]

That, for Locke, provided the main reason for setting up a political society in which there would be a single, common and stated, interpretation of the law of nature which would be impartially administered and by

---

[3] Henrik Syse, 'From Natural law to Human Rights – some reflections on Thomas Pogge and Global Justice' in A. Follesdal and T. Pogge (ed.), Real World Justice (Netherlnads: Springer, 2005): 229-237.

[4] Thomas D. A . Lloyd, Locke on Government (London: Rutledge, 1995): 18.

[5] Lloyd, Locke on Government, 18-9.

[6] Syse, 'From Natural law to Human Rights – some reflections on Thomas Pogge and Global Justice', 234.

[7] Peter Laslett, John Locke: Two Treatises of Government: A critical Edition with an introduction and Apparatus Criticus (Cambridge: Cambridge University Press, 1967): 97.

[8] Ibid., 98.

reference to which disputes would be settled. In addition, standard punishments would be imposed for those who violated the common rules. For Locke political power was "a right of making laws with penalties of death, and consequently all less penalties, for the regulating and preserving of property, and of employing the force of the community in the execution of such laws, and in the defence of the commonwealth from foreign injury, and all this only for the public good".[9] The state was a device that would ensure that the law of nature did in fact regulate people's relationships with each other.

Locke connected natural rights to government in three ways. First, the principal task of a government was to uphold the natural rights of its citizens. Second, government was created and given authority by individuals, each of whom possessed the same natural rights and the same moral status. Because of that equal moral status, political authority could be wielded only over those who had consented to it. Third, natural rights were given to each individual by God rather than by a government. Individuals held their natural rights 'against' government in that natural rights set limits to a government's authority. If a people believed that the government had broken its trust and had violated their natural rights, they could withdraw power from it. No government had the authority to deprive individuals of their natural rights and a government that violated, rather than upheld, natural rights could be removed by its subjects, as James II was removed in 1688. It was the idea of individuals holding rights 'naturally' and therefore independently of governments, which limited what governments might do to their subjects, that was the most important bequest of the idea natural rights to subsequent human rights thinking. It was also why much use was made of the idea of natural rights in justifying the French and American Revolutions of the eighteenth century.

During the 20th century the language of human rights replaced that of natural rights. As Thomas Pogge points out, this change in language signalled a move towards secularising the idea. Human rights thinkers differ over the way they believe human rights should be justified, but the idea of human rights itself has become detached from any particular theory or justification. For political purposes it has become, in Rawls's terms, a "political" rather than a "metaphysical" idea,[10] freed from contested claims about human nature.[11] Human rights are rights that all people are thought

[9] Lloyd, Locke on Government, 23.
[10] Syse, 'From Natural law to Human Rights – some reflections on Thomas Pogge and Global Justice', 235.
[11] Ibid.

to possess, whether or not those rights have been embodied in systems of positive law. They are rights that positive systems of law ought to recognise, but people's possession of human rights does not depend upon such formal recognition, which is why we can speak of governments and laws 'violating' human rights. For some thinkers, like Hart, human rights are 'general' rather than 'special' rights, since they are universal to all humanity,[12] and they are rights that individuals hold in any social context. Others, like Pogge, conceive human rights as rights individuals hold against governments and their officials, or against armies and large corporations and organisations, rather than against private individuals.[13] That usage of human rights departs from Locke's idea of natural rights, which he conceived as rights held against all-comers, including individuals taken singly.

The concept of human rights can be linked to a claim that they are God-given rights, but it does not have to be. While the idiom is meant to convey much the same idea as that of natural rights, namely, that these rights belong to humans qua humans, they can also be conceived as entirely human in origin and therefore as sharing in all the instability, uncertainty, and limitedness that characterise human affairs in general.[14]

Natural rights were generally conceived as negative in content; they imposed only negative duties upon others. They were rights to be left alone, by governments and others, to pursue one's own life as one chose within the bounds set by the laws of nature. Human rights, by contrast, have been given both negative and positive content. Negatively, they include rights such as those to freedom of speech, freedom of religion and freedom from arbitrary arrest. Positively, they have been said to include rights to goods and services such as personal security, a decent standard of living, and education and health care. They can also be rights that have both negative and positive dimensions. The right to freedom of assembly, for example, may seem to be a negative right in that it requires governments and others not to prevent individuals assembling together for political, religious or other purposes, but it may also impose upon governments a positive duty to provide protection against those who might disrupt meetings.[15]

---

[12] Jones, Rights, 81.

[13] Syse, 'From Natural law to Human Rights – some reflections on Thomas Pogge and Global Justice', 235.

[14] Ibid.

[15] James W. Nickel, Making Sense of Human Rights (London: University of California Press, 1987): 14.

The idea of human rights is not without its critics. Jeremy Bentham dismissed natural rights as 'simple nonsense' and Alasdair MacIntyre has rejected human rights in similar terms: 'there are no such rights and belief in them is one with belief in witches and in unicorns'.[16] However, the idea of human rights continues to survive that scepticism and has become very much a political reality. For instance, nowadays when a government is accused of violating its population's human rights, it typically responds by denying the alleged violation rather than by dismissing the idea of human rights.

The Universal Declaration of Human Rights, the first formal UN articulation of rights, reflected the conceptual change from 'natural' to 'human' rights. In the words of Kenneth Minogue, rights were no longer derived from the operation of natural reason, but rather from an idea of what it was to be human. We think that a person who is malnourished, tortured, wrongly imprisoned, illiterate and perhaps lacking in regular paid holidays is not living in a manner appropriate to a human being.[17] Over the last fifty years, human rights have acquired a legal or semi-legal status even though the very idea of human rights is fundamentally a non-legal one, for they are now embodied in a number of international declarations, conventions and covenants. Prior to 1945 human rights remained a national matter, but after the Second World War human rights language was written into the United Nations Charter. Member states of the United Nations negotiated an international bill of rights, which was then supplemented by other treaties and declarations codifying the fundamental legal rights that were to be respected. By the late 1990s about 140 states (in 1999 the UN membership was 185) had formally committed to the International Covenant on Civil and Political Rights and the companion International Covenant on Economic, Social and Cultural Rights. The 1949 Geneva Conventions were formally accepted by virtually all states; they enshrined the view that certain humanitarian values were to be respected even by parties engaged in armed conflict.[18] Other developments also indicated the central point that human rights were no longer a matter only for state domestic jurisdictions. In principle, states were to answer to the international community for their treatment of individuals. International relations included not only subjects like war and trade, but also human

---

[16] Ibid., 90.

[17] Walter. Loquer and B. Rubin (eds.), The Human Rights Reader (Philadelphia: Temple University Press, 1979): 14.

[18] Lynn H. Miller, Global Order: Values and Power in International Relations (Boulder, CO: Westview Press, 1994): 4.

rights. Human rights have been internationalised, and internationally recognised rights have become routinised.[19]

2.3 The Role of the UN on Human Rights

It may seem paradoxical that international human rights discourse emerged at a time when the dark side of Western modernity had culminated in an abhorrent and unprecedented negation of the rights of the individual. Historically, claims of right seem to emerge in contexts of extreme and widespread violations. Under the prevailing conditions it was impossible to establish a legal document reflecting the basic needs of all human beings. In 1948 the aim was not to create a charter for 'Western man'[20] but to follow the motto 'freedom from fear and want'. Its being recalled time and again in resolutions of international conferences at the world level[21] as well as in General Assembly Resolutions, shows that the UDHR has fulfilled its motto. Most recently in 2005, at the World Summit Outcome, the UDHR was acknowledged as a cornerstone of human rights in the world.[22]

Although it was 'the Charter of the United Nations ... that elevated human rights to the plane of international law and stipulated legal obligations on the part of the Member States of the United Nations',[23] the

---

[19] Ibid., 4-5.

[20] Because of the strong presence of socialist states, the Human Rights Commission and the General Assembly were not and could not be guided by an exclusively 'Western' understanding of human rights.

[21] The Vienna Declaration and Programme of Action, adopted by the World Conference on Human Rights on 25 June 1993, re-emphasised the importance of the UDHR as a 'common standard of achievement for all peoples and nations' (preamble, para.8). A/CONF.157/23: "World Conference on Human Rights: 12/07/1993
(http://www.unhchr.ch/huridocda/huridoca.nsf/(symbol)/a.conf.157.23.en, 10 April 2011) and General Assembly Resolution (A/RES/55/2) "55/2 United Nations Millennium Declaration" adopted by the General Assembly [without reference to a Main Committee (A/55/L.2) (8 September 2000).
(http://www.un.org/millennium/declaration/ares552e.pdf, 10 April 2011).

[22] General Assembly Resolution 60/1. "2005 World Summit Outcome" (24 October 2005) [adopted by the General Assembly without reference to a Main Committee] 1
(http://unpan1.un.org/intradoc/groups/public/documents/un/unpan021752.pdf, 2 March 2011): para.120.

[23] Anna Mamalakis Pappas, Law and the Status of the Child (New York: The United Nations Institute for Training and Research, 1983): xxx.

Charter was very soon identified as problematic as it did not define what was to be understood as a human right and a fundamental freedom under international law.[24] As a result, the UN members 'proceeded to prepare and promulgate the Universal Declaration of Human Rights, making specific the general Charter references to human rights and freedoms for all'.[25] Even though the UDHR was accepted with relative ease, it was not until 1966 that the recommendations laid out in the Declaration were introduced into international law, in the shape of the International Covenant on Civil and Political Rights (ICCPR), and the International Covenant on Economic, Social and Cultural Rights (ICESCR),[26] and not until a decade later that these Covenants became legally enforceable.[27] The main reason behind the Declaration's lack of binding power was the fact that it was introduced into a world dominated by realist politics, not least in respect of the Cold War, and it was not in the interests of the two emerging superpowers to have a legally binding document.[28] In Lauterpacht's view, the Declaration was devoid of any legal value or significance: by 'not being a legal instrument, the Declaration would appear to be outside international law', which in fact reflects the original intentions of the drafters who did not want the document to have any artificial legal significance.[29] For Lauterpacht states did not want the Declaration to have direct or indirect legal repercussions, let alone an effective enforcement mechanism. He details the various declarations made by state representatives on its adoption in the General Assembly,

---

[24] Louis Henkin, The International Bill of Rights: the Covenant on Civil and Political Rights (New York: Columbia Press, 1981): 8.

[25] B.G. Ramcharan, Human Rights: Thirty Years after the Universal Declaration (Dordrecht: Martinus Nijhoff, 1979):27ff.

[26] Today not only have European countries in large numbers adhered to the two Covenants, as well as Latin America and Africa, but also numerous Asian states. Only two poles of stubborn and tenacious resistance can be identified. On the one hand, the states of the Arabian peninsula (Bahrain, Oman, Qatar, Saudi Arabia and United Arab Emirates) and on the other hand, there is a small group headed by China, which comprises China and some nations linked to it by close ties of friendship (Laos and Singapore). Christian Tomuschat, Human Rights: Idealism and Realism (Oxford: OUP, 2008):75.

[27] Daren J. O' Byrne, Human Rights: An Introduction (London: Pearson Educations LTD, 2003): 87.

[28] Jochen von Bernstorff, 'The Changing Fortunes of the UDHR: Genesis and Symbolic Dimensions of the Turn to Rights in International Law' EJIL VOL19 (5) (2008): 906.

[29] Hersch Lauterpacht, International Law and Human Rights (London: Longmans, 1950): 416-7.

which had stressed the absence of legal obligations arising from the proclaimed 'common standard of achievement'.[30]

The purpose of the two Covenants was to spell out more clearly both the scope of each right and the conditions under which certain rights could be restricted in order to protect the rights of others or of the community, since the language used in the Declaration was broad and not easy to apply in concrete situations. But even when the Covenants were finally approved by the General Assembly, most observers of the international scene were rather pessimistic about their entry into force. Consequently, it was felt necessary to proceed step-by-step, to draft additional international instruments with respect to subjects which were of such interest to a large segment of the international community that one could hope that they would more quickly enter into force. There was also a justified feeling that even the Covenants were written in too broad language, and that more specificity would be desirable in several important areas.[31]

In short, because of the original lack of clarity about the status of the UDHR in international law, four levels of international obligations have been created – the UDHR, the Covenants, the other declarations and Conventions – each more specific than the other.[32] Each of them has a different level of specificity and separate levels of application.

The UDHR and the two Covenants taken together comprise the International Bill of Rights.[33] The two Covenants have a similar structure and, in some articles, adopt the same, or very similar wording.[34] One notable difference between the two Covenants is the principle of progressive realisation in Part II of the ICESCR. Article 2(1) specifies that a State Party "undertakes to take steps, [...] to the maximum of its available resources, with a view to achieving progressively the full realisation of the rights recognised in [the Covenant]". The principle of progressive realisation acknowledges the constraints that States Parties

---

[30] Von Bernstorff 'The Changing Fortunes of the UDHR: Genesis and Symbolic Dimensions of the Turn to Rights in International Law', 906.

[31] Louis B. Sohn, 'The Improvement of the UN Machinery Human Rights', International Studies Quarterly 23 (2) (1979):188.

[32] Ibid., 187.

[33] In a broader sense, the International Bill of Rights includes also the many declarations and conventions on human rights adopted by the General Assembly or by several specialised agencies of the United Nations. Ibid.

[34] Office of the United Nations: High Commissioner for Human Rights, 'Fact Sheet No.30. The United Nations Human Rights Treaty System: An Introduction to the core human rights treaties and the treaty bodies': 13-4 (http://www2.ohchr.org/english/bodies/docs/OHCHR-FactSheet30.pdf , 15 September 2008).

may face due to the limits of available resources. However, it also imposes an immediate obligation to take deliberate, concrete and targeted steps towards the full realisation of the rights of the Covenant. The Covenant also recognises the wider role of the international community (arts. 2(1), 11(2), 15(4), 22 and 23) building on the principles in articles 22 and 28 of the UDHR.[35]

The International Bill of Rights is effectively the definitive source of international human rights law. However, despite the establishment of the Human Rights Committee that is tasked with monitoring the ICCPR and the Committee on Economic, Social and Cultural Rights that monitors the ICESCR, the International Bill of Rights has suffered primarily from an inability to reconcile its liberal objectives with realist politics. Because no court exists that has the power to enforce the Covenants and to punish violators, international human rights law has had to rely upon nation-states for its promotion and maintenance.[36]

In addition to the ICCPR and the ICESCR, there are six more core human rights treaties that set international standards for the protection and promotion of human rights to which States can subscribe by becoming a party to each treaty.

The International Convention on the Elimination of All Forms of Racial Discrimination (ICERD), adopted in 1965 and entering into force in 1969, was one of the first human rights treaties to be adopted by the UN and is widely supported with more than 156 countries having ratified it. By ratifying it the States Parties among others undertake: (a) not to engage in any act or practice of racial discrimination against individuals, groups of persons or institutions and to ensure that public authorities and institutions do like likewise; (b) to prohibit and put a stop to racial discrimination by persons, groups and organisations and (c) to ensure effective protection and remedies for victims of racial discrimination.[37]

The Convention on the Elimination of All Forms of Discrimination against Women (CEDAW), adopted in 1979 by the UN General Assembly, is often described as an International Bill of Rights for women as, in its 30 articles, it defines what constitutes discrimination against women and sets up an agenda for national action to end such

---

[35] Office of the United Nations: High Commissioner for Human Rights, 'Fact Sheet No.30. The United Nations Human Rights Treaty System: An Introduction to the core human rights treaties and the treaty bodies': 15.

[36] O' Byrne, Human Rights: An Introduction, 90.

[37] 'The International Convention on the Elimination of All Forms of Racial Discrimination' Australian Human Rights Commission (www.hreoc.gov.au/racial_discrimination/guide_law/icerd.html , 10/12/2010).

discrimination.[38] The Convention against Torture and Other Cruel, Inhuman or Degrading Treatment (CAT) was adopted in1984 and entered into force in 1987. The International Convention on the Protection of the Rights of All Migrant Workers and Members of their Families (ICRMW) was adopted in 1990; it promotes the rights of both migrants and their families. The eighth and most recent Treaty is the International Convention on the Rights of Persons with Disabilities (ICRPD); it was adopted in 2006 and entered into force in 2008. The CRC is therefore one of a number of Conventions, each of which is designed to protect a specific sphere of human rights and each of which has the status of a legally binding treaty for the states who sign up to it. The developments that gave rise to the CRC and its place in the UN's efforts to secure and promote human rights are considered in Chapter 3 of this thesis.

Each State Party has an obligation to take steps to ensure that everyone in the State can enjoy the rights set out in the treaty. The treaty body (committee) helps them to do this by monitoring implementation and recommending further action. Each treaty is a separate legal instrument, which States may or may not choose to accept, and each treaty body is a committee of experts, independent from the other committees. The extent to which the treaties and the treaty bodies can function together as a system depends on two factors: first, states need to accept all of the core international human rights treaties systematically and to put their provisions into operation (universal and effective ratification); and, second, the treaty bodies need to coordinate their activities so as to present a consistent and systematic approach to monitoring the implementation of human rights at the national level.[39]

The first Committee to be established was the Committee on the Elimination of Racial Discrimination (CERD) in 1969, while the Human Rights Committee was created in 1976 and the CESCR in 1987. Special attention should be given to the CERD and CESCR, since they came into existence some time after the adoption of the Covenants in 1966. The remaining Committees have been created as part of the Conventions they oversee.

[38] 'United Nations Entity for Gender Equality and the Empowerment of Women' UN Women (http://www.unwomen.org/, 20/11/2010).
[39] Office of the United Nations: High Commissioner for Human Rights, 'Fact Sheet No.30. The United Nations Human Rights Treaty System: An Introduction to the core human rights treaties and the treaty bodies': 7.

Other UN organs that have some relevance to applicability of Human Rights both in direct and indirect way are: The Security Council[40], the Office of the Secretary-General, [41]the General Assembly,[42] the Economic and Social Council (ECOSOC)[43] and the International Court of Justice (ICJ)[44], followed by the major subsidiary bodies such as the Human Rights Commission, International Labour Organisation (ILO), and the High Commissioner for Refugees. All these organs have a common goal: the promotion and protection of human rights either through diplomatic measures or direct actions with the states in question.

The Convention on the Rights of the Child and its Committee are therefore part of a wider set of conventions and administrative machinery. The CRC has an implementation system similar to those of other Human Rights Conventions. Like them, the CRC's Committee is not empowered directly to enforce the standards that the CRC promulgates. However, the CRC differs from other Conventions in making formal provision for its Committee to cooperate with NGOs,[45] which constitutes an advance in the struggle for effective implementation procedures. [46] The machinery through which the UN seeks to implement the CRC and its Protocols is described in detail in Chapter 4.

One further factor that relates to the implementation and maintenance of internationally recognised human rights is the domestic legal system of a country. For these purposes we can distinguish between monist and dualist legal systems. In monist systems the treaties entered into by a state automatically become part of the domestic law of that state. Brazil, Estonia, Iran, Russia, Spain, and Romania are examples of countries that

---

[40] The most powerful of the UN organs, and is responsible for peacekeeping, interventions, and sanctions against warring or rogue states. See O' Byrne, Human Rights: An Introduction, 81.

[41] The office has around 8,900 staff from 160 states. 82.

[42] Each member state in represented, each with one vote; important decisions must be carried by a two-thirds majority, others by a simple majority; these decisions and resolutions are not enforceable by international law. Ibid., 81.

[43] Consists of 54 members elected for three-year period to oversee the work of certain specialist agencies dealing with economic, social and humanitarian issues. Ibid., 82.

[44] Based in The Hague its role is to seek to resolve conflicts between states by law rather than by force to be considered by the International Court and abide by its decision. Ibid.

[45] C. P. Cohen, 'The Role of Nongovernmental Organisations in Drafting of the Convention on the Rights of the Child', Human Rights Quarterly 12 (1990): 137ff.

[46] Michael Freeman, The Ideologies of Children's Rights (London; Martinus Nijhoff Publishers, 1992):77.

possess monist systems. In dualist systems, the treaties entered into by a state have to go through a separate process of incorporation before they become part of the state's domestic law. Australia, Britain, Canada, Finland and Mexico are examples of states where ratification has to be followed by a separate act of incorporation if a human rights treaty is to become part of their domestic law.[47] Prima facie one might expect that monist systems will do more to ensure compliance with human rights treaties than dualist systems, simply because dualist arrangements make it possible for governments not to incorporate their treaty obligations into domestic law and so avoid being held to account by their own judicial systems for their compliance with those obligations. However, as we shall see below, the distinction between monist and pluralist systems is only one of a number of domestic political factors that affect state's compliance with human rights treaties and not always the most important.

2.4 States and Human Rights

As has been already mentioned, states play a significant role in the implementation of the UDHR and the various Human Rights Treaties to which they are parties. Although in the contemporary world states are regarded as indispensable guarantors of human rights, the historical record also makes clear that states are also frequent violators of human rights.[48] In this section we shall examine the factors that are relevant to whether a state commits itself to a human rights treaty and to how far it complies with the obligations of the treaties it has ratified.

2.4.1 Commitment

There are five major factors that bear upon a state's opting to commit or not commit itself to a human rights treaty: its view of the human rights at stake, the band-wagon effect of these treaties, the nature of its regime, the domestic implications of ratifying, and the international regime to which it becomes subject.

---

[47] Christof Heyns and Frans Viljoen, 'The Impact of the United Nations Human Rights Treaties on the Domestic Level' Human Rights Quarterly 23.3 (2001):490. For a study that explores the translation of International Law into local practices see Sally Engle Merry, Human Rights and Gender Violence: translating international law into local justice (Chicago: The University of Chicago Press, 2006) who examines CEDAW.

[48] Tomuschat, *Human Rights: Idealism and Realism*, 97.

The first factor affecting commitment is a state's wish to join in promoting and securing the human rights contained in the treaty. What might be described as the 'culture' of human rights has become firmly entrenched in the international community and in the mores of particular societies. So in many cases we need not search beyond the simple explanation that a state commits itself to a human rights treaty because it embraces the values and goals embodied in the treaty. It is easy to be cynical and to dismiss this sort of explanation as naïve and unworldly. But, given that the UN is a body composed of states, the UN's adoption of declarations, covenants and conventions on human rights would be a complete mystery if a substantial number of states and their representatives were not genuinely committed to human rights. So often a state's ostensible reason for committing itself to a human rights treaty will also be its actual reason: it wants to, or believes it should. However, there are other factors of a more 'realist' nature that can affect whether a state does or does not commit itself to a human rights treaty.

Some states commit to a human rights treaty because they do not want to find themselves on the 'wrong' list of countries and so opt to jump on the human rights band-wagon. Hathaway suggests that many states ratify as a way of publicly manifesting their commitment to human rights. Through ratification they escape the pressure put on them by international actors, so that paradoxically ratifying a human rights treaty can reduce international pressure to promote human rights standards.[49] Through ratification, states reap "expressive" benefits, which reward them 'for positions rather than for effects'.[50]

Commitment also depends on the relative costs and benefits of complying with the treaty.[51] Andrew Moravcsik has discovered, counter intuitively, that potentially unstable democracies or newly established democracies are likely to be the strongest advocates for a binding human rights regime, while established democratic nations and dictatorships are more likely to resist such a regime. The reason is that unstable or recent democracies are keen to preserve their democratic status by tying it into international treaty obligations. More established regimes lack this

[49] Oona A. Hathaway, 'Do Human Rights Treaties Make a Difference?' 112 Yale L.J (2002): 2002-7.

[50] Ibid., 2007 and Beth A. Simmons, Mobilising for Human Rights: International Law in Domestic Politics (NY: Cambridge University Press, 2009): 59.

[51] Oona Hathaway, 'Why do countries commit to human rights treaties?' Conflict Resolution 51.4 (2007): 590.

incentive.[52] Another reason is that, by showing their strong support for international human rights treaties, newly established democracies show to the international community that they are breaking from their past and looking forward to a brighter future where the human rights values will prevail.

The decision whether to ratify can also be affected by the implications of ratification for a state's internal arrangements, that is, by whether the treaty will change its national system of rules, statutes, customs, and judicial decisions. Unlike nonbinding political agreements, treaties may be relevant to judicial processes in the countries that formally accept them. As previously mentioned, some states have 'monist' legal systems in which treaties to which the state is a party become part of the state's domestic law. Governments in these states have to consider not only whether they want the obligations of a treaty to be part of their domestic law, but also how far externally generated treaty law, with its attendant legal concepts, comports with their domestic legal system.[53] From a government's point of view, the incorporation of treaty law in its domestic system may result in more uncertainty as the rules become subject to judicial interpretation and the courts gain greater competence to review administrative actions and to hold governments accountable for their infractions of constitutional or treaty-based human rights. Admittedly, this is likely to be true only in countries in which the rule of the law is generally taken seriously; nonetheless, for a large number of countries, it is essential to think through the implications of an international legal obligation for domestic law.[54]

In many jurisdictions, treaty ratification makes possible the initiation of individual legal claims based on the treaty's substantive guarantees. As a consequence, it encourages lawyers and their clients to express their complaints in terms of the newly established treaty obligations. For that reason, a state may appear to be less respectful of human rights after ratification than it was before. Just as more expansive sexual violence laws are likely to result in statistically higher levels of rape claims, irrespective of whether the actual rate of rape remains constant or declines, so the domestic implementation of treaties involving civil and political rights may create the appearance of an increase in human rights

[52] Andrew Moravcsik, 'The Origins of Human Rights Regimes' International Organisation 54 (2000): 228-9.
[53] Simmons, Mobilising for Human Rights: International Law in Domestic Politics, 72-3.
[54] Ibid., 68&75.

violations.[55] Formal institutional arrangements accompanying ratification are also likely to increase the awareness and documentation of human rights. Ratification of a universal human rights treaty creates a special array of relationships, between a government and the UN treaty system. As a result, the more a country engages with the treaty system, the more its actual human rights record will be exposed.[56] Thus, other things being equal, the smaller the adjustments required by a treaty at the domestic level, the higher the chances of a state's committing to the treaty.

Finally, the comparative weakness of global institutions for the monitoring and enforcement of human rights has a bearing on states' willingness to commit to human rights treaties. That weakness can provide an inducement for states to commit to human rights treaties, since they are unlikely to be held closely to account after ratification. Their ratification, rather than signalling a serious commitment to implementing human rights, may be little more than window dressing. Moreover, these international agreements may at times provide governments with a shield for increasingly repressive behaviours, since treaty ratification confers on them a human rights legitimacy and makes it difficult for others to pressure them for further action. As external pressures decrease, governments often spiral into worse repression after ratification, and the human rights legal regime remains powerless to stop this process.[57] Hathaway has proposed that governments ratify treaties because this allows a costless expression of support for the principles they contain.[58] Because human rights agreements are not effectively monitored, countries will enjoy the "expressive" benefits of ratification "regardless of whether they actually comply with the treaty's requirements".[59]

There are therefore a variety of factors that affect the likelihood of a state's committing to a human rights treaty and, accordingly, states exhibit a variety of forms of conduct in relation to ratification. In her study of the factors affecting whether a state does or does not ratify a human rights treaty, Beth Simmons identifies four different types of state: sincere ratifiers, strategic ratifiers, false positives and false negatives. Sincere

[55] Ryan Goodman and Derek Jinks, 'Measuring the Effects of Human Rights Treaties' EJIL 14(2003), 176.
[56] Heyns and Viljoen, 'The Impact of the United Nations Human Rights Treaties on the Domestic Level', 487-8.
[57] Emilie M. Hafner-Burton, 'Human Rights in a Globalising Word: The Paradox of Empty Promises' American Journal of Sociology 110.5 (2005):1378.
[58] Hathaway, 'Do Human Rights Treaties Make a Difference?', 2007 and Simmons, Mobilising for Human Rights: International Law in Domestic Politics, 59.
[59] Ibid.

ratifiers are states that are genuinely committed to the human rights provided for in a treaty and who fully intend to comply with the obligations they assume through ratification. Strategic ratifiers are those who are less fundamentally committed to the content of the treaty but who ratify for strategic reasons and who also expect to comply for strategic reasons. False positives are states who ratify treaties but who have no genuine intention to remain bound by them. False negatives are states who do not ratify, not because they will not comply with the treaty but because they are already largely in compliance with its obligations and see no point in taking on international treaty obligations to do what they do already. They are 'false negatives' because their failure to commit to a human rights treaty might suggest, falsely, that they stand in a negative relation to the human rights at issue.[60]

2.4.2 Compliance

If commitment need not entail compliance, what are the factors that encourage states to comply with their treaty obligations? There are both international and domestic factors that provide states with incentives to honour the treaty obligations that they have taken on.

We previously noted that an important reason why many states commit themselves to human rights treaties is their genuine commitment to the values embodied in those treaties. They are 'sincere ratifiers'. If that is their reason for ratification, it is also likely to be their reason for compliance. If a state wants to, or believes that it should, participate in the securing and promoting of human rights, it would be odd if that played no part in motivating its compliance with the treaty. Of course, there may be more to its motives than a pure desire to do the right thing. When individual persons engage in 'right conduct', they often do so because they accept that it is the right thing to do, but their compliance might also helped by a concern for their reputation and a reluctance to be seen by others as acting shamefully. Doubtless, a concern to be seen as a well-behaved state and a desire not to incur international opprobrium plays a similar role in helping those who act on behalf of states to comply with treaty obligations.[61]

---

[60] Simmons, Mobilising for Human Rights: International Law in Domestic Politics, 57-9.

[61] George W. Downs and Michael A. Jones 'Reputation, Compliance and International Law' Journal of Legal Studies XXXI (2002): 96, Hathaway, 'Do Human Rights Treaties Make a Difference?'2007 and Simmons, Mobilising for Human Rights: International Law in Domestic Politics, 59.

However, as with commitment, so with compliance, there can also be more instrumental reasons that induce states to comply.

First, a state's failure to comply will provide other states with evidence of its unreliability and so damage its cooperative relationships with other states and reduce their willingness to enter into future agreements with it.[62] According to the traditional theory, a state's general reputation for cooperativeness determines its attractiveness to other states as treaty partners, both now and in the future. Because a defection will bring reputational costs that affect their current and future agreements, states are motivated to comply with their commitments even in circumstances in which they would otherwise defect.[63] Abram and Antonia Chayes believe that the power of reputational concerns to promote compliance is considerable and rivals the deterrent effect of expectations about reciprocal defection: "But in international organisations, as in other political settings, specific reciprocity is not the only or even the most important form of exchange. When a member of an organisation goes back on a commitment, it compromises in some degree its reputation as a reliable partner and jeopardises its ability to continue to reap organisational benefits".[64] Similarly Oran Young argues that the forces of "social opprobium" and "the sense of shame or social disgrace" work to induce treaty compliance.[65]

A state's propensity to comply with human rights treaties is also affected by its domestic politics. For example, a recent study suggests that fully democratic states that ratify the CAT have lower rates of torture than those that have not ratified. Similarly, fully democratic states that ratify the ICCPR have lower rates of violation than those who have not ratified. By contrast, nondemocratic states that ratify have higher rates of violation.[66] Of course, regimes that have not fully embraced human rights norms are not usually willing to parade their non-compliance. They often censor their local media, restrict the number and access of international reporters, and harass or threaten local individuals who might otherwise document violations. After describing these types of practices, sociologist

[62] Downs and Jones 'Reputation, Compliance and International Law', 96.
[63] Ibid., 99.
[64] Ibid., 100.
[65] Abram Chayes and Antonia H. Chayes, The New Sovereignty: Compliance with International Regulatory Agreements (United States of America: Library of Congress, 1995): 273 and Downs and Jones 'Reputation, Compliance and International Law', 100.
[66] Eric Neumayer, 'Do International Human Rights Treaties improve respect for human rights?' Journal of Conflict resolution 49.6 (2005): 926.

Kenneth Bollen concludes, 'ironically, it is possible that a nation which is relatively open may appear lower in human rights and liberties simply because violations are more likely to be reported to the outside world'.[67]

When we turn to factors that might induce states not to comply with their treaty obligations, these again include both domestic and international factors. Domestically, regimes can find respect for human rights 'inconvenient'. If, for example, they want to secure their own position against internal threats of subversion, they may be able to do so more effectively if they are willing to set human rights aside. Once again, it is easier for an undemocratic than for a democratic regime to set aside human rights as suits its purposes and to obscure the fact that it is doing so.

There can also be more prosaic domestic reasons why a state is less than fully compliant with its treaty obligations. International and national systems are not usually synchronised. There is typically a lack of coordination within governments (among departments on the national level, and between national and local levels) in respect of their formal human rights obligations. Domestic NGOs can provide governments with a spur for treaty compliance but their activities might provide a rather patchy check on governments' performance. Making a treaty the exclusive responsibility of a certain government department limits its reach. Existing treaties cover eight areas of human rights but government departments are not usually structured according to those seven areas of obligation and it can be difficult to pinpoint responsibility for a particular treaty obligation. In addition, widespread ignorance of the treaty system in government circles, among lawyers and in civil society around the world, diminishes the impact that the treaties might otherwise have.[68]

Turning to international factors, the most obvious circumstance that is relevant to states' non-compliance is that the international world remains a world of states, each of which considers itself sovereign over its internal affairs and each of which is reluctant to cede that sovereignty to others. States are therefore reluctant to subordinate themselves to any rigorous form of international policing. It is not the case that states can act as completely free agents in the international domain. Nowadays they

---

[67] Kenneth A. Bollen, 'Political Rights and Political Liberties in Nations: An Evaluation of Human Rights Measures, 1950 to 1984' *Human Right Quarterly* 8.4 (1986): 567-591.

[68] Heyns and Viljoen, 'The Impact of the United Nations Human Rights Treaties on the Domestic Level', 517-8.

generally find themselves enmeshed in global governance.[69] Mostly by their own consent, they are parts of international legal regimes that generate diplomatic pressure to conform to human rights standards. While direct international protection or enforcement of human rights is mostly absent, attempts at indirect international implementation of human rights are frequently present.[70] States have been willing to use their sovereignty to restrict their sovereignty in the name of human rights and, in general, the importance of internationally recognised human rights is increasing, and the value placed on full national independence decreasing.[71] Not infrequently, in order to gain internal as well as international legitimacy, governments simply bow to external pressures, following verbally a strong current which they feel they cannot resist.[72] There are instances of sheer hypocrisy, but such a faked attitude of law-compliance is certainly not the norm and should therefore not be depicted as such.[73]

All that said, it remains the case that states have been and remain unwilling to subordinate themselves to an international body that has anything like the authority that domestic governments wield over their populations. The possibility that states should be subjected to international regulation to ensure their compliance with international rules remains a 'hot potato' just because it constitutes a significant challenge to the sovereignty of states.[74] According to David Forsythe, "Most states, in negotiating human rights agreements, do not want authoritative international agreements, do not want authoritative international means of protections".[75] Jurgen Habermas has observed that "the discrepancy between, on the one hand, the human rights content of classical liberties and, on the other hand, their form as positive law, which initially limits them to a nation-state, is just what makes one aware that the discursively grounded 'system of rights' points beyond the constitutional state in the singular toward the

---

[69] Mark W. Zacher, 'The Decaying Pillars of the Westphalian Temple: Implications for International Order and Governance' in James N. Rosenau and Ernst-Otto Czempiel, eds., Governance without Government: Order and Changes in World Politics (Cambridge: Cambridge University Press, 1992): 58-101.

[70] David P. Forsythe, Human Rights in International Relations (Cambridge: Cambridge University Press, 2004): 56.

[71] Ibid.

[72] Tomuschat, Human Rights Between Idealism and Realism, 72.

[73] Ibid.

[74] Hans-Joachim Heintze "The UN Convention and the Network of the International Human Rights Protection by the UN" in Michael Freeman and P. Veerman The Ideologies of Children's Rights (London: Martinus Nijhoff, 1992), 71

[75] David P. Forsythe, Human Rights and World Politics (Lincoln: University of Nebraska Press, 1989): 46.

globalisation of rights".[76] But that globalisation of rights still depends largely upon the good will of states and states are unlikely to disappear from the international scene any time soon. The compliance of states with human rights agreements remains largely a 'good faith' exercise. It is that state of affairs that provides the rationale of this thesis: in the absence of rigorous enforcement mechanisms, how far do states actually comply with the obligations of human rights treaties, such as those that relate to the CRC and OPAC?

For many states, the UN can often seem a remote, invisible and anonymous body, one that speaks in foreign languages, with little knowledge of local conditions and customs. This partly explains the greater popularity of regional systems, which are "closer to home". The Jamaican report[77] refers to a perception that members of the UN committees have no appreciation of local circumstances or difficulties. The UN is seen as distant and it lacks a domestic profile and the discrepancies among the ways in which different committees operate are further confusing.[78]

Such international compliance mechanisms as the UN has established for human rights treaties seem to have had a limited and variable impact. They have taken a number of decades to develop and they are prey to inefficiencies (backlogs, overlaps, vagueness in findings, etc.). Some countries are highly engaged with the system. They submit substantial reports, their NGOs bring individual complaints, etc. For these countries, the implementation system can and does have an impact. However, the system has a very weak hold over other countries. Disengaged countries – those that do not submit reports and ignore recommendations – can largely escape criticism from the treaty system, which is, after all, based on consent. One unfortunate consequence is that those countries that most often end up being singled out as human rights violators are those that are most engaged, while the disengaged escape criticism.[79] This thesis is devoted to examining states' compliance with their reporting obligations as parties to the CRC and OPAC. It examines how far states comply with their obligation to submit reports at particular times and how fully their reports provide the information required by the CRC Committee guidelines. Once we have completed that examination, we shall return, in Chapter 9,

---

[76] Mathieu Deflem, Habermas, Modernity and Law (London: Sage, 1996): 143.

[77] UN Doc. CRC/C/70/Add.15, 2003. Second Periodic Report of Jamaica to the Un Committee on the Rights of the Child.

[78] These are some of the cases that appear to be mentioned by Colombia and Australia in their periodic reports to the CRC Committee. Heyns and Viljoen, 'The Impact of the United Nations Human Rights Treaties on the Domestic Level', 520.

[79] Ibid., 488-9 and 508-10.

to the issue of state compliance in considering how the UN's monitoring systems might be improved.

2.5 NGOs and Human Rights

A decade ago, Antonio Donini, writing about the United Nations, declared that "the Temple of States would be a rather dull place without nongovernmental organisations".[80] His observation was apt and is suggestive of a more general thesis: had NGOs never existed, international law would have played a less vital role in human progress. Although the study of NGOs is not new, they have received much greater attention in recent years by scholars of international law and international relations.

Baldwin together with other legal scholars of his time reflected upon the blossoming of private international associations.[81] In 1908 Wilhelm Kaufmann pointed to three possible purposes of international regulation of non-state international associations:[82] (1) to preserve the international general interest; (2) to effectuate the formation and functioning of non-state international associations; and (3) to ensure that a single state "cannot retard and hinder through state acts or state norms the existence and activity within its competence of the non-state international association".[83]

One fairly new aspect of NGOs is their geographic range. Thirty years ago, many countries lacked significant NGO activity. The range of activity was even smaller 145 years ago when Francis Lieber wrote about the role of associations and found that "all-pervading associative spirit"[84] only in England and America. Today, the associative spirit is nearly universal.

---

[80] Antonio Donin, 'The Bureaucracy and the Free Spirits: Stagnation and Innovation in the Relationship Between the UN and NGOs' Third Wold Quarterly 16.3 (1995): 421-439.

[81] In 1907 Simeon E. Baldwin observed that "we shall commonly find that the initiative has been found in individual action, prompted by considerations sometime commercial, sometimes scientific or philosophic, sometime altruistic. So, and for similar reasons, it has often been found that he public progress of moment to the world has been the immediate consequence of a private progress". Simeon E. Baldwin, The International Congress and Conferences of the Last Century as Forces Working Toward the Solidarity of the World, AJIL 1.3 (1907): 565, 576.

[82] Steve Charnovitz, 'Non-governmental Organisations and International Law' The American Journal of International Law 100.2 (2006): 349.

[83] Ibid.

[84] Francis Lieber, On Civil Liberty and Self-Government (http://files.libertyfund.org/files/1943/Lieber_1382_EBk_v5.pdf 129, 10/11/2010).

As the UN's provisions for human rights have developed, so has the number of NGOs concerned to promote human rights. NGOs and their advocacy of human rights ideas are directed both to the creation and application of human rights norms. Thus, when we talk of 'regulating human rights', we cannot now refer only to formal political and legal bodies, such as the state, the United Nations, or the structures and institutions of international law. Non-governmental organisations and global social movements are beginning to form an increasingly important sector, both as spokespersons for citizens' demands, and as respected advisors to policy-makers. This is not to say that nation-state politics are either dead or insignificant. It is fair to say that the shift away from nation-state-based politics towards these global, issue-based concerns reflects a growing awareness among people that the things which most directly affect our lives are not, in most cases, those which fall into the restricted politics of the nation-state; rather, they are matters that transcend the nation-state and that impact upon the entire globe, regardless of borders.[85]

There are perhaps 250 private organisations[86] consistently active across borders that take as their raison d'etre the advocacy of some part of the international law of human rights and/or humanitarian affairs on a global basis.[87]

The oldest and best-funded human rights NGOs are based in the west and concern themselves primarily with civil and political rights in peace time and international humanitarian law in war or similar situations. Western societies have manifested the civil rights, private wealth, leisure time and value structures that allow for the successful operation of major human rights NGOs. To advocate human rights via a truly independent and dynamic NGO, there must be respect for civil rights and a civil society to start with. With the spread of liberal democracy and more open societies following the Cold War, one might have expected that the number of NGOs concerned with human rights would have increased but, relative to the total number of NGOs active in international relations, their number

---

[85] O' Byrne, Human Rights: An Introduction, 94.

[86] They are also called relief or development agencies as well as PVOs (private voluntary agencies) or VOLAGs (Voluntary agencies). A classic example is Oxfam. These actors are crucial especially for grass roots action that directly or indirectly attends to social and economic rights. Forsythe, Human Rights in International Relations, 163.

[87] Jackie Smith, Ron Pagnucco and George A. Lopez, 'Globalizing Human Rights: the work of Transnational Human Rights NGOs in the 1990s' Human Rights Quarterly 20. 2 (1998): 379-412.

has remained rather stable.[88] NGOs may be involved in promoting human rights, either generally or with a focus on a specific issue. A framework exists for the participation of NGOs in many UN human rights mechanisms, such as the granting of consultative status with ECOSOC, which allows them to participate in the Commission on Human Rights. Both international and national NGOs follow the work of the treaty bodies closely and most of the treaty bodies provide an opportunity for them to make an input into the reporting process through the submission of, for example, additional information relating to the implementation of the treaties in a particular country (sometimes referred to as "shadow" or "parallel reports").

In theory, the CESCR Committee has granted official standing to NGOs. According to Article 69 of its Rules of Procedure, NGOs are free to make submissions to the Committee 'that might contribute to full and universal recognition and realisation of the rights contained in the Covenant'. Likewise, the CAT Committee, the Committee Against Torture (Rules of Procedure, Rule 62), the CEDAW Committee (Rules of Procedure, Rule 47), the Committee on the Elimination of Discrimination against Women (Rules of Procedure, Rule 47), and Committee on Migrant Workers (Rules of Procedure, Rule 28) grant NGOs some right of participation to provide written information and even make oral statements.[89]

In reality, links between NGOs and treaty bodies vary among the committees. Neither CERD nor CAT has pre-sessional working groups that meet with NGOs, nor (formal or informal) meetings with NGOs scheduled during the time period of the session. They meet NGOs on an ad-hoc basis, either as individual members in the case of CAT, or in the case of CERD over lunch-times when few members attend and others refuse to go systematically. CERD has also ceased its former practice of soliciting information from NGOs.

CESCR permits NGOs to speak at an open meeting on the first day of the session for which there are no summary records. The Committee permits NGOs to use the time to speak about states which are not on the agenda for the session, and outside the context of a state report. In the past, states parties have sometimes not been informed such submissions have been scheduled, although such submissions have led to specific requests from the Committee to states parties.

While CEDAW does not formally solicit information from NGOs, it sets aside time to meet with NGOs both during the pre-session working

---

[88] Margaret E. Keck and Kathryn Sikkink, Activities beyond Borders: Advocacy Networks in International Politics (Ithaca: Cornell University Press, 1998): 11.

[89] Tomuschat, Human Rights Between Idealism and Realism, 184.

group and on the second day of the session. It also has a close working relationship with a number of international women's NGOs which closely follow the work of the Committee, and with UNICEF which has characterised the Convention as a fundamental charter for its own work. NGOs routinely submit shadow reports which relate to Convention articles, and women from the national level frequently attend the actual dialogue with the assistance of leading international NGOs, such as International Women's Rights Action Watch (IWRAW)-Asia Pacific, together with United Nations Development Fund for Women (UNIFEM).[90]The CRC is the only Convention, though, that has included the participation of NGOs in its principles, hence, is the only Committee with the closest working relationship with NGOs.

There are differences in the way in which the treaty bodies treat NGO information. In practice, NGO information has been most helpful to the treaty bodies when: a) it has been prepared through some degree of coordination or coalition-building at the national level, b) international NGOs have endeavoured to play a facilitator's role: alerting national NGOs to reporting expectations of the state party, providing information about the treaty's substantive requirements and procedural rules, and encouraging and facilitating the direct participation by national level NGOs, c) efforts have been made to follow committee or other guidelines on the preparation of NGO "shadow" reports, particularly tailoring information to the provisions of the treaty, and suggesting concrete proposals, both with respect to questions for the lists of issues or dialogue and recommendations for specific future national action.[91]

The truth remains that both international and national NGOs also have an important role in following up on implementation of recommendations contained in treaty bodies' concluding observations at the national level and in promoting national public debate on human rights implementation during the report writing process and afterwards. NGOs have also made an important contribution to promoting the ratification of the human rights treaties worldwide.[92] An analysis and assessment of the role of NGOs in relation to the rights of children in war and armed conflict will therefore be conducted in Chapter 8.

---

[90] Anne. F. Bayefsky, 'The Human Rights Treaty System: Universality at the Crossroads' (http://www.bayefsky.com/report/finalreport.pdf, 15 September 2009): 4.
[91] Ibid., 48.
[92] Office of the United Nations: High Commissioner for Human Rights, 'Fact Sheet No.30. The United Nations Human Rights Treaty System: An Introduction to the core human rights treaties and the treaty bodies': 51.

CHAPTER THREE

THE RIGHTS OF THE CHILD: THE HISTORICAL AND CONTEMPORARY CONTEXT

3.1 Introduction

The Convention on the Rights of the Child (CRC) adopted in 1989 gave international recognition to children's rights. This chapter looks at how these rights have evolved since the early twentieth century. The chapter is divided into four sections. The first section examines the evolution of children's rights as part of Human Rights Law. Children's rights in armed conflict and the application of International Humanitarian Law is examined in the second section. The third section examines the two International Treaties, the CRC and its Optional Protocol on the Participation of Children in Armed Conflict. The last section looks at the post 1989 developments of the UN, General Assembly, Security Council and the International Criminal Court (ICC) in relation to the protection of children's rights.

3.2 The Evolution of Children's Rights

The UN gave its fullest recognition of children's rights with the drafting of the United Nations Convention on the Rights of the Child in 1979, which was named as United Nation's Year of the Child.[1] On the eve of the 1979, the government of Poland took the lead and formally proposed a draft text for a Convention, which was essentially the 1959 Declaration of the Rights of the Child with the addition of legal text on implementation of the ten-point-declaration.[2]

---

[1] United Nations Special Session on Children (8-10 May 2002) http://www.unicef.org/specialsession/rights/path.htm.
[2] Ibid.

However the adoption of the CRC was the culmination of a long history of international concern with children's rights. This section describes a series of instruments relating to children, some aimed directly at children caught up in an armed conflict and others aimed at children more generally. This shows clearly that children's rights have been in the minds of regional and international drafting bodies since the end of the First World War. Children's rights have been recognised in both 'declarations' and 'conventions'. These two sorts of documents are significantly different in nature. The most crucial difference relates to implementation, as a declaration is understood as a recommendation or a moral guideline, while a convention has a more binding character and demands an active decision on the part of individual states to ratify it.[3] Thus, a mechanism for monitoring a nation's compliance is usually an integral part of a Convention.[4]

The International Convention for the Suppression of the Traffic in Woman and Children 1922 can be regarded as the first instrument to incorporate measures for the protection of trafficked children and to punish those accused of being engaged or having attempted to commit such a crime.[5] In the same year, the International Council of Women (ICW)[6], in response to resolutions of the Women's Councils of Italy and the United States requesting the formulation of a Children's Rights Charter with minimum rights for children of all countries, produced a Charter that consisted of seven sections, each divided into a number of paragraphs. The Charter covered a wide range of topics, such as *Prenatal*

---

[3] Lassa Oppenheim and Ronald Roxburgh International Law (Lawbook Exchange Ltd, 2006) p. 665, Charon Detrick, Jaap Doek, The United Nations Convention on the Rights of the Child: A Guide to the Travaux Preparatoires (Martinus Nijhoff, 1992) p.49.

[4] 'Convention on the Rights of the Child' Population and Development Review 15 (1989): 779.

[5] The International Convention for the Suppression of the Traffic in Women and Children was adopted on 30 September 192, enetered into force on 15 June 1922. 'The International Convention for the Suppression of the Traffic in Women and Children' articles 2-3 (http://www.vilp.de/Enpdf/e158.pdf , 10 October 2009).

[6] The International Council of Women (ICW) was founded in 1888 in Seneca Falls (NY) as an umbrella organisation for women's movements. The ICW enjoys consultative status with the UN and its Permanent Representatives to: ECOSOC, ILO, FAO, WHO, UNDP, ENEP, UNESCO, UNICEF, UNCTAD, UNIDO, etc. 'International Council of Women' Global Hand (http://www.globalhand.org/data /organisation.2007-06-30.7154102560/, 12 September 2009).

Care (Section I)[7], *Care of mothers and children up to school age (Section II)*[8], *Children of School Age (Section III)*[9], *Children in Employment (Section IV)*. Paragraphs 1 and 2 of section IV demanded "prohibition of the employment of boys and girls under eighteen at night and in dangerous trades," which corresponds to the fifth and sixth Convention of the International Labour Organisation (ILO). The other subjects discussed concern 'Delinquent Children' (Section V)[10], 'Children born out of wedlock' and 'Children of aliens to different countries'. The latter two subjects proved to be so controversial that no consensus was reached on them; therefore no reference to them was made in the Charter.[11] The content of this Charter shows that the ICW showed great interest in the authorities' initiatives and financial investments for the improvement of children's quality of life.

Two year's later in 1924, the Declaration of Geneva, also known otherwise as the Declaration of the Rights of the Child, was adopted by the Fifth Assembly of the League of Nations. The Declaration was the first international document entirely devoted to the protection of children's rights and recognised a more extensive list of children's rights than the previous document.[12] According to the Declaration, children's normal

[7] Section I aimed to prevent the spread of venereal diseases leading to degeneration and also demanded that the causes of mother and child mortality be explained. Philip E. Veerman, The Rights of the Child and the Changing Image of Childhood (Netherlands: Martinus Nijhoff, 1992): 326.

[8] Section II, Care of mothers and children up to school age, demands, among other things, treatment of eye diseases in order to prevent infantile blindness that pertains to the conservative mode of the physical subsystem And (Convalescent homes) holiday homes for mothers and young children who need to regain strength belongs in the integrative mode of the physical subsystem. For the first time in 1922 importance is attached to play and recreation under the guidance of professional teachers. Play is classifiable in the expressive mode of the personality subsystem. Recreation relates to the adaptive mode of the personality subsystem. Veerman, *The Rights of the Child and the Changing Image of Childhood,* 327.

[9] The main concern of Section III, is the physical health and education.

[10] Demands provisions preventing the delinquent, abnormal, defective and neglected child from drifting into crime. Ibid.

[11] Ibid.

[12] Tabatha Abu El-Haj and Carolyn Hamilton, 'Armed Conflict: The Protection of Children under International Law' The International Journal of Children's Rights 5 (1997) and D, Hodgson, 'The Historical Development and 'internationalisation' of the Children's Rights Movement' *Australian Journal of Family Law* 6 (1992): 260-261.

development required both material and spiritual involvement[13], and they must be protected against every form of exploitation[14] and be the first to receive relief in times of distress.[15]

In 1938 the International Conference of the Red Cross asked the International Committee of the Red Cross to cooperate with the International Union for Child Welfare to study the possibility of providing protection for children under a convention, and in 1939 they produced a draft Convention for the Protection of Children in Emergency and Armed Conflict. Although the draft was accepted on 12 January 1939, the work to secure its adoption was overtaken by the outbreak of World War Two.[16]

It was not until 24 October 1945 and the establishment of the United Nations that human rights were fully recognised as universal rights. The 51 initial country members of the UN accepted the Charter of the United Nations which contains not only the guiding principles of the organisation but also very important human rights provisions. According to the Charter, one of the many roles of the UN is "to save succeeding generations from the scourge of war".[17] Human rights are conceived as universal rights that belong to people by virtue of their being human, encompassing civil, political, economic, social and cultural rights and freedoms, and are based on the notion of personal dignity and human worth. Articles 1, 2 and 3 of the Universal Declaration of Human Rights (1948) states that 'all human beings are born free and equal in dignity and rights' are 'entitled to all the rights and freedoms set forth in the Declaration, without discrimination of any kind' and 'have the right to life, liberty and security of person'. [18] In particular, Article 25 (2) states that 'Motherhood and childhood are entitled to special care and assistance' and that 'all children, whether in or

[13]Article 1 of the Geneva Declaration of the Rights of the Child, adopted on 26 September 1924, League of Nations. 'Geneva Declaration of the Rights of the Child' *UN Document: Gathering a Body of Global Agreements(* http://www.un-documents.net/gdrc1924.htm, 8 September 2009).

[14] Ibid., Article 4.

[15] Ibid., Article 3.

[16] Geraldine Van Bueren, 'The International Legal Protection of Children in Armed Conflict' International Comparative Law Quarterly 43 (1994): 811.

[17] The Charter of the United Nations was signed on 26 June 1945 and came into force on 24 October 1945. The Charter of the United Nations, 'Preamble of the Charter of the United Nations' The United Nations (http://www.hrweb.org/legal/unchart.html, 19 August 2009).

[18] On December 10, 1948 resolution 217A (III) the General Assembly of the United Nations adopted and proclaimed the Universal Declaration of Human Rights (UDHR) 'The Universal Declaration of Human Rights' The United Nations (http://www.un.org/en/documents/udhr/, 5 August 2009).

out of wedlock, shall enjoy the same social protection'[19] and should be among its beneficiaries by giving them 'the right to special care and assistance'.[20] In Article 26 (3) parents are given the right to choose the kind of education that their children shall receive.[21] Although the UDHR does recognise children as possessors of human rights, it does not go into much detail.

The 1959 Declaration on the Rights of the Child, in its preamble acknowledges the principles of the Geneva Declaration (1924) and their recognition by the UDHR and the specialised agencies and international organisations concerned with children's welfare and proclaims the rights and freedoms set forth in this Declaration to promote a happy childhood.[22] The Declaration contains ten principles that have been universally accepted as being applicable to all children as "…mankind owes to the child the best it has to give".[23] The ten principles do provide a broader and strengthened range of rights for the protection of children. Specifically Principle 8 of the Declaration provides: "The child shall in all circumstances be amongst the first to receive protection and relief"[24] and "shall not be subject of any form of traffic".[25]

The 1966 International Covenant on Economic, Social and Cultural Rights[26] and the International Covenant on Civil and Political Rights[27] provide in greater detail the rights that individuals and nations have. In

---

[19] Ibid., Article 25 (2).

[20] Ibid., Article 25.

[21] Ibid., Article 26 (3).

[22] The Declaration of the Rights of the Child (1959) was drafted by the UN Commission on Human Rights and adopted by the General Assembly of the UN on 20 November 1959. U.N. Doc. A/4354, 'Declaration of the Rights of the Child (1959)' The Circumcision Reference Library (http://www.cirp.org/library/ethics/UN-declaration/, 7 July 2009).

[23] Ibid., Preamble.

[24] Ibid., Principle 8.

[25] Ibid., Principle 9.

[26] International Covenant on Economic, Social and Cultural Rights (ICESCR). Adopted and opened for signature, ratification and accession by General Assembky resolution 2200A (XXI) of 16 December 1966. Entered into force 3 January 1976, in accordance with article 27.

[27] International Covenenant on Civil and Political Rights (ICCPR). Adopted and opened for signature, ratification and accession by General Assembky resolution 2200A (XXI) of 16 December 1966. Entered into force 3 January 1976, in accordance with article 49.

addition, both Covenants[28] have measures that guarantee children's rights and prohibit any type of discrimination[29] against them as well as their exploitation.[30]

The 1974 Declaration on the Protection of Women and Children in Emergency and Armed Conflict came into existence as a result of the increasing suffering of women and children who in situations of emergency or armed conflict are "too often the victims of inhuman acts"[31] as "grave attacks are still being made on fundamental freedoms and the dignity of the human person and colonial and racist foreign domination Powers continue to violate international humanitarian law".[32]

The adoption of the 1989 Convention on the Rights of the Child can be seen as a natural consequence of these earlier developments, for the Convention is designed to shed light onto some of the grey areas when basic human rights are applied to the realities of childhood. It marks the culmination of a long legislative process initiated by the Polish government in 1978.[33] In short, the Convention establishes a legal framework that

---

[28] The 'covenant' is a binding agreement between states; used synonymously with Convention and Treaty. Nancy Flowers, 'Human Rights Here and Now: Celebrating the Universal Declaration of Human Rights' (http://www1.umn.edu/humanrts/edumat/hreduseries/hereandnow/Part-5/6_glossary.htm, 10 July 2009).

[29] ICCPR, Article 24 (1) states "Every child shall have, without any discrimination as to race, colour, sex, language, religion, national or social origin, property or birth, the right to such measures of protection as are required by his status as a minor, on the part of his family, society and the State".

[30] ICESCR, Article 10 (3) states that "Special measures of protection and assistance should be taken on behalf of all children and young persons without any discrimination for reasons of parentage or other conditions. Children and young persons should be protected from economic and social exploitation. Their employment in work harmful to their morals or health or dangerous to life or likely to hamper their normal development should be punishable by law. States should also set age limits below which the paid employment of child labour should be prohibited and punishable by law".

[31] Declaration on the Protection of Women and Children in Emergency and Armed Conflict was proclaimed by the General Assembly resolution 3318(XXIX) of 14 December 1974. 'Declaration on the Protection of Women and Children in Emergency and Armed Conflict' *Office of the United Nations High Commissioner for Human Rights* (http://www2.ohchr.org/english/law/protectionwomen.htm, 10 April 2009).

[32] Ibid.

[33] Francois Krill, 'The Protection of Children in Armed Conflict', in Michael Freeman and Philip Veerman (ed.), The Ideologies of Children's Rights (London: Martinus Nijhoff, 1992): 347.

greatly extends the previous recognition of children as the direct holders of rights and acknowledges their distinct legal personality.

3.3 International Humanitarian Law and Armed Conflict

Another area of international law that relates to the protection of children in armed conflict is International Humanitarian Law. The relevant Treaty sources are the 1949 four Geneva Conventions and their Additional Protocols of 1977. For non-international armed conflicts, article 3, common[34] to all the Geneva Conventions, and the 1977 Additional Protocol II are the only instruments in force.[35] The Four Geneva Conventions and their Additional Protocols are the most important International Humanitarian Law treaties (IHL). IHL, otherwise known as the law of armed conflict, is the body of international law, which governs the conduct of war, for it sets out the parameters of what is legally permissible during hostilities. It also regulates the treatment of people who are not, or who are no longer, in time of war participating in hostilities (e.g. prisoners of war or injured

[34] Art. 3. In the case of armed conflict not of an international character occurring in the territory of one of the High Contracting Parties, each Party to the conflict shall be bound to apply, as a minimum, the following provisions:(1) Persons taking no active part in the hostilities, including members of armed forces who have laid down their arms and those placed hors de combat by sickness, wounds, detention, or any other cause, shall in all circumstances be treated humanely, without any adverse distinction founded on race, colour, religion or faith, sex, birth or wealth, or any other similar criteria. To this end, the following acts are and shall remain prohibited at any time and in any place whatsoever with respect to the above-mentioned persons: (a) violence to life and person, in particular murder of all kinds, mutilation, cruel treatment and torture; (b) taking of hostages; (c) outrages upon personal dignity, in particular humiliating and degrading treatment; (d) the passing of sentences and the carrying out of executions without previous judgement pronounced by a regularly constituted court, affording all the judicial guarantees which are recognized as indispensable by civilized peoples. (2) The wounded and sick shall be collected and cared for. An impartial humanitarian body, such as the International Committee of the Red Cross, may offer its services to the Parties to the conflict. The Parties to the conflict should further endeavour to bring into force, by means of special agreements, all or part of the other provisions of the present Convention. The application of the preceding provisions shall not affect the legal status of the Parties to the conflict. 'Common Article 3' ICRC (http://www.icrc.org/Web/eng/siteeng0.nsf/htmlall/genevaconventions#a1, 15 May 2009).

[35] 'International Humanitarian Law and International Human Rights Law: Similarities and Differences' ICRC (http://www.icrc.org/Web/Eng/siteeng0.nsf/htmlall/57JR8L/$File/IHL_and_IHRL.pdf, 15 June 2009).

soldiers).[36] These treaties still apply to today's warfare[37], even though they were drafted and adopted soon after the end of the World War II.

The First Geneva Convention refers to the protection and treatment of the members of the armed forces who are wounded or sick in the field.[38] The Second Convention refers to the protection and treatment of the members of the armed forces who are shipwrecked or wounded and sick at sea.[39] The Third Convention deals with prisoners of war and how they should be treated and protected.[40] Finally, the main function of the Fourth Geneva Convention[41] is "to protect a strictly defined category of civilians from arbitrary action on the part of the enemy, and not from the dangers

---

[36] Rachel Harvey 'Children and Armed Conflict: A guide to International Humanitarian and Human Rights Law' Children and Armed Conflict Unit (http://www.essex.ac.uk/armedcon/story_id/000044.pdf, 10 July 2009): 6.

[37] 194 States have acceded the Geneva Conventions, which signifies their universal acceptance. 'The Geneva Conventions of 1949' ICRC (http://www.icrc.org/Web/eng/siteeng0.nsf/htmlall/genevaconventions#a1, 15 May 2009).

[38] Geneva Convention I for the Amelioration of the Condition of the Wounded and Sick people in Armed Forces in the Field. Adopted pn 12 August 1949 by the Diplomatic Conference for the Establishment of International Conventions for the Protection of Victims of War, held in Geneva from 21 April to 12 August 1949. Entry into force 21 October 1950. (http://www.icrc.org/ihl.nsf/7c4d08d9b287a42141256739003e636b/fe20c3d903ce27e3c125641e004a92f3, 15 May 2009).

[39] Convention II for the Amelioration of the Condition of Wounded, Sick and Shipwrecked Members of the Armed Forces at Sea. Adopted on 12 August 1949. by the Diplomatic Conference for the Establishment of International Conventions for the Protection of Victims of War, held in Geneva from 21 April to 12 August 1949. Entry into force 21 October 1950. (http://www.icrc.org/ihl.nsf/7c4d08d9b287a42141256739003e636b/44072487ec4c2131c125641e004a9977 , 15 May 2009).

[40] Convention III relative to the Treatment of Prisoners of War. Adopted on 12 August 1949. by the Diplomatic Conference for the Establishment of International Conventions for the Protection of Victims of War, held in Geneva from 21 April to 12 August 1949. Entry into force 21 October 1950. (http://www.icrc.org/ihl.nsf/7c4d08d9b287a42141256739003e636b/6fef854a3517b75ac125641e004a9e68, 15 May 2009).

[41] Convention IV relative to the Protection of Civilian Persons in Time of War. Adopted on 12 August 1949. by the Diplomatic Conference for the Establishment of International Conventions for the Protection of Victims of War, held in Geneva from 21 April to 12 August 1949. Entry into force 21 October 1950 (http://www.icrc.org/ihl.nsf/7c4d08d9b287a42141256739003e636b/6756482d86146898c125641e004aa3c5 , 15 May 2009).

due to military operations themselves".[42] Children are among those considered in need of special protection due to their inherent weakness. Article 24 makes specific reference to children "under fifteen, who are orphaned or are separated from their families as a result of the war"[43]; they are not to be left alone and are to be protected by the Parties to the conflict. However, this protection does not extend to children over fifteen. Furthermore, Convention IV makes reference to more than one age group and the rights they should enjoy. For instance, children under seven have an additional right to be with their mothers, if in such a safety zone[44], while an occupying power may not compel a child under the age of eighteen to work[45] or pronounce the death penalty against a protected person who committed an offence while under the age of eighteen[46]

Here, it should be acknowledged that in the 1930s and 1940s there were attempts to draft a separate instrument of IHL relating to children[47], however, it was decided that provisions for the protection of children should be incorporated into the Fourth Geneva Convention rather than push for a Fifth Convention. Pictet, in his comment at of the Fourth Convention, says little about the fate of this Fifth Convention but hints at the need for compromise throughout the negotiation process.[48] There is no doubt that the failure to obtain a separate Fifth Convention has had serious consequences for children caught up in armed conflict. The specific and very different needs of children, instead, have been subsumed into the general need for protection of the civilian population.

After nine years of negotiations (1968-1977), the two Additional Protocols to the Geneva Convention came into existence. Their development coincided with the bitter experience of the Vietnam War, the use of new weapons of war and the ongoing suffering of the civilians who fought in the name of self-determination.[49]

---

[42] Abu El-Haj and Hamilton, 'Armed Conflict: the Protection of Children Under International Law'.

[43] Convention IV relative to the Protection of Civilian Persons in Time of War, Art. 24.

[44] Ibid., Article 14.

[45] Ibid., Art 51.

[46] Ibid., Art. 68.

[47] Krill , ' The Protection of Children of Children in Armed Conflict', 350.

[48] Jean Pictet, Development and Principles of International Humanitarian Law (Lancaster: Martinus Nijhoff, 1985).

[49] Abu El-Haj and Hamilton 'Armed Conflict: The Protection of children under International Law', 17.

The adoption of the Additional Protocol I marked a development of the law of armed conflict[50] as it widened the protection afforded to civilians and applied to international conflicts and granted protection to all civilians. Previously, protection had been given only to specific categories of protected persons, while now the whole civilian population was granted protection from the conduct of hostilities.[51]

Protocol I has set two main requirements for the protection of civilians. First, at all times fighting parties must distinguish between combatants and civilians and between military objectives and civilian objects.[52] Second, civilians and civilian objects shall not be the object of attack.[53] The only legal targets of attack are military objectives, which are "those objects which by their nature, location, purpose or use make an effective contribution to military action and whose total or partial destruction, capture or neutralisation, in the circumstance ruling at the time offers a definite military advantage".[54]

Protocol I also incorporates protective measures for children in times of international conflict. They should be the object of special respect and should be protected from any form of indecent assault. In addition, it is the responsibility of the Parties to the conflict to provide them with the care and aid that they require.[55] Moreover, Protocol I is the first binding international document that addresses the issue of child soldiers, for it sets the minimum age of 15 for recruitment by armed forces and for the direct participation of children in hostilities.[56]

---

[50] Protocol Additional to the Geneva Convention of 12 August 1949, relating to the Protection of Victims of International Armed Conflicts (Protocol I), 8 June 1977 (http://www.icrc.org/ihl.nsf/7c4d08d9b287a42141256739003e636b/f6c8b9fee14a77fdc125641e0052b079, 15 May 2009).

[51] Such protection does not exist in either Hague Law or the Fourth Geneva Convention. The only protection from hostilities afforded to the civilian population in traditional Hague Law are to be found in 1907 Hague Convention IV, Respecting the Laws and Customs of War on Land and its annexed Regulations, in which there are a few provisions. Abu El-Haj and Hamilton 'Armed Conflict: The Protection of children under International Law', 18 footnote 41.

[52] Additional Protocol I to the Geneva Convention, Art 52 (1) and Art 52 (3).

[53] Ibid.

[54] Ibid., Art 53 (2).

[55] Ibid., Art77 (1).

[56] Ibid., Art 77 (2) "The Parties to the conflict shall take all feasible measures in order that children who have not attained the age of fifteen years do not take a direct part in hostilities and, in particular, they shall refrain from recruiting them into their armed forces. In recruiting among those persons who have attained the age of fifteen years but who have not attained the age of eighteen years, the Parties

Unlike Protocol I, Protocol II applies in non-international armed conflicts and addresses mainly the conduct of parties in an armed conflict as defined in Article 1[57] and provides some protection to civilian population as stated in Common Article 3. It is the first time, since Common Article 3 of the Geneva Conventions, that protection was granted in internal armed conflicts, which was a significant development in the law.

Furthermore, Protocol II is the first humanitarian law that addresses children as children. Article 4 (3) states that children are entitled to be provided with the care and aid that they require. In particular, children have the right to education[58], to be reunited with their families when they have been temporary separated[59] and to be removed from conflict zones to safer areas in the country.[60] Of great significance is the fact that Protocol II does recognise the need for children under the age of 15 to be protected from being recruited by both government and opposition armed groups.[61]

---

to the conflict shall endeavour to give priority to those who are oldest". And Article 77 (3) "If, in exceptional cases, despite the provisions of paragraph 2, children who have not attained the age of fifteen years take a direct part in hostilities and fall into the power of an adverse Party, they shall continue to benefit from the special protection accorded by this Article, whether or not they are prisoners of war".

[57] Article 1 states that Protocol II applies to all conflicts, which are not covered by Protocol I, that take place in the territory of a State that is party to the Protocol, between its armed forces and rebel armed forces or other organised groups. Non-governmental groups must be under responsible command and exercise enough control over part of the State's territory as to enable them to, firstly, carry out sustained and concerted military operations, and second to implement Protocol II. There are therefore internal conflicts in which both Common article 3, discussed above, and Protocol II apply, and internal conflicts in which only Common Article 3 applies. In particular, Common Article 3 does not require State armed forces to be involved in the conflict, unlike Protocol II, and it is applicable at a much lower level of intensity e.g. non-government forces do not need to be in control of the territory. Protocol Additional to the Genaeva Conventions of 12 August 1949, and relating to the Protection of Victims of Non-International Armed Conflicts (Protocol II), 8 June 1977.
(http://www.icrc.org/ihl.nsf/7c4d08d9b287a42141256739003e636b/d67c3971bcff1c10c125641e0052b545, 15 May 2009).

[58] Ibid., Art 4 (3)a.

[59] Ibid., Art 4 (3)b.

[60] Ibid., Art 4 (3)e.

[61] Ibid., Art 4 (3)c.

3.4 The Convention on the Rights of the Child and its Protocols

The Convention on the Rights of the Child (CRC) and the Optional Protocol to the Convention on the Involvement of Children in Armed Conflict (OPAC), are the perfect example of the overlap between IHL and HR law, as they incorporate both bodies of law.

Both IHL and HR Law strive to protect the lives, health and dignity of individuals, though from different angles. For example, the two bodies of law aim to protect human life, prohibit torture or cruel treatment, prescribe basic rights for persons subject to a criminal justice process, prohibit discrimination, make provision for the protection of women and children, and regulate aspects of the right to food and health. On the other hand, IHL deals with many issues that are outside the purview of human rights law, such as the conduct of hostilities, combatant and prisoner of war status and the protection of the Red Cross and Red Crescent emblems. Similarly, human rights law deals with aspects of life in peacetime that are not regulated by IHL, such as freedom of the press, the right to assembly, to vote and to strike.[62] Nevertheless, HR Law also applies in conflict situations that fall below the level of armed conflict, the threshold of which can be difficult to determine.[63]

The final draft of the CRC was produced in 1988 and submitted to the Commission on Human Rights for approval in 1989. It was finally adopted by the General Assembly in November 1989 and entered into force in 1990. The CRC has been ratified by 192 countries and is the most widely ratified international treaty. Due to its binding obligations for the individual States that ratify it and an integral monitoring mechanism that strengthens Conventions existing powers,[64] the Convention establishes a legal framework that greatly extends the previous recognition of children as the direct holders of rights and acknowledges their distinct legal personality.

The rights listed cover the broad spectrum of children's needs and aspirations. Its 54 articles, some 40 of which are concerned with substantive rights, cover civil, political, economic and social issues. Unlike other international human rights treaties, notably the International Covenant on Civil and Political Rights (ICCPR) and the International Covenant on

---

[62] 'International Humanitarian Law and International Human Rights Law: Similarities and differences'.

[63] Jenny Kuper, Military Training and Children in Armed Conflict: Law, Policy and Practice (Netherlands: Martinus Nijhoff Publishers, 2005): 21.

[64] 'Convention on the Rights of the Child', 779.

Economic, Social and Cultural Rights (ICESCR), the Convention contains both sets of rights in one single document. The Convention applies to 'every human being below the age of eighteen years'[65], and by including all the traditional civil and political rights, such as freedom of expression[66], religion[67], association and assembly[68], it departs radically from the earlier international documents which primarily aimed to address children's immaturity and need for care. By including children's social welfare rights, the Convention also emphasises that states must not only protect children and safeguard their fundamental freedoms, but also devote resources to ensuring that they realise their potential for maturing into a healthy and happy adulthood.

Furthermore, the Convention contains provisions specifically related to armed conflict (Articles 38, 39). Article 38 is significant because it brings together humanitarian law and human rights law, showing their complementarity. Its provisions require that State Parties undertake to respect and to ensure respect for rules of international humanitarian law applicable to children in armed conflicts, and paragraph 4 states that: "In accordance with their obligations under international humanitarian law to protect the civilian population in armed conflict, States Parties shall take all feasible measures to ensure protection and care of children who are affected by an armed conflict".

On the other hand, a major controversy in drafting the Convention focused on the issue of participation that can be exacted from children in armed conflicts. The controversy ended with a compromise: states should not recruit anyone under age 15 into armed forces. If the Convention on the Rights of the Child were to be fully implemented during armed conflicts, this would go a long way towards protecting children. Children's right to special protection in these situations has long been recognised. The Convention has no general derogation clause and, in light of this, the Committee on the Rights of the Child stresses that the most positive interpretation be adopted with a view to ensuring the widest possible respect for children's rights. In particular the Committee has stressed that, in view of the essential nature of article 2, 3 and 4, they do not admit any kind of derogation (A/49/41).

---

[65] Unless the age of majority is attained earlier. 'Convention on the Rights of the Child', Article 1.
[66] Ibid., Art. 13.
[67] Ibid., Art. 14.
[68] Ibid., Art. 15.

There is an issue of what age some of these rights (e.g. freedom of expression) become effective for children, but the Committee takes no view on this.

The role of the Committee on the Rights of the Child, mentioned above, pursuant to Article 43 of then Convention, when formed was to review reports submitted at regular interval by States Parties and to make recommendations on how States can better implement the Convention's provisions. After the adoption of the two Optional Protocols – Optional Protocol on the Sale of Children, Child Prostitution and Child Pornography[69] and the Optional Protocol on the Involvement of Children in Armed Conflict – the Committee's mandate was extended to include monitoring the implementation of these treaties.

3.4.1 The Optional Protocols

Ten years after the CRC came into force, the General Assembly adopted the OPAC (May 2000), which came into force on 12 February 2002. The Optional Protocol (OPAC) was adopted as a response to the widespread phenomenon of children's recruitment and use by states and non-state armed groups all over the world. Significantly, OPAC raised the minimum age from 15 years to 18 years of age for both compulsory and voluntary recruitment and deployment by (non) state forces. A detailed analysis of both CRC and OPAC will be provided in Chapter 3.

The Optional Protocol on the Sale of Children came into force on 18 January 2002 in accordance with article 14 (1) and addresses the growing problem of sex trafficking, sexual exploitation and abuse, and outlines steps for the protection of child victims' rights during all phases of the criminal justice process. [70]

3.5 Post-1989 Developments

Since the adoption of the CRC in 1989, there have been several other developments relating to the protection of children in armed conflicts.

---

[69] 'Optional Protocol on the Sale of Children, Child Prostitution and Child Pornography. Adopted and opened for signature, ratification and accession by General Assembly resolution A/54/RES/263 of 25 May 2000, entered into force on 18 January 2002' Child Rights Information Network (http://www.crin.org/law/Instrument.asp?InstID=1002 , 10 April 2009).

[70] Ibid.

3.5.1 Special Representative of the Secretary General for Children and Armed Conflict -SRSG(CAC)

Prior to referring to the role and duties of the SRSG (CAC), it is worth mentioning the significant contribution of the Graça Machel report[71] (1996) to the UN General Assembly on the impact of armed conflict on children. Machel's report was the first comprehensive human rights assessment of war-affected children that used the CRC as a guiding framework of analysis and that contained a comprehensive agenda for action by Member States and the International Community to improve the protection and care of children in situations of conflict.[72] Following Machel's recommendation, in 1996, the General Assembly adopted the 51/77[73] Resolution which addressed the prevention of the involvement of children in armed conflict[74], and recommended the Secretary-General to appoint a Special Representative on the impact of armed conflict on children, for a three years term with a chance to be renewed[75]. The Assembly called upon institutions concerned, in collaboration with States to ensure that the necessary support is made available to the Special Representative for the effective performance of his/her mandate.[76] Since 1996 the mandate has been extended three times by the General Assembly[77]. In 1997 Olara Otunnu was first to be appointed as Special Representative, and in recognition of his work his term in office was extended until 2006, when Ms Radhika Coomarasawamy took over.[78]

---

[71] Her report was submitted at 51st session of the General Assembly "Promotion and Protection of the Rights of Children: Impact of Armed Conflict on Children" A/51/306 (26 August 1996) (http://www.unicef.org/graca/a51-306_en.pdf , 15 February 2009).

[72] Ibid.

[73] General Assembly Resolution A/RES/51/77) "The Rights of the child" adopted by the General Assembly [on the report of the Third Committee (A/51/615) (20 February 1997) without a vote at 82nd plenary meeting on December 12, 1996. (http://www.un.org/documents/ga/res/51/ares51-77.htm , 10 March 2009).

[74] Ibid. art13.

[75] Ibid. art35.

[76] Ibid.

[77] General Assembly Resolution 60/231. "Rights of the Child" (23 December 2005) [adopted by the General Assembly on the report of the Third Committee] (http://www.endcorporalpunishment.org/pages/pdfs/GA-Res_Dec2005.pdf, 10 March 2009).

[78] 'Office of the Special Representative of the Secretary-General for Children and Armed Conflict' UN (http://www.un.org/children/conflict/english/theoffice.html , 10 March 2009).

The mission of the Special Representative is i) to be an advocate on behalf of war-affected children; ii) to propose measures to protect the rights of children in war; iii) to bring together UN and non-UN actors to think of more effective responses; and iv) to undertake humanitarian and diplomatic roles for overcoming difficult political situations. [79]

By submitting annual reports to the GA and the Commission on Human Rights, the Special Representative has succeeded in placing the issues of children and armed conflict high on the international agenda. Children are not only recognised as being in need of special protection and assistance, but it is now also accepted that children should be more central to peace processes, security issues in general and post-conflict reconstruction. The Special Representative has also secured commitments for child protection from both State and rebel leaders.[80]

3.5.2 Security Council

It was not till the late 1990s that the Security Council in its Resolutions made any reference to children affected by armed conflict. Since 1999 four very important resolutions has been adopted on this topic, all of which call on all actors that might influence or affect the conflict to take measures to provide protection for children. The actors include the Security Council, UN bodies, Member States, corporate actors, regional organisations, and international financial institutions. [81]

Prior to 1999 the Security Council resolutions were more specific to situations that the Council was dealing with: in 1996 the situation in Liberia[82] and in 1998-9 the case of Sierra Leone[83].

---

[79] As appears at the official website of the Office of the Special Representative of the Secretary-General for Children and Armed Conflict. http://www.un.org/children/conflict/english/theoffice.html and Protection of Children Affected by Armed Conflict: Report of the Special Representative of the Secretary-General for Children and Armed Conflict, annexed to Protection of Children Affected by Armed Conflict: Note by the Secretary-General, UN Doc. A/53/482 (12 October 1999), paras.13, 14-17, 40.

[80] Matthew Happold "Child Soldiers in International Law", pp.40-42 and Harvey, "Children and Armed Conflict: A guide to International Humanitarian and Human Rights Law", p.15.

[81] Rachel Harvey, "Children and Armed Conflict: A Guide to International Humanitarian and Human Rights Law"p.15.

[82] The Council condemned the practice "of recruiting, training and deploying children for combat" SC Res. 1071 of 30 August 1996 On the Situation in Liberia, para. 9; and SC Res. 1083 of 27 November 1996 On the Situation in Liberia, para.6 and Happold, p.42.

The four resolutions that refer to war-affected children are:

3.5.2.1 Security Council Resolution 1261

The 1999 resolution on children and armed conflict[84] was the first to formally recognise that the protection and security of children affected by armed conflict is an international peace and security issue, and therefore, within the responsibility of the Security Council. It recognises and condemns the deliberate targeting of children in places protected by IHL, such as schools.[85] Furthermore, the resolution provides States with a list of calls for action on the issues of proliferation of small arms[86], recruitment of children[87] and access of humanitarian and UN personnel.[88]

3.5.2.2 Security Council Resolution 1314[89]

This resolution was adopted in 2000 and could be seen as an expanded version of the 1261 resolution. It does state though that in places where there is a systematic and widespread violation of IHL and HR Law, including children's rights violations, the Security Council sees that as a threat to international peace and security and therefore, is ready when needed to take special measures.[90]

---

[83] In 1998 and 1999 the Council adopted two resolutions that urged the prosecution and punishment of those responsible for such violations. SC Res. 1181 of 13 July 1998 On the Situation in Sierra Leone and SC Res. 1231 of 11 March 1999 On the Situation in Sierra Leone. Para.3.

[84] Adopted by the Security Council at it 4037th meeting, on 25 August 1999 http://www.securitycouncilreport.org/atf/cf/%7B65BFCF9B-6D27-4E9C-8CD3-CF6E4FF96FF9%7D/CAC%20SRES%201261.pdf.

[85] Ibid. para.2.

[86]Ibid. para.14.

[87] Paras.2, 13.

[88] Paras.11, 13.

[89] Adopted by the Security Council at its 4185th meeting, on 11August 2000 http://www.mineaction.org/downloads/S%20RES%201314%20Protection%20of%20Children.pdf.

[90] Ibid and Rachel Harvey, "Children and Armed Conflict: A Guide to International Humanitarian and Human Rights Law"p.16.

3.5.2.3 Security Council Resolution 1379[91]

This resolution, adopted in 2001, in addition to the concerns raised in the previous resolution, addressed the issue of HIV/AIDS and its link with armed conflict. Amongst those actors who play a significant role in starting and maintaining an armed conflict, the resolution identifies the corporate actors who engage in illicit trade in natural resources and small arms.[92] The Security Council urges them to stop such activities as they are in breach of relevant Security Council resolutions and the Charter of the UN.[93]

Finally the Security Council requested that the Secretary-General provide the Council with a list of parties to armed conflict that recruit or use children in violation of international peace and security.[94]

3.5.2.4 Security Council Resolution 1460[95]

This Resolution was adopted in 2003 and reiterates the previous three resolutions and supports the Secretary-General's call for "an era of application" of international norms and standards for the protection of children affected by armed conflict.[96]

3.5.3 International Criminal Court (ICC)

The ICC was created on 1 July 2002S when the ICC Statute entered into force.[97] The Court is not part of the UN, but an independent institution

---

[91] Adopted by the Security Council at its 4423rd meeting, on 20 November 2001 http://www.mineaction.org/downloads/S%20RES%201379%20Protection%20of%20Children.pdf .

[92] Ibid. paras.9 (c)&(d).

[93] Para. 9(d).

[94] Para.16.

[95] Adopted by the Security Council at its 4695th meeting, on 30 January 2003 http://www.securitycouncilreport.org/atf/cf/%7B65BFCF9B-6D27-4E9C-8CD3-CF6E4FF96FF9%7D/CAC%20SRES%201460.pdf .

[96] Ibid. para.1.

[97] On April 11th 2002, at a special event at the United Nations when 10 countries simultaneously deposited their instruments of ratification and within 60 days the ICC had to be created.
http://www.icc-cpi.int/NetApp/App/MCMSTemplates/Index.aspx?NRMODE=Published&NRNODEGUID={D788E44D-E292-46A1-89CC-

based in The Hague, the Netherlands. It consists of four organs: the Presidency, the judicial Divisions, the Office of the Prosecutor and the Registry.[98] With the creation of the ICC the perpetrators of the core crimes of genocide, crimes against humanity and war crimes, can be brought to justice. The Court's jurisdiction can be exercised over crimes of aggression, once a provision is adopted defining the crime and setting out the conditions under which the court shall exercise its jurisdiction with respect to it.[99]

The Rome Statute that governs the ICC states that an act of war crime among other things involves "conscription and enlistment of children under the age of fifteen years into the national armed forces or using them to participate actively in hostilities".[100] Acts committed against children are also mentioned in the Statute when defining 'genocide' and 'enslavement'. For the ICC an act of genocide involves "forcible transfer of children of the group to another group"[101]. While "enslavement" among other things means "the exercise of any or all of the powers attaching to the right of ownership over a person and includes the exercise of such power in the course of trafficking in persons, in particular women and children".[102]

The Court's first case is against the leader of the Union of Congolese Patriots, Thomas Lubanga, who has been charged with war crimes as he trained child soldiers to kill, pillage and rape.[103] The hearings of the case began in November 2006 and in January 2009 it was announced that he will stand trial.[104]

D03637A52766}&NRORIGINALURL=/Menus/ICC/About+the+Court/Frequently+asked+Questions/&NRCACHEHINT=Guest#id_1 .

[98] ICC "Structure of the Court" http://www.icc-cpi.int/Menus/ICC/Structure+of+the+Court/.

[99] http://www.icc-cpi.int/NetApp/App/MCMSTemplates/Index.aspx?NRMODE=Published&NRNODEGUID={D788E44D-E292-46A1-89CC-D03637A52766}&NRORIGINALURL=/Menus/ICC/About+the+Court/Frequently+asked+Questions/&NRCACHEHINT=Guest#id_1 .

[100] Article 8(2)(xxvi).Rome Statute of the International Criminal Court entered into force 1 July 2002 http://untreaty.un.org/cod/icc/statute/romefra.htm.

[101] Article 6 (3) Ibid.

[102] Article 7 (2)(c) Ibid.

[103] BBC NEWS "International Court in first case" http://www.bbc.co.uk/2/hi/europe/6131198.stm .

[104] Euronews "International Court of Justice: ICC hears of child soldiers hell in first case" 26/01/09 http://www.euronews.net/en/article/26/01/2009/icc-hears-of-child-soldier-hell-in-first-case/.

3.6 Conclusion

The CRC and its Protocol are the culmination of several decades of attempts to provide international protection for children. But the CRC goes much further than previous efforts, both in the comprehensive set of rights it accords children and in the attempt to secure those rights in reality. There have been some significant developments on children's rights since the CRC, especially the foundation of the ICC. Nevertheless, the CRC remains the principle effort of the international community to provide children with rights.

CHAPTER FOUR

THE CRC, OPAC AND THEIR IMPLEMENTATION

4.1 Introduction

This chapter will examine in detail the provisions of the CRC relating to armed conflict, namely Article 38, the content of the OPAC, and the machinery established for the implementation of the CRC and the OPAC – the Committee on the Rights of the Child.

The chapter is divided into three main sections. The first section will examine article 38, with a brief reference to articles 22 and 39 and their provisions regarding children's rights during and after periods of armed conflict. The second section will focus on the scope of the OPAC. The final section will examine the CRC's implementation machinery, in particular, the role of the Committee on the Rights of the Child, States Parties' duties and obligations, and how the Committee compares with other Human Rights Committees.

4.2 The CRC: Article 38

Article 38 is the only article of the Convention that focuses on providing protection for children in armed conflict, and states that:

1. *States Parties undertake to respect and to ensure respect for rules of International Humanitarian Law applicable to them in armed conflicts which are relevant to the child.*
2. *States Parties shall take all feasible measures to ensure that persons who have not attained the age of fifteen years do not take a direct part in hostilities.*
3. *States Parties shall refrain from recruiting any person who has not attained the age of fifteen years into their armed forces. In recruiting among those persons who have attained the age of fifteen years but have not attained the age of eighteen years, States Parties shall endeavour to give priority to those who are oldest.*

4. In accordance with their obligations under international humanitarian law to protect the civilian population in armed conflicts, States Parties shall take all feasible measures to ensure protection and care of children who are affected by an armed conflict.

Article 38 combines both IHL and HR Law. On the one hand, this article is part of a human rights instrument and is therefore monitored by a human rights body, namely the CRC Committee.[1] On the other hand, the content of Article 38 is inspired by IHL and is structured in a typical IHL manner: its first paragraph contains a general provision on the applicability of IHL, the second and third paragraphs deal with the protection of children from participation in hostilities or recruitment in the armed forces, and the fourth paragraph reminds the States Parties to protect the civilian population.[2]

Paragraph 1 makes it clear to all States Parties that they are bound by instruments of the IHL to which they are party. In other words, paragraph 1 serves as a 'safety net' provision, which means that the rules regulating the treatment of child combatants, being part of the rules of IHL relevant to the child, are fully applicable to the States Parties, as long as they are party to those rules.[3]

In the original draft of the CRC there were no provisions regarding the protection of children in armed conflicts, which was seen by NGOs as a gap in the treaty. During the 1985 and 1986 session, the "open-ended" Working Group[4] received a significant number of proposed articles dealing with this issue, and at the 1986 session the Working Group adopted a draft article that failed to live up to the existing IHL standards, let alone develop them.[5] Due to the dissatisfaction expressed by a number

[1] Rachel Brett, 'Child Soldiers: law and practice' *International Journal of Children's Rights* 4(2) (1996): 116.

[2] Fiona Ang, *A Commentary on the United Nations Convention on the Rights of the Child: Article 38 Children in Armed Conflict* (Leiden [The Netherlands]: Martinus Nijhoff, 2005): 13.

[3] Ang, *A Commentary on the United Nations Convention on the Rights of the Child: Article 38 Children in Armed Conflict*, 28.

[4] Established by the UN Commission on Human Rights (UNCHR) in 1979. The "open-ended" nature of the Working Group meant that any of the forty-three states represented on the Commission could participate, while all the other Member States of the UN could send "observers" with the right to take the floor, as could inter-governmental organisations. Non-governmental organisations could participate but with no absolute right to speak. Detrick and Doek, '*The UN Convention on the Rights of the Child: A guide to the "Travaux Preparatoires'* 21-2.

[5] Happold, *Child Soldiers in International Law,* 70.

of states and NGOs, the Chairman of the Working Group at the 1988 session stated that the new text should incorporate improved international standards by making use of Article 77 (2)[6] of the Additional Protocol I (AP I) to the Geneva Conventions.[7]

Taking this into consideration, the Working Group at the 1989 session was provided with two versions of paragraph 2 and was asked to adopt one of them. The two versions were:

> (a) *States Parties shall take all feasible measures to ensure that no child takes a direct part in hostilities. With regard to persons who have attained majority before the age of 18 years, States Parties shall endeavour to prevent them from taking part in hostilities. Persons who have not attained the age of 15 years shall not be allowed to take part in hostilities.*[8]
>
> *(b)States Parties shall take all feasible measures to ensure that persons who have not attained the age of fifteen years do not take a direct part in hostilities*

A majority of states represented in the Working Group favoured the first version, with the exception of USSR and USA who completely rejected it, while the UK and India were happy to go along with the first version but with reservations. In particular the representative of the USA stated his unwillingness to join a consensus in favour of the first.[9] After a lengthy debate, the Chairman of the Working Group stated the second version was adopted, due to lack of opposition from the participants to the provisions of the second version, and in order to secure the maximum level of consensus.[10] Although, the decision was followed by threats to reopen the issue at a higher level, either in the Commission on Human Rights or in the General Assembly, the text was adopted unmodified with

---

[6] Art77 (2) of Additional Protocol I states that "the Parties to the conflict shall take all feasible measures in order that children who have not attained the age of fifteen years do not take a direct part in hostilities and, in particular, they shall refrain from recruiting them into their armed forces. In recruiting among those persons who have attained the age of fifteen years but who have not attained the age of eighteen years, the Parties to the conflict shall endeavour to give priority to those who are oldest".

[7] Happold, *Child Soldiers in International Law,* 70-1.

[8] Ibid.,73.

[9] Ibid., 73.

[10] The Working Group operated on the basis of consensus. At no time during its work a proposal was taken to vote. Detrick and Doek, '*The UN Convention on the Rights of the Child: A guide to the "Travaux Preparatoires'* , 22.

restrictions on the recruitment of children and their participation in hostilities that were identical to those of the AP I.[11]

In the adopted version of paragraph 2, the concept of 'direct participation' in hostilities is open to different interpretation. Apparently the majority of the drafters of this article found that the insertion of 'against his or her will' would be 'contrary to the spirit of the Convention'.[12] It is highly unfortunate that this paragraph by implication allows children under the age of 15 years to take an 'indirect part' in hostilities. Many delegations belonging to the Working Groups drafting this article had expressed themselves in favour of the deletion of the word 'direct', but in the end the paragraph was considered adequate to prevent the participation of 15-18 years old in hostilities even though children of that age could be legitimately recruited to the military.[13]

In paragraph 3, the term 'recruitment' is meant to encompass both compulsory and voluntary recruitment, that is, both conscription and enlistment. Thus, 'recruitment' covers different ways in which recruitment may take place.[14]

There are some important differences between paragraphs 2 and 3. While paragraph 3 creates obligations only for the States Parties themselves, paragraph 2 extends the obligation beyond the States Parties' own armed forces. States Parties should make sure that no child is used in hostilities by any other armed group, guerrilla and paramilitary groups present in their territory,[15] no matter how great the de facto control of these groups may be.[16] Nevertheless, paragraph 3 sets a higher standard than paragraph 2 as, even in the absence of hostilities, recruitment is prohibited,[17]whereas paragraph 2 applies only to 'hostilities'.

Finally, paragraph 4, requires States to take 'all feasible' measures to ensure the protection and care of war-affected children. This formulation

---

[11] Happold, *Child Soldiers in International Law,* 73.

[12] Detrick and Doek, '*The UN Convention on the Rights of the Child: A guide to the "Travaux Preparatoires'*, 506.

[13] Ibid., 509-513.

[14] Ang, *A Commentary on the United Nations Convention on the Rights of the Child: Article 38 Children in Armed Conflict*, 49.

[15] E.g. UN Doc, CRC/C/15/Add.137, 2000: Concluding Observations of the Committee on the Rights of the Child: Colombia, para.54: the CRC Committee 'expresses deep concern at the very high numbers of children who have been forcibly recruited into guerrilla paramilitary groups'.

[16] E.g. UN Doc. CRC/C/15/Add.190, 2002: Concluding Observations of the Committee on the Rights of the Child: Sudan, para.6.

[17] E.g. UN Doc. CRC/C/15/Add.2, 1993: Concluding Observations of the Committee on the Rights of the Child: Sweden, paras.8 and 11.

has been received with disappointment as it does not impose an absolute duty on the states.[18]

Article 38 is the only section of the CRC that includes provisions extending protection only to children under 15 years old, as opposed to all children up to the age of 18 years[19]. Moreover, it is unclear whether or not a child combatant is protected by these provisions, for the second, third and fourth paragraphs deal exclusively with the legal framework applicable to child civilians[20] which means that child combatants do not explicitly benefit from the protection provided by the article.

The positive aspect of Article 38 is that it applies to all types of armed conflict especially if we take into consideration the manipulation of the IHL thresholds by States. In the current IHL, 'armed conflict' implies the exclusion of lower-intensity conflicts[21]; in the AP II 'armed conflict' is identified as either 'international' or 'high-intensity non-international'; and in Common Article 3 of the GC it includes 'low-intensity non-international' conflict. [22] Article 38 encompasses all of these forms of conflict.

On the other hand, Article 38 is weaker than Article 4 (3)(c) of AP II[23] as it does not explicitly prohibits the use of children under the age of fifteen either by the armed forces or by paramilitary groups, which came as a disappointment to a number of states and NGOs involved in the negotiation of the CRC.[24] Moreover, a number of state parties to the CRC (Andorra, Argentina, Austria, Colombia, Ecuador (upon signature), Germany, the Netherlands, Spain and Uruguay) made declarations that they considered Article 38 failed to prohibit the use of all persons under 18 in armed conflicts. They stated they would apply their own more demanding national legislation rather than the principles laid down in the

---

[18] Abu El-Haj and Hamilton, 'Armed Conflict: the Protection of Children Under International Law', 36.

[19] Happold, *Child Soldiers in International Law,* 72.

[20] Ang, *A Commentary on the United Nations Convention on the Rights of the Child: Article 38 Children in Armed Conflict*, 28.

[21] Christopher Greenwood, 'Scope of Application of Humanitarian Law' in Dieter Flack (ed.), *The Handbook of Humanitarian Law in Armed Conflicts* (Oxford: OUP, 1995): p.47.

[22] Theodor Meron, 'The Humanisation of Humanitarian Law' *American Journal of International Law* 94 (2) (2000): 260-1.

[23] Art 4 (3) (c) states: " children who have not attained the age of fifteen years shall neither be recruited in the armed forces or groups nor allowed to take part in hostilities".

[24] Happold, *Child Soldiers in International Law,* 72.

CRC to regulate the recruitment of persons into their national armed forces.[25]

Article 38 has also been criticised for its departure from the general age limit of 18 years that applies to the other articles of the Convention and, with respect to the prohibition against recruitment and participation, for largely repeating Article 77 of Additional Protocol I to the Geneva Conventions, applicable in international armed conflict. In so doing, it not only brought nothing new, but also distracted attention from the stronger standard contained in Additional Protocol II to the Geneva Conventions, which provides a more absolute and comprehensive prohibition for non-international armed conflict.[26]

4.2.1 The CRC: Articles 22 and 39

Articles 22 and 39 bear some relation to Article 38 as their provisions aim to provide protection to post-war child victims.

Article 22 provides protection to refugee children. In particular, children have the right to special protection and help if they are refugees (if they have been forced to leave their home and live in another country), as well as all the other rights of the Convention.[27] Article 39 takes care of the rehabilitation of child victims. In particular, children who have been neglected, abused or exploited in armed conflict should receive special help to aid their physical and psychological recovery and reintegration into society. Particular attention should be paid to restoring the health, self-respect and dignity of the child.[28]

In view of the way they are related to Article 38, these articles are grouped together by the Committee on the Rights of the Children under the 'Special Protection Measures' section in States' reports to the Committee.

---

[25] Ibid., 73-4.

[26] Art.4 para.3 "Children shall be provided with the care and aid they require, and in particular: (…) (c) children who have not attained the age of fifteen years shall be neither recruited in the armed forces or groups nor allowed to take part in hostilities (…)".

[27] 'Fact Sheet: A summary of the Rights under the Convention on the Rights of the Child' (http://www.unicef.org/crc/files/Rights_overview.pdf , 10 June 2009).

[28] Ibid.

4.3 Scope of the OPAC

Despite the fact that the Convention is a major new tool that ensures increased respect for the provisions of international law, its provisions are the result of a compromise.[29] So too is Article 38.

The dissatisfaction with Article 38, in particular, was noticed by the Committee on the Rights of the Child itself. In 1992, at its second session, the Committee proposed a "preliminary drafting of a future Optional Protocol to the Convention on the Rights of the Child raising the age of recruitment of children into the armed forces to 18 years of age".[30] In 1993 the Committee appointed one of its members to prepare a preliminary draft of the Optional Protocol raising the minimum age of recruitment to 18.[31] The draft of the Optional Protocol was submitted to the Commission on Human Rights[32] and examined at its fiftieth session.[33] The Commission then established an open-ended inter-sessional Working Group that would "meet for a period of two weeks prior to the fifty-first session of the Commission in order elaborate a draft Optional Protocol".[34]

The Committee's concern for Article 38 was supported by the World Conference on Human Rights, which, in the Vienna Convention and Programme of Action adopted on 25 June 1993, urged the Committee "to study the question of raising the minimum age of recruitment into armed forces".[35]

The conviction behind the OPAC was that the treaty would contribute effectively to the implementation of the principle that the best interests of

---

[29] Freeman, *The Ideologies of Children's Rights*, 355.

[30] UN Doc. CRC/C/10, 1992: Committee on the Rights of the Child: Report adopted by the Committee at its 46th Meeting, on 9 October 1992.

[31] UN Doc. CRC/C/16, para.176 (b) (Sessional/Annual Report of Committee): Report of the third session of the Committee on the Rights of the Child:.05/03/93.

[32] The Commission on Human Rights was established by Economic and Social Council Resolution 5(1) of 16 February 1946 and reported to the ECOSOC. The Commission concluded its 62nd and final session on 27 March 2006 and its work now is continued by Human Rights Council.

[33] UN Doc. E/CN.4/1994/91: Commission on Human Rights: Rights of the Child.

[34] E/CN.94/RES/1994/91, notes 13-15: Office of the High Commissioner for Human Rights on the Implementation of the Convention on the Rights of the Child.

[35] J.K. Kleffner (ed.), *Yearbook of International Humanitarian Law* (Universiteit van Amsterdam: Cambridge University Press, 2006): 299 and
UN Doc. A/CONF.157/24 (Part I): World Conference on Human Rights Report of the World Conference on Human Rights, Report of the Secretary-General, Vienna, 14-25 June 1993: Ch III, s. II, para.50.

the child are to be a primary consideration in all actions concerning children.[36] In 2000 the Working Group completed its work and on 25 May 2000 the UN General Assembly adopted the Optional Protocol. The Protocol became legally binding on 12 February 2002[37], once it had received its first 10 ratifications[38]

Overall, the OPAC has managed to achieve a 'straight-18' protection.[39] Nevertheless, 18 years has not been set as minimum threshold for all recruitment, deployment and practices due, in particular, to the USA's objections. Even States that are signatories to OPAC are allowed to recruit under-18s provided those recruits volunteer to join the national army.

The Optional Protocol consists of thirteen articles and its provisions address issues such as direct participation in hostilities (Art1), military recruitment by state (Arts 2, 3) and by non-state armed forces (Art 4).

Although Article 1 of the Protocol states that "States Parties shall take all feasible measures to ensure that members of their armed forces who have attained the age of 18 years do not take a direct part in hostilities",[40] no definition is provided of the concept of direct 'participation', nor regarding the difference between 'direct' and 'indirect' participation.[41] The final text was the result of a compromise that accommodated the interests and concerns of the states, where recruitment of children under 18 years old was permitted by national laws.[42] In fact, in the view of the United Kingdom and Viet Nam, the Article permitted deployment of

---

[36] Ibid.,61-77,

[37] Tiny Vandewiele, *Optional Protocol: The Involvement of Children in Armed Conflicts* (Leiden: Martinus Nijhoff Publishers, 2006): 20.

[38] The number of ratifications needed for its entry into force. The first 10 states to ratify it were: Andorra, Austria, Bangladesh, Canada, Democratic Republic of the Congo, Holy See, Iceland, New Zealand, Romania and Sri Lanka.

[39] A Sheppard 'Child soldiers: Is the Optional Protocol evidence of an emerging "straight-18" consensus?' *The International Journal of Children's Rights* 8 (2000): 38 and Vandewiele, *Optional Protocol: The Involvement of Children in Armed Conflicts*, 20.

[40] OPAC.

[41] UNICEF, Coalition to Stop the Use of Child Soldiers, Guide to the Optional Protocol on the involvement of children in armed conflict (New York: UNICEF and Coalition to Stop the Use of Child Soldiers, 2003): 13-14.

[42] UNICEF, Coalition to Stop the Use of Child Soldiers, Guide to the Optional Protocol on the involvement of children in armed conflict , 14 and E/CN.4/2000/74, 2000: Report of the Working group on a draft optional protocol to the Convention on the Rights of the Child on involvement of children in armed conflicts on its sixth session., paras.57-59.

under-18s in certain exceptional circumstances, and for that reason they made declarations on this article.[43]

Moreover, instead of children's participation in 'armed conflicts', the article refers to 'hostilities'. According to the definition given by the International Committee of the Red Cross, an armed conflict 'is usually a situation during which there are periods of hostilities, interspersed with periods of truce'.[44] At the Diplomatic Conference of Geneva of 1974-1977[45] 'hostilities' were defined as "acts of war that by their nature or purpose [strike] at the personnel and material of enemy armed forces".[46] Thus 'hostilities' describe a narrower range of circumstances than 'armed conflicts'.

Overall, the language used in this Article can be seen as a combination of that of Article 38(2) of the CRC and Article 77(2) of the AP I to the Geneva Conventions.

Compulsory recruitment of children into national armed forces is the main concern of Article 2 of the Protocol. States Parties "shall ensure that persons under the age of 18 years are not compulsorily recruited into their

---

[43] The declarations are the following: The United Kingdom declared:

> "The United Kingdom understands that Article 1 would not exclude the deployment of members of its armed forces under the age of 18 to take a direct part in hostilities where:
>
> -there is a genuine military need to deploy their unit or ship to an area in which hostilities are taking place
>
> - by reason of nature and urgency of the situation
>
> - it is not practicable to withdraw such persons before deployment, or
>
> -to do so would undermine the operational effectiveness of their ship or unit, and thereby put at risk the successful completion of the military mission and/or the safety of the personnel" Viet Nam declared: "Those who are under the age of 18 shall not be directly involved in military battles unless there is an urgent need for safeguarding national independence, sovereignty, unity and territorial integrity".
>
> —Vandewiele, Optional Protocol: The Involvement of Children in Armed Conflicts, 21.

[44] International Committee of the Red Cross, 'Optional Protocol to the Convention on the Rights of the Child concerning the Involvement of children in armed conflicts: position of the international committee of the red cross Geneva, 27 October 1997, International Review of the Red Cross 322 (1998): 107-125.

[45] 'Diplomatic Conference on the Reaffirmation and Development of International Humanitarian Law applicable in Armed Conflicts, Geneva, 1974-1977' Human Rights Library (http://www1.umn.edu/humanrts/instree/1977d.htm , 12 May 2009).

[46] Vandewiele, Optional Protocol: The Involvement of Children in Armed Conflicts, p.22 note 111.

national forces".[47] Some of the successes of the Optional Protocol are that it prohibits compulsory recruitment below the age of 18 by government forces, and raises the minimum age for direct participation in hostilities from 15 years to 18 years [48] and the minimum age for voluntary recruitment by government forces from 15 years to 16 years. However, lack of precise definition arises once again, this time in relation to the concept of 'compulsory recruitment' and how it can be differentiated in practice from 'voluntary' recruitment, given that lack of food, poverty, revenge and the need for physical protection[49] are significant reasons for individuals 'volunteering' to join the armed forces. Also, it should be noted here that, although Article 1 of the CRC has defined a child as "every human being below the age of eighteen years unless under the law applicable to the child, majority is attained earlier"[50], Article 2 refers to 'persons'. This could imply that the provisions of Article 2 of the OPAC are also applicable to adults younger than 18 years, for those States Parties where adulthood starts before the age of 18.

While compulsory recruitment is dealt with by Article 2, Article 3 of the Optional Protocol in its five paragraphs provides for voluntary recruitment. Although Article 3 paragraph 1 has been seen as a success for raising the minimum age for voluntary recruitment, in reality it is a compromise. Many participants were in favour of a straight 18 years as minimum age for all recruitment[51], while others were in favour of 17 years as minimum age for voluntary recruitment.[52] Paragraph 3 lists the four criteria that a volunteer should fulfil in order to be accepted. While three of the criteria are very clear and straightforward, the very first criterion raises some questions, as the "the recruitment must be genuinely voluntary".[53] First, no definition of 'genuine' has been given and second, it is not easy to establish whether or not this criterion has been fulfilled. According to the Committee's reporting guidelines for Article 3(3), States Parties should give a detailed description of the procedure used for

[47] OPAC, Article 2.

[48] Which has been set by CRC and other legal instruments.

[49] UNICEF, Coalition to Stop the Use of Child Soldiers, Guide to the Optional Protocol on the involvement of children in armed conflict , 16.

[50] CRC, Article 1.

[51] Vandewiele, Optional Protocol: The Involvement of Children in Armed Conflicts, note 169.

[52] Ibid., note 170.

[53] OPAC, Art3 (3)(a).

recruitment, i.e. from the expression of intention to volunteer until the physical integration into the armed forces.[54]

The significance of Article 4 lies in the fact that it addresses armed groups, in contrast with the CRC which applies only to States Parties. Armed groups often recruit large numbers of child soldiers in internal conflicts and therefore need to be held accountable. However what constitutes an 'armed group' has not been defined. According to M. Happold, the definition of 'armed forces' is "wide enough to encompass armed groups allied with a State Party's government but not part of or under the control of its armed forces".[55] Pursuant to Article 1 of the AP II to the Geneva Conventions, a group must fulfil four criteria in order to be treated as an armed group: it must be organised with a responsible command, control a part of the territory, carry out sustained and concerted military operations, and be able to implement the Additional Protocol.[56]

Of the remaining articles of the Optional Protocol, Article 6 is crucial as it deals not only with the implementation, enforcement and dissemination of the Protocol, but also with the demobilisation and recovery of child soldiers (Art 6 (3)). Article 39 of the CRC was the first to raise the issue of the rehabilitation and reintegration of children, but it was not until the adoption of the Optional Protocol that an international agreement explicitly imposed the obligation to demobilise, rehabilitate and reintegrate children who have been recruited or used in hostilities.[57]

Overall, the provisions of the Optional Protocol are more protective than the AP to the Geneva Conventions and the CRC. First, Art 77 (2) of the AP I is concerned with children under the age of 15, and Art 38 of the CRC does nothing more than repeat the provisions of the APs to the Geneva Conventions, while the Optional Protocol extends the protection to all children under the age of 18.

Second, the Optional Protocol applies to all parties to the conflict, in contrast with the CRC and the APs that are directed only to the States Parties. Although Art 77 (2) refers to all parties to the conflict, the fact the Additional Protocols deal with international armed conflicts means that Art 77(2) is applicable to States Parties only.

Third, the Optional Protocol explicitly focuses on the demobilisation and recovery of child soldiers.

---

[54] Vandewiele, Optional Protocol: The Involvement of Children in Armed Conflicts, note 191 and M. Happold, Child Soldiers in International Law, 239.

[55] Happold, Child Soldiers in International Law, 239.

[56] AP II to the Geneva Conventions, Art1(1).

[57] Vandewiele, *Optional Protocol: The Involvement of Children in Armed Conflicts*, 50.

The common element that the APs to the Geneva Convention, the CRC and the OPAC share is that all three address only direct participation in hostilities and require States Parties to take 'all feasible measures'.

4.4 Implementation Machinery

This section examines, first, the Committee on the Rights of the Child – referred to hereafter as the Committee – by outlining its composition, mandates and the role it serves in the protection of children's rights. The duties and obligation of States Parties towards the Committee will be outlined in the second part of this section. The constitution and role of other Human Rights Committees will be examined in the final part of this section.

4.4.1 The Committee on the Rights of the Child

Pursuant to Article 43 of the Convention, the Committee was formed to review reports submitted at regular interval by States Parties and to make recommendations on how States can better implement the Convention's provisions. After the adoption of the two Optional Protocols – OPSC and the OPAC – to supplement the rights supported by the Convention, the Committee's mandate was extended to include monitoring the implementation of these treaties. In addition to these main activities, the Committee undertakes activities that promote international cooperation on securing children's rights among multilateral agencies, donor countries and developing countries. Every two years, the Committee reports on its activities to the UN General Assembly through the UN Economic and Social Council.[58]

Currently the Committee is made up of 18 independent experts, though from its first meeting in 1991 until 2003 the Committee consisted of only 10 members.[59] Members of the Committee are elected by States Parties[60] for a four year term and are eligible for re-election if re-nominated.

---

[58] 'FACT SHEET: THE Committee on the Rights of the Child' (http://www.unicef.org/crc/files/Committee_fact_sheet.pdf, 10 February 2009).

[59] GA Resolution A/RES/51/77 section 5 urged that the States Parties accept the amendment to Article 43 (2) of the Convention to increase the membership from ten to eighteen experts. UN Doc. CRC/C/33, 1994: Overview of the reporting procedures.

[60] UN Doc. Child CRC/C/4/REV.1, 2005: Committee on the Rights of the Child, Provisional Rules of Procedure, see rules 11, 12 and Article 43 (6) of the Convention.

Several Committee Members have been re-elected, such as Ms. Sandra Prunella Mason (Barbados) and Mr. Youri Kolosov (Russia).[61] Each member is required to be an experienced lawyer in the Human Rights sphere and to be of high moral character. For instance, Vuckovic Sahovic Nevena, a current Committee member, is an experienced lawyer and has a wide range of experience on children rights, and has written a series of independent reports on the exercise of the rights of the child in FRY and Serbia.[62] Despite being elected by States Parties, Committee members are meant to be accountable to the children of the world, whose rights they are elected to safeguard, rather than to their countries.[63]

The Committee holds three sessions a year: in January, May and September, for a period of three weeks each, in Geneva, where States Parties reports are reviewed. Each session is followed by a week of preparations for the next session by a pre-sessional working group. The country files of the pre-sessional working group are prepared by the secretariat and contain not only the relevant information for each of the reports to be examined but also documentation from relevant UN bodies and specialised governmental and non-governmental agencies and organisations that has been submitted to the secretariat beforehand.[64] The purpose of the working group is both to identify in advance the most important issues that will be discussed in the plenary session[65] and to provide States Parties with advance notice on the principal issues that might arise in the examination of their reports.[66] The meetings with the working group are closed to the public and there are no official records, but any decisions taken by the working group are reported to the Committee at its next plenary session. At the end of the discussion of the

[61] The names used are just an example, see 'Past Membership of the Committee on the Rights of the Child (1991-2003) (http://www2.ohchr.org/english/bodies/crc/docs/MembersCVs/PastMEMBERSHIP.pdf , 12 February 2008).

[62] All the information has been taken from the Ms Vuckovic CV published by the Committee on the Rights of the Child. 'Ms Vuckovic CV' (http://www.see-educoop.net/experts/data/0147e.htm , 15 July 2007).

[63] Article 43 (2) of the Convention states that "...The members of the Committee shall be elected by States Parties among their nationals and shall serve in their personal capacity, consideration being given to equitable geographical distribution as well as to the principal legal systems".

[64] UN Doc. CRC/C/33, 1994, sections 9-10.

[65] Which usually takes place between 3 and 4 months after the working group.

[66] UN Doc. CRC/C/33, 1994, section 8.

State's report with the working group, a "List of Issues"[67] is drawn up by the working group which is sent to the relevant government through diplomatic channels.[68] A List of Issues usually asks a State Party for information additional to that provided in its report. The Committee requests the State Party to provide the answers to its Lists of Issues in writing, by including any additional or updated information requested in advance of the session, so as to facilitate the effectiveness of the dialogue[69], and to provide an opportunity to consider questions relating to any technical assistance and international cooperation that might be needed.

During the plenary session of the Committee, the States Parties Representatives, who have been invited by the Committee to attend the meeting at which their reports are examined, are able to answer any questions raised by the Committee and to make statements on reports already submitted by their State, and may also provide additional information if that is necessary[70] - as long as the representative present at the meeting is authorised to respond. In practice, some States Parties do not send a representative who is fully authorised. The Committee appoints two of its member to act as "country rapporteurs"[71] to lead the discussions with the delegation of the State Party, whose report is being examined. Once a short introductory statement has been made by the head of the delegation, an interactive dialogue begins, with the Chairperson of the Committee requesting the country rapporteurs to provide a brief overview of the state of children's rights in their country. Then Committee members are allowed to question or comment on aspects of the reports that need to be clarified, and the delegation may respond. Towards the end of the discussion, the country rapporteurs summarise their observations on the report and the discussion itself, and may also make suggestions and recommendations. The final statement of the session belongs to the State delegation.[72]

---

[67] Is a list of issues that the working group considers highly possible to be discussed during the plenary session, and in the giver State report have either not been stated accordingly or there was lack of evidence to prove progress achieved.

[68] UN Doc. CRC/C/33, 1994, sections 12-13.

[69] Ibid., Also it gives enough time to the Committee for the text to be translated into the working languages of the Committee.

[70] UN Doc. Child CRC/C/4/REV.1, 2005, see rule 68.

[71] Rapporteur's role will be extensively discussed in a separate paragraph later

[72] Illustration of dialogue process between the Committee monitoring Children's Rights and States Parties, found in Mertus, A. Julie, *The United Nations and Human Rights: A Guide for a New Era* (London: Routledge, 2005), 83 and a

The Convention is the only international human rights treaty that expressly gives NGOs a role in monitoring its implementation. In accordance with Article 45(a) of the Convention, "representatives of the specialised agencies, such as, the United Nations Children's Fund and other United Nations organs shall be entitled to be represented at the consideration of the implementation of such provisions of the Convention as fall within the scope of their mandate and may participate in private meetings of the Committee or its subsidiary bodies, when invited by the Committee to do so."[73] Furthermore, representatives of other competent bodies concerned may participate in public or private meetings of the Committee or its subsidiary bodies, when invited to do so.[74] These agencies can issue their own version of reality in a "shadow report" or "alternative report."[75] Such a report is regarded as the Committee's independent and effective tool during the assessment of a State's fulfilling its obligations to promote and protect children's rights. NGO shadow reports provide an in-depth knowledge of their home countries that are invaluable for the Committee members who, due to lack of time, cannot focus on selected areas or issues that require extra attention.[76]

Once discussion with the State Party has taken place, the Committee, in a closed meeting, will agree on written Concluding Observations which include suggestions and recommendations[77] that are made public on the last day of a Committee session during adoption of the report, of which they form a part. Article 44 (6) of the Convention requires that the

---

complete version can be found in 'Committee on the Rights of the Child- Working Methods, "Overview of the Working Methods of the Committee on the Rights of the Child"' (http://www.ohchr.org/english/bodies/crc/workingmethods.htm, 19 December 2008).

[73] UN Doc. Child CRC/C/4/REV.1, 2005, see rule 34.

[74] UN Doc. Child CRC/C/4/REV.1, 2005, see Rule 34 (2).

[75] Mertus, The United Nations and Human Rights: A Guide for a New Era, 84.

[76] See Guidelines of International Human Rights Law Group for Preparing a Shadow Report for the CERD. 'International Human Rights Law Group: Guidelines on preparing shadow reports for the CERD' http://docs.google.com/viewer?a=v&q=cache:kwMIJ8gtNiAJ:action.web.ca/home/narcc/attach/USA%2520-%2520CERD%2520shadow%2520report%2520guide%2520-%2520IHRMG%2520-%25202001.pdf+Human+Rights+Law+Group+GUIDELINES+FOR+PREPARING+A+SHADOW+REPORT+FOR+THE+CERD&hl=en&gl=uk&sig=AHIEtbQe-JzOp6gEst4LI21jqDcKHBB9og, 20 August 2007).

[77] 'Committee on the Rights of the Child- Working Methods, "Overview of the Working Methods of the Committee on the Rights of the Child"' (http://www.ohchr.org/english/bodies/crc/workingmethods.htm, 19 December 2008).

Concluding Observations are made widely available in the State Party concerned.[78] The purpose of the Concluding Observations is to make the relevant State Party aware of additional information required by the Committee, in accordance with the Article 44 of the Convention, so that it can better assess the situation in the State Party.[79] In practice, though, the Concluding Observations are used for more than that; for instance, they recommend States Parties to sign up to International Treaties, the ICC and the ILO, and also to adapt their national legislation so that it accords more fully with the Treaties they are party to.

Finally, it is the Secretary–General's responsibility to inform the Committee of all cases of non-submission of reports, both the initial and periodic, by the States Parties.[80] After this, the Committee sends a reminder to the State Party concerning the submission of such reports(s) and undertakes any other efforts in a spirit of dialogue between the State concerned and the Committee.[81] However, if after a number of reminders have been sent there is still no response from a State Party, the Committee "shall consider the situation as it deems necessary"[82] and shall mention this in its report to the General Assembly. The Committee also considers the possibility of the need for technical assistance and advisory services to be provided to a State by the UN Centre for Human Rights. In case of persistent failure to respond by a State Party and taking account of all available information, the Committee may decide to consider the situation in the country in the absence of a report.[83]

The phrase "as it deems necessary" is open to broad interpretation. However, the Committee lacks any coercive powers and therefore cannot apply sanctions against those States Parties that fail to meet their reporting obligations. Moreover, as we shall see in later chapters, the great majority of States Parties fail to meet their deadlines and to comply fully with the reporting requirements, though some fail more seriously than others.

---

[78] UN Doc. CRC/C/33, 1994, Sections 21-2.

[79] Ibid., A deadline for submission of such written information is determined by the Committee. The Concluding Observations usually contain the following aspects: introduction; positive aspects (including progress achieved); factors and difficulties impending the implementation; principal subjects for concern; suggestions and recommendations addressed to the State Party.

[80] In accordance with the Article 44 of the Convention.

[81] UN Doc. Child CRC/C/4/REV.1, 2005, see rule 67.

[82] Ibid.

[83] UN Doc. CRC/C/33, 1994, see article 32. The State Party will be notified about such a decision in advance of the event.

4.4.2 States Parties' Duties and Obligations

The Committee has developed comprehensive guidelines for the preparation of initial and periodic reports by States Parties in an attempt to achieve its goal of dealing in a methodical and informative manner with the States Parties. Of the two Optional Protocols, here we shall consider only the OPAC. For both the CRC and OPAC there are two sets of guidelines,[84] one governing the form and content of the initial reports and the other governing those of the periodic reports.[85]

Pursuant to Article 44 of the Convention[86], governments are obliged to submit the initial report on their implementation of the Convention within two years of ratification and to report thereafter every five years. Similarly, according to Article 8 (1) of the Optional Protocol, each State Party is required to submit an initial report to the Committee within two years of the entry into force of the Optional Protocol. Thereafter, States Parties shall include in the reports they submit to the Committee, in

84 These Guidelines are contained in the UN Doc.CRC/C/5: General Guidelines regarding the content of Initial Reports to be submitted by States Parties under Article 44, paragraph 1 (a), of the Convention and UN Doc. CRC/C/58, 1996: General Guidelines regarding the form and contents of periodic reports to be submitted by states Parties under Article 44, paragraph 1 (b), of the Convention respectively. And CRC, Article 44(1)(a).

85 Under Article 44(1)(a) and in the UN. Doc. CRC/OP/AC/1, 2001: Guidelines Regarding Initial Reports to be submitted by states parties under Article 8(1) of the Optional Protocol to the Convention on the Rights of the Child on the Involvement of Children in Armed Conflicts.

86 Article 44 states: 1. States Parties undertake to submit to the Committee, through the Secretary-General of the United Nations, reports on the measures they have adopted which give effect to the rights recognised herein and on the progress made on the enjoyment of those rights: (a) Within two years of the entry into force of the Convention for the State Party concerned; (b) Thereafter every five years. 2. Reports made under the present article shall indicate factors and difficulties, if any, affecting the degree of fulfilment of the obligations under the present Convention. Reports shall also contain sufficient information to provide the Committee with a comprehensive understanding of the implementation of the Convention in the country concerned. 3. A State Party which has submitted a comprehensive initial report to the Committee need not, in the subsequent reports submitted in accordance with paragraph 1 (b) of the present article, repeat basic information previously provided. 4. The Committee may request from States Parties further information relevant to the implementation of the Convention. 5. The Committee shall submit to the General Assembly, through the Economic and Social Council, every two years, reports on its activities. 6. States Parties shall make their reports widely available to the public in their own countries.

accordance with Article 44 (1) (b) of the Convention, any further information with respect to the implementation of the Optional Protocol. States Parties to the Optional Protocol, who are not parties to the CRC (currently only the USA), must submit a report every five years, after the submission of the initial comprehensive report.[87]

In their reports, States Parties are required to provide "relevant legislative, administrative and other information, including statistical data" that will provide the Committee with adequate data for its analysis, and also information about "factors and difficulties encountered", "progress achieved", "implementation priorities" and "specific goals for the future".[88]

Second, with reference to the States Parties' reports for the CRC, the Committee has proposed a structured order for the contents of reports that serves as the agenda for the discussions with the States and enables every single article of the Convention to be covered in the report and presented in a logical order.[89]

Third, States Parties are required to provide information on measures taken to implement the Optional Protocol, such as the procedure for determining whether a potential recruit to the armed forces meets the age requirement. States are also asked to report any difficulties or special circumstances that affect their implementation of the Optional Protocol.

The Committee discusses the State Party report in open and public meetings, where other relevant information may be requested, such as copies of principal legislative texts and judicial decisions, administrative and other instructions to the armed forces, statistical information, indicators and other research. The State should also describe the process involved in preparing the report, including the role of governmental actors and non-governmental organisations in drafting and disseminating the report.

---

[87] UN. Doc. CRC/OP/AC/1, 2001.

[88] 'Committee on the Rights of the Child- Working Methods, "Overview of the Working Methods of the Committee on the Rights of the Child"' .

[89] The order that has to be followed in the report is as follows: (a) General measures of implementation; (b) Definition of the child; (c) General Principles; (d) Civil Rights and Freedoms; (e) Family environment and alternative care; (f) Basic health and welfare; (g) Education, leisure and cultural activities; (h) Special Protection measures: (i) Children in situations of emergency; (ii) Children in conflict with law; (iii)Children in situations of exploitation, including physical and psychological recovery and social reintegration; (iv)Children belonging to a minority or an indigenous group. This order applied both for the reports to the Convention and the Optional Protocol. For more details concerning each of the sections see UN Doc. CRC/C/33, 1994.

In its reviews, the Committee considers not only compliance with each article of the Optional Protocol but also adherence to the Convention's general principles – non-discrimination, the best interests of the child, the right to life, survival and development, and respect for the views of the child.

The reporting guidelines are useful tools as they provide details on steps required to implement the Optional Protocol, and enable children's rights advocates to point to specific measures required for States to fulfil their obligations.[90]

In addition to the duties and obligations described above, States Parties have implicit duties and obligations, for instance, managing the monitoring process by harmonising national law with international requirements, as well as encouraging cooperation and coordination between different governmental and non-governmental bodies of the state to speed up the process of data collection and report presentation.

4.4.3 Other Human Rights Committees

The Committee on the Rights of the Child is just one of eight Human Rights Committees, otherwise known as 'human rights treaty bodies' established by Human Rights treaties for holding States accountable for their Treaty commitments.

The other seven Committees share many similarities, with, as well as some differences from, the Committee on the Rights of the Child. First, all the Committees, except CESCR, were created by their corresponding instruments and their members are elected by the States Parties to the relevant Treaty. CESCR was created by the Economic and Social Council (ECOSOC) and its members are elected by the ECOSOC. As such CESCR is a subsidiary organ of ECOSOC, from whom it derives its authority from.[91]

Second, the members of these committees are independent experts (ranging in number from 10 to 23 members). They can be re-elected if nominated.

---

[90]UN Doc. CRC/OP/AC/1, 2001.

[91] 'Fact Sheet No.16 (Rev.1), The Committee on Economic, Social and Cultural Rights' (http://www.ohchr.org/Documents/Publications/FactSheet16rev.1en.pdf , 15 February 2008).

Table 4.1 Major International Human Rights Committees

Initials	Date Estab.	HR treaties	No. of Members	Initial Reports	Periodic reports
CERD	Dec 1965	International Convention on the Elimination of All Forms of Racial Discrimination (ICERD)	18	Within 1 yr	Every 2 yrs
CCPR	Dec 1966	International Covenant on Civil and Political Rights (ICCPR) and its Optional Protocols	18	Within 1 yr	Whenever requested (usually every 4 yrs)
CESCR	Dec 1966	International Covenant on Economic, Social and Cultural Rights (ICESCR)	18	Within 2 yrs	Every 5 yrs
CEDAW	Dec 1979	Convention on the Elimination of All Forms of Discrimination against Women (CEDAW) and its Optional Protocol (OP-CEDAW)	23	Within 1 yr	Whenever requested (usually every 4 yrs)
CAT	Dec 1984	Convention against Torture and Other Cruel, Inhuman or Degrading Treatment (CAT)	10	Within 1 yr	Every 4 yrs
CRC	Nov 1989	Convention on the Rights of the Child (CRC) and its Optional Protocols (OP-CRC-AC), (OP-CRC-SC)	18	Within 2 yrs	Every 5 yrs

CMW	Dec 1990	International Convention on the Protection of the Rights of All Migrant Workers and Members of their Families (ICRMW)	14	Within 1 yr	Every 5 yrs
CRPD	Dec 2006	International Convention on the Rights of Persons with Disabilities (ICRPD)	12	Within 2 yrs	Every 4 yrs

Third, the primary function of all the treaty bodies is to monitor States Parties' implementation of the relevant treaty. In particular, all treaty bodies consider reports submitted by States Parties in accordance with the treaty provisions. The process followed for the consideration of State reports by the treaty bodies has some essential common features, such as: i) submission of an initial report and subsequent periodic reports by a State Party; ii) the drafting of a list of issues and questions by a working group of the Committee which the State Party is to respond; iii) a written response to list of issues by the State Party; iv) formal consideration of the report by the Committee and the conduct of a constructive dialogue between the Committee and the State Party; v) the drafting of Concluding Observations and Recommendations by the Committee and, finally, vi) the implementation of Concluding Observations by the State Party.[92] CCPR, CERD, CAT and CEDAW are the only four Committees that can under certain conditions receive petitions from individuals who claim that their rights under the Treaties have been violated.[93] Finally, if a State Party fails to report to the Committee and does not respond to the Committee's request to report, the Committee can review the situation in the State concerned based on the information they have gathered, in the absence of any report from the State. This procedure is sometimes called a "review

[92] Office of the United Nations: High Commissioner for Human Rights, 'Fact Sheet No.30. The United Nations Human Rights Treaty System: An Introduction to the core human rights treaties and the treaty bodies': 29-31.

[93] 'Human Rights Treaty Bodies: Monitoring the core international human rights treaties', Office of the UN High Commissioner for Human Rights (http://www2.ohchr.org/english/bodies/treaty/index.htm, 18 October 2008).

procedure".[94] None of the Committees have the power to impose sanctions on a State Party for failing to comply with its treaty obligations, including its failure to submit reports or to report adequately.

Given the highly similar constitutions, power and roles of the Human Rights Committees, the study of the CRC Committee conducted in this thesis can function in some measure as a case study of the working of the Human Rights Committees in general. However, a full comprehensive study of the eight Committees falls outside the scope of this thesis.

4.5 Conclusion

Although the modest ambitions of article 38 of the CRC are unduly modest for many of its critics, the article has set a standard for the use of child soldiers, which all but two of the UNs member states have ratified. OPAC has set much more demanding standards in relation to children and war and armed conflict, and more than half of the UN's member states have ratified the Protocol. No less significant is the machinery the UN has established to monitor states' compliance with the CRC and OPAC, so that states' compliance with the Convention and the Protocol are not left merely to the good faith of states themselves. But how effectively has that machinery actually worked? It is to that question that we now turn.

[94] Office of the United Nations: High Commissioner for Human Rights, 'Fact Sheet No.30. The United Nations Human Rights Treaty System: An Introduction to the core human rights treaties and the treaty bodies': 33.

CHAPTER FIVE

STATES PARTIES' PERFORMANCE IN SUBMITTING REPORTS

5.1 Introduction

This chapter will begin the examination of the effectiveness of the UN's processes for monitoring children's rights. It examines the States Parties' reporting performance for the Convention on the Rights of the Child (CRC) and the two Optional Protocols to the Convention. The data used as the basis for this research is taken from sessions of the Committee of the Rights of the Child up to its forty-fourth session, which took place from 15/01/2007 to 2/02/2007. This was the most recent data available at the time the research was conducted.

The first part of the chapter will provide an analysis of states' reporting performance for the Convention and the Optional Protocols. Performance rates for the initial, second and third periodic reports for the CRC will be assessed along with those for the initial reports for OPAC and OPSC. The fourth periodic reports for the CRC are not examined since the due dates for these reports fall after 2007, so that the performance of states in submitting that report cannot yet be assessed.

Each of the reports will be assessed individually, and tables will show the performance of States Parties in relation to the deadline by which they were supposed to submit their reports. The due dates for each of the States Parties vary, for a treaty has a binding power over a state not when the state concerned signed the document, but after the act of ratification, acceptance, accession, or succession has taken place. For instance, Belgium signed the Convention on 26 January 1990 but it was not until 16 December 1991 that Belgium ratified the Convention and became bound by it. Pursuant to Article 49 of the Convention, "the Convention shall enter into force on the thirtieth day after the deposit by such State of its instrument of ratification or accession". Therefore, the due date for Belgium's initial report was not till January 1994. In short, the main reason for such a wide range of deadlines is the different times taken by individual states to ratify or accept the Convention. The same principle applies for the Optional Protocols, pursuant to Article 10 (2) (OPAC) and Article 14 (2) (OPSC).

5.2 Report Submission Rates

States Parties, as already stated, have clearly specified obligations in respect of both the CRC and its Optional Protocols. Prominent amongst these is their obligation to submit reports at regular intervals on the state of children's rights in their countries and on the measures they have taken to implement and maintain those rights. As a contribution to assessing the effectiveness of the UN's processes for promoting children's rights, we will now examine how promptly states meet their obligations to submit reports by the stipulated deadlines.

5.2.1 Initial Report Submission Rates

Table 5.1 Initial Report Submission Rates

Submission groups	No.	%
By the deadline	3	1.54
Within 3 months	26	13.33
Over 3 and within 6 months	10	5.13
Over 6 and within 12 months	17	8.72
Over 1 year and within 3 years	50	25.64
Over 3 and within 5 years	36	18.46
Over 5 and within 10 years	39	20.00
Over 10 years	4	2.05
Not submitted	10	5.13

States' initial report[1] performance shows that only three states, constituting 1.54%, actually met the deadline. Nearly 30% (28.72%) submitted their reports within twelve months of the deadline and just over half (54.36%)

[1] As at November 1, 2006 the Convention has been ratified or acceded to by 192 States. However the number of states that we have used for the analysis of initial reports is 195 due to the fact that Netherlands (Netherlands Antilles), Netherlands (Aruba) and United Kingdom of Great Britain and Northern Ireland (overseas territories) have submitted those reports. However these three cease to appear as independent States Parties for subsequent reports. For full details of States Parties' deadlines ad the dates on which they submitted their Initial Reports, see the volume of Supporting Data, pp. 15-23.

submitted their reports within three years of the deadline. But that leaves a large proportion of states (45.64 %) who submitted more than three years late and more than a quarter of states (27.18%) submitted their reports over five years late. Ten states, constituting 5.13% of the total, had still not submitted their initial reports.

5.2.2 Second Periodic Report Submission Rates

Table 5.2 Second Periodic Report Submission Rates

Submission groups	No.	%
By the deadline	4	2.08
Within 3 months	12	6.25
Over 3 and within 6 months	8	4.17
Over 6 and within 12 months	10	5.21
Over 1 year and within 3 years	24	12.50
Over 3 and within 5 years	20	10.42
Over 5 and within 10 years	24	12.50
Granted permission to consolidate (2nd, 3rd and 4th)	28	14.58
Consolidated reports that are overdue	4	2.08
Not submitted	56	29.17
Submission date later than 2007	2	1.04

As in the case of the initial report, a very small number of states (four, constituting 2.08%) actually met the deadline. Less than a fifth (17.70%) submitted within one year and about a third (30.20%) submitted within three years of the deadline. Two states have deadlines that fall after 2007, but that still leaves more than two-thirds of states (68.76%) who have been more than three years late with their submissions and over half (58.34%) who have been more than five years late. Excluding the two states which have still to reach their deadlines, fifty-six states (29.16%) have not submitted at all. Thus performance rates for submitting the second report have been significantly poorer than for the initial report. Some states have been granted permission to consolidate their reports. That is, some States Parties have been allowed to combine two or more of their reports and to submit them as a single document at a new deadline approved by the Committee. The criteria used for granting states the permission to consolidate their reports are unclear. However, the fact that states resort to consolidation is a sign of poor performance, since it results from their failure or inability to submit the second report by the deadline originally stipulated.

For over half of the states who have been granted permission to consolidate their reports, the new deadline is up to ten years later. Some of the states in this category are Israel, Turkmenistan, Guyana, Congo and Brazil. The deadlines for those states that have not yet submitted their reports vary. For example, Barbados, Gambia, Holy See, Zimbabwe are some of the states whose deadline was in 1997, while Bulgaria, Cote d'Ivoire, Kuwait, Nigeria and a number of other states had their deadline in 1998. On the other hand, the Cook Island and United Arab Emirates (UAE) whose deadline was in 2004 have still not submitted their reports. The above cases show that the failure of to submit their second periodic report cannot be due to their having unduly limited time within which to prepare their reports. Instead, it raises questions of whether other factors might impact upon their performance.

5.2.3 Third Periodic Report Submission Rates

Table 5.3 Third Periodic Report CRC

Submission groups	No.	%
By the deadline	2	1.04
Within 12 months	11	5.73
Over 1 year and within 3 years	7	3.65
Over 3 and within 5 years	2	1.04
Granted permission to consolidate (3rd and 4th)	96	50.00
Not submitted	60	31.25
Submission date later than 2007	14	7.29

Similarly to the initial and second periodic report, only two states, constituting 1.04%, actually met the deadline for the third report. 6.7% submitted within one year and only a further 4.69% within five years. The due date for fourteen states, amongst them Turkey, Netherlands, Serbia, Timor-Leste and UAE, falls during or after 2007, which leaves a third of states (31.25%) who have still not submitted. These include Cote d'Ivoire, Cambodia, Democratic Republic of Congo, Sierra Leone, Venezuela, Portugal, Greece and Monaco. For this report, the number of states consolidating their reports (50.00%) has almost doubled in comparison with the second periodic report. Amongst them are many European states, such as Germany, France, Italy, Estonia, Cyprus, Belgium, Luxembourg, Romania, United Kingdom, as well as many non-European states, for instance, Iran, Indonesia, Israel, Kiribati, Philippines, Solomon Islands,

United Republic of Tanzania and Uzbekistan. It is difficult to discern any pattern amongst those states that have consolidated their reports and those that have not.

5.2.4 Optional Protocols

Table 5.4 Submission Rates for (OPAC)

Submission groups	No.	%
By the deadline	2	1.82
Within 12 months	18	16.37
Over 1 year and within 3 years	8	7.27
Not submitted	59	53.64
Submission date later than 2007	23	20.90

As in the case of reports on the CRC, very few states actually met the deadline for their initial report on the OPAC: only New Zealand and Denmark (1.82%) did so. Almost a sixth (16.37%) submitted within one year, including Andorra, Costa Rica and Bangladesh. Eight states (7.27%) submitted within three years of the deadline. In contrast to the tables 5.1, 5.2 and 5.3, no table is given for states that have submitted over three years and within five years after the deadline, since for most states the due date was in 2004 or later. This leaves over half of the states (53.64%) that, more than two years after the deadline, have not submitted at all. Among these states are a significant number of European states, including Greece and Romania as well as non-European states, such as Sierra Leone, USA and Uganda. The remaining states (20.90%) have deadlines that fall during or after 2007.

By way of comparison, we might look at performance rates for the submission of reports on OPSC.

Table 5.5 Submission Rates (OPSC)

Submission groups	No.	%
By the deadline	0	0.00
Within 12 months	12	11.21
Over 1 year and within 3 years	8	7.48
Not submitted	67	62.62
Submission date later than 2007	20	18.69

No states met their deadline for the initial report for the OPSC. Only twelve states (constituting 11.21%) submitted their reports within a year. Qatar and Italy were among the states that submitted their reports within a few months of their deadline. Eight states (7.48%), including Denmark and France, submitted their reports within three years. The number of states that still have not submitted reports for the OPSC (62.62%) is much higher that for the OPAC. This leaves us with only twenty states (18.69%) to have their deadline for the reports during or after 2007, just three states less than for the OPAC. In short, table 5.5 shows that the reporting rates for OPSC are even poorer than for the OPAC.

Given the optional nature of the Protocols, we might expect that the states who are signatories to them to be more punctilious in meeting their reporting obligations. Yet, the data we have at present does not suggest that reporting performances for the Optional Protocols will be significantly better than for the Convention.

5.3 The Patterning of Submission Performances

5.3.1 Introduction

Given the wide variations in reporting performance that we have seen and given that almost all countries in the world are signatories to the CRC and a majority to the Optional Protocols, we can ask whether there is any pattern to these variations in reporting performance. Are the variations randomly spread across countries or do some categories of country perform better than others? In the remainder of this chapter, we shall examine how reporting performances for the CRC and OPAC correlate with geographical region (using continents as regions), income level and regime type. In addition, for OPAC, we shall examine whether variations in reporting performance relate to whether use of child soldiers is an issue for a country.

As always, there is a danger of moving too easily from correlations to causal relationships. For example, in so far as there are correlations between reporting performance and average income level, we might suppose those arise because richer countries are better equipped to produce reports than poorer countries. Similarly, we might expect regimes that have a better general human rights record to be more concerned to fulfil their human rights obligations in respect of the CRC and the Optional Protocol than countries who have shown less respect for human rights. However, the data presented here can be no more than suggestive of those possibilities. Moreover, we shall see that correlations are often far from strong.

The percentage tables give the percent of countries falling within each category (continent, income level, regime type) for each time-period (by the deadline, within one year of the deadline, etc.)

5.3.2 'States Parties' Submission Performance and Geographical Region

For the following analysis, the States Parties to the CRC and the OPAC have been examined as part of the geographical region they belong to[2]. Some states can be assigned to two different continents, for instance Russia spans Northern Asia and Easter Europe, while Turkey and Cyprus might be assigned to Western Asia and Middle East as well as to Southern Europe. For the purpose of this research all the three states have been assigned to Europe.

The United Kingdom of Great Britain and Northern Ireland Overseas Territories have submitted an initial report to the CRC, which contained reports relating to the Crown Dependencies of Antiguilla, Bermuda, the British Virgin Islands, the Cayman Islands, Montserrat, Pitcairn Island, St. Helena and its dependencies, the Turks and Caicos Islands. Since the body responsible for drafting and submitting the report (UK) is in Europe, they are included in Europe as well.

On the other hand, Netherlands Antilles and Netherlands Aruba which are geographically located in the Caribbean, and because the Charter for the Kingdom of the Netherlands represents an end to the colonial relations and the acceptance of the new legal system in which each nation will look after their own interests independently[3], they are regarded in this analysis as part of the Americas.

---

[2] Based on the division of the Nationsonline, 'The Continents of the World' (http://www.nationsonline.org/oneworld/continents.htm, 2 June 2007).

[3] US Department of States, 'Background Note: Netherlands Antilles' (http://www.state.gov/r/pa/ei/22528.htm, 2 June 2007).

5.3.2.1 Geographical Analysis of States Parties' Submission Performance for Initial Reports

Table 5.6 Numbers

Continents	By deadline	Within 1 y.	1-3 y.	3-5 y.	5-10 y. and over	Not submitted
Africa	1	9	7	13	22	0
America	0	11	8	9	8	0
Asia	1	13	16	7	4	4
Europe	1	17	15	6	6	1
Oceania	0	3	4	1	3	5

Table 5.7 Percentages

Continents	By deadline	Within 1 y.	1 -3 y.	3- 5 y.	5-10 y. and over	Not submitted
Africa	1.92	17.31	13.46	25.00	42.31	0.00
America	0.00	30.56	22.22	25.00	22.22	0.00
Asia	2.22	28.89	35.56	15.56	8.89	8.89
Europe	2.17	36.96	33.33	13.04	13.04	2.17
Oceania	0.00	18.75	25.00	6.25	18.75	31.25

The geographical performance analysis for the initial report for the CRC shows some differences in performance level according to continent. If we take reports that were submitted within three years of the deadline, the pattern is as follows: Europe (72.46%), Asia (66.67%), America (52.78%), Oceania (43.75%) and Africa (32.69%). This reveals a significant variation between continents. But it should also be noted that a significant number of countries in all continents submitted reports more than three years late and more than five years late. Moreover, while all countries in Africa and America have submitted their initial reports, these have still not submitted by one European country (2.17%), four Asia countries (8.89%) and five Oceanic countries (31.25%).

5.3.2.2 Geographical Analysis of States Parties' Submission Performance for Second Periodic Reports

Table 5.8 Numbers

Cont/s	By dead/ne	Within 1 y.	1- 3 y.	3- 5 y.	5-10 y. and over	Granted perm/ion to consolidate (2nd, 3rd, 4th)	Consolidated rep/s that are overdue	Not Sub/ed	Submission date later than 2007
Afr.	0	4	4	2	10	9	1	22	0
Am.	1	7	5	3	4	6	1	7	0
As.	2	7	6	9	5	4	1	10	1
Eur.	1	11	9	5	4	5	1	8	1
Ocea.	0	1	0	1	1	4	0	9	0

Table 5.9 Percentages

Cont/s	By dead/ne	Within 1 y.	1- 3 y.	3- 5 y.	5-10 y. and over	Granted perm/ion to consolidate (2nd, 3rd, 4th)	Consolidated rep/s that are overdue	Not Sub/ed	Submission date later than 2007
Afr.	0.00	7.69	7.69	3.85	19.23	17.31	1.92	42.31	0.00
Am.	2.94	20.59	14.71	8.82	11.76	17.65	2.94	20.59	0.00
As.	4.44	15.56	13.33	20.00	11.11	8.89	2.22	22.22	2.22
Eur.	2.22	24.44	20.00	11.11	8.89	11.11	2.22	17.78	2.22
Ocea.	0.00	6.25	0.00	6.25	6.25	25.00	0.00	56.25	0.00

For the second periodic reports, geographical analysis shows that within three years of the deadline, the continents' performances are as follows: Europe (46.66%), America (38.24%), Asia (33.33%), Africa (15.30%) and Oceania (6.25%). As with the initial report, the numbers reflect a significant variation between continents. It is worth remarking that, for the second report, an even larger proportion of all continents have either submitted their reports more than three years late or not submitted at all.

5.3.2.3 Geographical Analysis of States Parties' Submission Performance for Third Periodic Reports

Table 5.10 Numbers

Continents	By deadline	Within 1 y.	1- 5 y.	Granted permission to consolidate (3rd and 4th)	Not submitted	Submission date later than 2007
Africa	0	0	1	25	25	1
America	0	5	5	14	10	0
Asia	2	0	3	26	10	4
Europe	0	5	0	26	10	4
Oceania	0	1	0	5	5	5

Table 5.11 Percentages

Continents	By deadline	Within 1y.	1- 5 y.	Granted permission to consolidate (3rd and 4th)	No submitted	Submission date later than 2007
Africa	0.00	0.00	1.92	48.08	48.08	1.92
America	0.00	14.71	14.7	41.18	29.41	0.00
Asia	4.44	0.00	6.67	57.78	22.22	8.89
Europe	0.00	11.11	0.00	57.78	22.22	8.89
Oceania	0.00	6.25	0.00	31.25	31.25	31.25

For third periodic reports, geographical analysis for reports submitted up to five years late shows that continents' performances are: America (23.53%), Asia (11.11%), Europe (11.11%), Oceania (6.25%) and Africa

(1.92%). Since only a small number of third reports have been submitted, the submission of reports up to five years late, rather than up to three years late, has been used as the basis for comparison. In view of the recentness of deadlines for third reports, it is not possible at the moment to make inclusive assessments for these reports. However the existing figures reveal a very low performance rate from all continents.

5.3.2.4 Geographical Analysis of States Parties' Submission Performance for OPAC

Table 5.12 Numbers

Continents	By deadline	Within 1 y.	1- 3 y.	Not submitted	Submission date later than 2007
Africa	0	0	0	18	4
America	0	4	0	15	3
Asia	0	4	2	13	7
Europe	1	10	6	13	8
Oceania	1	0	0	0	1

Table 5.13 Percentages

Continents	By deadline	Within 1 y.	1- 3 y.	Not submitted	Submission date later than 2007
Africa	0.00	0.00	0.00	81.82	18.18
America	0.00	18.18	0.00	68.18	13.64
Asia	0.00	15.38	7.69	50.00	26.92
Europe	2.63	26.32	15.79	34.21	21.05
Oceania	50.00	0.00	0.00	0.00	50.00

Geographical analysis of OPAC initial reports submitted up to three years late shows that the ordering of continents is: Oceania (50%), Europe (44.74%), Asia (23.07%), America (18.18%) and Africa (0%). It should be noted that only two states from Oceania are States Parties to the OPAC, therefore the 50% for Oceania constitutes one country. Over half of the American and African states and over a third of European states have not submitted their reports. As with the third periodic CRC report, the deadlines for the initial report for the OPAC are relatively recent.

5.3.3 Overall Assessment

The data reveal some significant variations in states' performances by continent for submitting reports. Europe emerges as having the best record for both the initial and second reports, while America and Asia have better general records than Africa and Oceania. However, even Europe does not emerge with a very creditable record, given the proportion of European countries who have submitted their reports more than three years late. The variations amongst continents is great enough to suggest they are of some significance, but mere geography is, in itself, unlikely to have much explanatory power. The income level and regime types of states may have greater explanatory potential.

5.4 Income Level Analysis of States Parties' Submission Performance

Using the World Bank's classification of 184 member countries of the Bank and all other economies with populations of more than 30,000 (total 208), States Parties to the CRC and the OPAC, in this research, have been classified as high income (HI), upper middle income (UMI), lower middle income (LMI) or low (LI).[1] The percentage given for each type of income level is the percentage of countries falling within that income level for the relevant category. The percentages are designed to show how the reporting performances of the states of different income levels compare with one another. For this analysis, those states have been omitted for which no data is available.

5.4.1 Income Level Analysis of States Parties' Submission Performance for Initial Reports

Table 5.14 Numbers

Income Level (IL)	By deadline	Within 1 y.	1- 3y.	3 -5y.	5 – 10 y. and over	No submitted
HI	1	18	13	6	5	1
UMI	0	9	13	4	7	1
LMI	1	20	11	9	16	2
LI	0	6	12	17	15	2

[1] 'Country Classifications' *World Bank* (http://web.worldbank.org, 8 May 2007).

Table 5.15 Percentages

Income Level (IL)	By deadline	Within 1 y.	1 -3y.	3-5y.	5-10 y. and over	No submitted
HI	2.33	41.86	30.23	13.95	11.63	2.33
UMI	0.00	26.47	38.24	11.76	20.59	2.94
LMI	1.67	33.33	18.33	15.00	26.67	3.33
LI	0.00	11.54	23.07	32.69	28.85	3.85

The income level analysis for the initial report for the CRC shows a clear correlation between income level and reporting performance. In particular, the correlation is more obvious if we use the period of up to three years late, again, as a bench mark: HI 74.42%, UMI 64.71%, LMI 53.33%, LI 34.615%. The same type of correlation is evident in the figures for five years and over.

5.4.2 Income Level Analysis of States Parties' Submission Performance for Second Periodic Reports

Table 5.16 Numbers

IL	By deadline	Within 1 y.	1- 3 y.	3- 5 y.	5- 10 y.and over	Granted permission to consolidate (2nd, 3rd, 4th)	Consolidating reports that are overdue	Not submitted	Submission date later than 2007
HI	1	11	8	3	2	7	1	7	0
UMI	0	6	5	4	6	5	1	11	0
LMI	2	11	6	7	5	10	1	13	1
LI	1	2	5	6	11	6	1	20	1

Table 5.17 Percentages

IL	By deadline	Within 1 y.	1-3y.	3 – 5 y.	5- 10 y. and over	Granted permission to consolidate (2nd, 3rd, 4th)	Consolidating reports that are overdue	Not submitted	Submission date later than 2007
HI	2.50	27.50	20.00	7.50	5.00	17.50	2.44	17.50	0.00
UMI	0.00	15.79	13.16	10.53	15.79	13.16	2.63	28.95	0.00
LMI	3.57	19.64	10.71	12.50	8.93	17.86	1.82	19.64	1.82
LI	1.89	3.77	9.43	11.32	20.75	11.32	1.89	37.74	1.89

Using the same time frame of up to three years late, the order of reporting performance in terms of states parties' income level is: HI 50%, UMI 28.95%, LMI 30.25% and LI 15.09%. This clearly shows the existence of the same sort of correlation but less steeply and less smoothly than for the Initial report. The figures for those states that have been granted permission to consolidate their reports show: seven (17.50%) HI, five (13.16%) UMI, ten (17.86%) LMI and six (11.32%) LI. Hence, requests for permission to consolidate reports bear no relation to income levels.

5.4.3 Income Level Analysis of States Parties' Submission Performance for Third Periodic Reports

Table 5.18 Numbers

IL	By deadline	Within 1 y.	1-3 y.	3-5 y.	Granted permission to consolidate (3rd and 4th)	Not submitted	Submission date later than 2007
HI	0	5	0	0	23	8	4
UMI	0	2	2	1	19	8	4
LMI	1	4	4	1	26	20	2
LI	1	0	1	0	28	22	1

Table 5.19 Percentages

IL	By deadline	Within 1 y.	1-3 y.	3-5 y.	Granted permission to consolidate (3rd and 4th)	Not submitted	Submission date later than 2007
HI	0.00	12.50	0.00	0.00	57.50	20.00	10.00
UMI	0.00	5.56	5.53	2.8	52.78	22.22	11.11
LMI	1.72	6.89	6.9	1.72	44.83	34.48	3.45
LI	1.88	0.00	1.88	0.00	52.83	41.51	1.88

Due to very small numbers of States Parties that have submitted their third periodic report, it is hard to make any meaningful comparison between the income levels of States Parties and their submission dates. The limited data shows no particular correlation between submission dates and income level, although LI countries seem to be doing less well than countries at other income levels.

5.4.4 Income Level Analysis of States Parties' Submission performance for OPAC

Table 5.20 Numbers

IL	By deadline	Within 1 y.	1- 3y.	Not submitted	Submission date later than 2007
HI	2	11	5	9	5
UMI	0	1	2	14	3
LMI	0	4	0	19	9
LI	0	2	1	16	6

Table 5. 21 Percentages

IL	By deadline	Within 1 y.	1-3y.	Not submitted	Submission date later than 2007
HI	6.25	34.38	15.63	28.13	15.63
UMI	0.00	5.00	10.00	70.00	15.00
LMI	0.00	12.50	0.00	59.38	28.13
LI	0.00	8.00	4.00	64.00	24.00

Over half (56.26%) of the HI states submitted their report within three years of the deadline, followed by UMI 15%, LMI 12.50% and finally LI 12%. There is a relatively small difference between UMI, LMI and LI states reporting performance.

5.4.5 Overall Assessment

The analysis of the states parties' income level and reporting performance shows at times the existence of a clear correlation, especially for the initial report to the CRC and the OPAC. The correlation is less smooth for the second and third periodic reports. The contrast is more marked between HI states and other states. Differences between UMI, LMI and LI states are much less significant.

5. 5 Regime Types and States Parties' Submission Performance

5.5.1 Introduction

Regime type analysis of the States Parties reporting performance to the CRC and OPAC is designed to show how the reporting performances of different types of regime compare with one another. The percentage given for each regime type is the percentage of countries falling into that regime type for the relevant category. The data used is from two independent sources, 'The Economist Intelligence Unit's Democracy Index' (EIUDI)[1] and the Freedom House classifications[2].

The EIUDI data is based on five categories: electoral process and pluralism; civil liberties; the functioning of the government; political participation; and political culture. The five categories are interrelated and form a coherent conceptual whole. The EIUDI provides a snapshot of the current state of democracy worldwide for the majority of independent states and divides them in full democracies (FD), flawed democracies (fD), authoritarian regimes (AR) and finally, hybrid regimes (HR).

The Freedom House data is a comparative assessment of political rights and civil liberties and cover a total of 192 countries of which 14 have related and disputed territories. The related territories include Hong Kong in China and Puerto Rico in the United States, while the disputed territories are Nagorno-Karabakh in Armenia/Azerbaijan, Tibet in China, Northern (Turkish) Cyprus in Cyprus, Abkhazia in Georgia, Kashmir in India, Israeli-Occupied Territories Palestinian Authority – Administered Territories in Israel, Transnitria in Moldova, Western Sahara in Morocco, Kashmir in Pakistan, Chechnya in Russia, Kosovo in Serbia, and Somaliland in Somalia [3] Each country has been assigned a numerical rating based on a 1 to 7 scale, with 1 representing the highest and 7 the lowest level of freedom. Each pair of political rights and civil liberties

[1] Laza Kekic, 'The Economist Intelligence Unit Index of Democracy" *The Economist* (http://www.economist.com/media/pdf/DEMOCRACY_INDEX_2007_v3.pdf, 15 March 2007).

[2] 'Freedom in the World 2006' *Freedom House Organisation* (http://www.freedomhouse.org/uploads/press_release/fiw07_charts.pdf, 22 March 2007).

[3] Ibid.

ratings is averaged[4] to determine an overall status of "Free" (F), "Partly Free" (PF), or "Not Free" (NF).

Data was not available data for all the member states of the CRC and the OPAC. The calculated percentages apply only to those countries for which the data on regime type was available.

5.5.2 Regime Types and States Parties' Submission Performance for Initial Reports

Table 5.22 EIUDI Data – Numbers

Regimes	By deadline	Within 1 y.	1-3y.	3-5y.	5-10 y. and over	Not submitted
FD	2	15	10	1	1	0
fD	0	17	13	8	8	4
HR	0	5	8	8	9	0
AR	2	14	14	9	15	1

Table 5.23 EIUDI Data – Percentages

Regimes	By deadline	Within 1 y.	1-3y.	3-5y.	5-10 y. and over	Not submitted
FD	0.00	55.56	37.04	3.70	3.70	0.00
fD	0.00	34.00	26.00	16.00	16.00	8.00
HR	0.00	16.67	26.67	26.67	30.00	0.00
AR	3.64	24.45	25.45	16.36	27.27	1.82

EIUDI Regime type analysis shows that 92.6% (56) FD states submitted their initial reports up to three years late, followed by 60.00% fD, 43.34% HR and 53.54% AR states. This leaves us with FD 7.4%, fD 32.00%, HR 56.67% and AR 43.63% states that submitted their initial reports over five and up to ten years late.

[4] The numbers that have been given for the Civil Liberty and Political Rights have been added up and calculated in a scale 1 to 14 in order to end up with the final statement of the status.

Table 5.24 Freedom House– Numbers

Regimes	By deadline	Within 1 y.	1-3y.	3 - 5y.	5-10 y. and over	Not submitted
F	1	29	26	13	15	4
PF	3	10	13	11	19	4
NF	0	14	10	10	9	0

Table 5.25 Freedom House Data – Percentages

Regimes	By deadline	Within 1 y.	1 -3y.	3 - 5y.	5-10 y. and over	Not submitted
F	1.14	32.95	29.55	14.77	17.05	4.55
PF	5.00	16.67	21.67	18.33	31.67	6.67
NF	0.00	32.56	23.25	23.25	20.93	0.00

Freedom house regime type analysis, using the three year cut-off point, yielded a similar picture to EIUDI: F 63.64%, PF 43.34%, NF 55.81%. This reveals the existence of a clear correlation between FD and F countries. Differences between other types of regime have relatively little significance.

5.5.3 Regime Types and States Parties' Submission Performance for Second Periodic Reports

Table 5.26 EIUDI DATA – Numbers

Regimes	By deadline	Within 1 y.	1- 3 y.	3- 5 y.	5-10 y. and over	Granted permission to consolidate (2nd, 3rd, 4th)	Consolidating reports that are overdue	Not submitted	Submission date later than 2007
FD	1	12	4	3	7	1	0	2	0
fD	1	6	11	7	8	6	1	8	2
HR	1	5	2	0	7	6	0	9	0
AR	1	7	6	9	3	5	2	22	0

Table 5.27 EIUDI Data – Percentages

Regimes	By deadline	Within 1 y.	1- 3 y.	3- 5 y.	5-10 y. and over	Granted permission to consolidate (2nd, 3rd, 4th)	Consolidating reports that are overdue	Not submitted	Submission date later than 2007
FD	3.70	44.44	14.82	11.11	25.93	3.70	0.00	7.41	0.00
fD	2.00	12.00	22.00	14.00	16.00	12.00	2.00	16.00	4.00
HR	3.33	16.67	6.67	0.00	23.33	20.00	0.00	30.00	0.00
AR	1.82	12.73	10.91	16.36	5.45	9.09	3.64	40.00	0.00

EIU data shows that 62.96% (17) FD states submitted their second periodic report up to three years late, followed by fD 36.00%, HR 26.67 % and AR 25.46%. It is worth remarking that a significant number of FD and fD states submitted their report over three and up to ten years late, as well as that almost the same number of states from all regime types have been granted permission to consolidate their reports.

Using up to three years as a bench mark, again, shows that F 34.48%, PF 29.31% and NF 25% submitted their reports. The categories used by Freedom House therefore reveal much less striking correlations than those used by EIU.

Table 5.28 Freedom House Data–Numbers

Regimes	By dead line	Within 1y.	1-3 y.	3-5 y.	5- 10 y. and over	Granted permission to consolidate (2nd, 3rd, 4th)	Consolidating reports that are overdue	Not submitted	Submission date later than 2007
F	1	15	14	10	14	12	1	19	1
PF	3	9	5	1	7	10	2	20	1
NF	0.00	6	5	9	3	6	1	14	0

Table 5.29 Freedom House Data–Percentages

Regimes	By dead line	Within 1y.	1-3 y.	3-5 y.	5- 10 y. and over	Granted permission to consolidate (2nd, 3rd, 4th)	Consolidating reports that are overdue	Not submitted	Submission date later than 2007
F	1.15	17.24	16.09	11.49	16.09	13.79	1.15	21.84	1.15
PF	5.17	15.52	8.62	1.72	12.07	17.24	3.45	34.48	1.72
NF	0.00	13.64	11.36	20.45	6.82	13.64	2.27	31.82	0.00

5.5.4 Regime Types and States Parties' Submission Performance for Third Periodic Reports

Table 5.30 EIUDI Data– Numbers

Regimes	By deadline	Within 1 y.	1-3 y.	3-5 y.	Granted permission to consolidate (3rd and 4th)	Not submitted	Submission date later than 2007
FD	0	6	0	0	14	6	1
fD	0	2	3	2	28	11	4
HR	0	3	2	0	14	10	1
AR	2	0	1	0	27	23	2

Table 5.31 EIUDI Data– Percentages

Regimes	By deadline	Within 1 y.	1- 3 y.	3- 5 y.	Granted permission to consolidate (3rd and 4th)	Not submitted	Submission date later than 2007
FD	0.00	22.22	0.00	0.00	51.85	22.22	3.70
fD	0.00	4.00	6.00	4.00	56.00	22.00	8.00
HR	0.00	10.00	6.67	0.00	46.67	33.33	3.33
AR	3.64	0.00	1.82	0.00	49.09	41.82	3.64

Using, as with the previous reports, the benchmark of up to three years late, the regime type performance analysis is: FD 22.22%, fD 10.00%, HR 16.67% and AR 5.46%. The majority of states from all regime types have either been granted permission to consolidate their reports or have not submitted them at all.

Table 5.32 Freedom House Data - Numbers

Regimes	By deadline	Within 1 y.	1-3 y.	3-5 y.	Granted permission to consolidate (3rd and 4th)	Not submitted	Submission date later than 2007
F	0	6	2	1	49	23	6
PF	1	4	4	1	25	22	4
NF	1	1	1	0	22	14	2

Table 5.33 Freedom House Data - Percentages

Regimes	By deadline	Within 1 y.	1-3 y.	3-5 y.	Granted permission to consolidate (3rd and 4th)	Not submitted	Submission date later than 2007
F	0.00	6.9	2.3	1.15	56.32	26.44	6.9
PF	1.64	6.56	6.56	1.64	40.98	36.06	6.56
NF	2.44	2.44	2.44	0.00	53.66	34.15	4.88

The freedom house analysis compared to EIU shows that for the same period of time the results are: F 9.2%, PF 14.76%, and NF 7.32%. The small percentage of states of all types that have submitted their reports within three years of the deadline makes comparison less meaningful than for the earlier reports.

5.5.5 Regime Types and States Parties' Submission Performance for OPAC

Table 5.34 EIUDI Data – Numbers

Regimes	By deadline	Within 1 y.	1-3y.	Not submitted	Submission date later than 2007
FD	2	10	4	7	3
fD	0	4	1	25	9
HR	0	1	0	11	3
AR	0	2	2	13	6

Table 5.35 EIUDI Data – Percentages

Regimes	By deadline	Within 1 y.	1-3y.	Not submitted	Submission date later than 2007
FD	7.69	38.46	15.38	26.92	11.54
fD	0.00	10.26	2.56	64.10	23.07
HR	0.00	6.67	0.00	73.33	20.00
AR	0.00	8.70	8.70	56.52	26.09

The regime type analysis of the reporting performance of the states parties for the OPAC showed that for up to three years late the figures are: 61.53% (16) FD states, 12.82% fD, 6.67% HR, and 17.4% AR. This shows a marked contrast between FD states and other regime types, but no correlation beyond that.

Table 5.36 Freedom House Data – Numbers

Regimes	By deadline	Within 1 y.	1-3y.	Not submitted	Submission date later than 2007
F	2	13	6	28	11
PF	0	3	0	21	5
NF	0	2	2	9	7

Table 5.37 Freedom House Data – Percentages

Regimes	By deadline	Within 1 y.	1-3y.	Not submitted	Submission date later than 2007
F	3.33	21.67	10.00	46.67	18.33
PF	0.00	10.34	0.00	72.41	17.24
NF	0.00	10.00	10.00	45.00	35.00

Freedom House data for the same time-frame showed F 35%, PF 10.34 %, NF 20%. This shows a very obvious contrast between the F and PF and NF states. As with the EIUDI data, F states have the best level of performance though the contrast is less stark for the F states than for FD states. But also as noted the EIUDI, there is no 'sliding scale' correlation beyond that.

5.6 Child Soldiers and States Parties' Submission Performance for OPAC

This section examines whether the issue of child soldiers might have a bearing on the relative performances of states in reporting on OPAC. We might hypothesise that states in which child soldiering is an issue will be more reluctant to report since reporting involves exposing their position to the world. The data on child soldiering used here is drawn from a report published by the Coalition to Stop the Use of Child Soldiers published in 2004. The report covers the period from April 2001 to March 2004. It used a wide range of resources: UN agencies and peacekeeping missions, other intergovernmental organisations, news media, academic sources, and human rights and humanitarian organisations.[1]

Tables 5.38 and 5.39 show how reporting performances relate to the presence of child soldiering as an issue both for the state's own government forces and for political groups operating is a state's territory. The abbreviations used here are: I (indicated recruitment of child soldiers); P (possible recruitment of child soldiers); N (No issue of child soldiering reported) and L (legal possibility of recruitment or use of child soldiers in cases with no reported practice, but with a legal minimum recruitment age below 18). The percentages given for each type (I, P, N, L) is the percentage of countries falling within that type for the relevant category.

Table 5.38 Numbers

a) In Government Forces

Regimes	By deadline	Within 12 m.	1-3 y.	Not submitted	Due date during 2007 and later
I	1	4	0	8	5
P	0	0	0	2	2
N	1	8	4	30	6
L	0	3	3	11	8

[1] For more details look at 'Child Soldiers Global Report 2004' *Coalition to Stop the Use of Child Soldiering* (http:www.child-soldiers.org/library/global-reports?root_id=159&category_id=165, 15 January 2007).

b) Political groups

Regimes	By deadline	Within 12 m.	1-3 y.	Not submitted	Due date during 2007 and later
I	0	0	0	8	5
P	0	0	0	2	0
N	0	1	0	7	0
L	0	0	0	0	0

Table 5.39 Percentages

a) In Government Forces

Regimes	By deadline	Within 12 m.	1-3 y.	Not submitted	Due date during 2007 and later
I	3.70	14.81	0.00	29.63	18.52
P	0.00	0.00	0.00	22.22	22.22
N	1.29	10.38	5.19	38.96	7.79
L	0.00	6.39	6.38	23.40	17.02

b) Political groups

Regimes	By deadline	Within 12 m.	1-3 y.	Not submitted	Due date during 2007 and later
I	0.00	0.00	0.00	30.77	19.23
P	0.00	0.00	0.00	15.38	0.00
N	0.00	7.14	0.00	50.00	0.00
L	0.00	0.00	0.00	0.00	0.00

For the purpose of this analysis, we have divided the table in two sections based on where the child soldiers may be deployed, either in the government forces or in political (militia) groups. Using up to three years late as a basis for comparison, the analysis for the government forces section provides us with the following sequence: I 18.51%, P 0%, N 16.86% and L 12.76%. This results show that the largest percentage of states with indicated recruitment of children in their government forces have submitted their report. On the other hand, thirty states (38.96%) with no reported child recruitment in the army have not submitted their report – the largest percentage of any category. The data for political groups is far too sparse to make any comparison possible. Even the data for government forces consists of a relatively small number of countries. However, what the existing data shows is that there is no correlation between the presence or absence of child soldiers and the States Parties' reporting performance on the OPAC, so there is nothing in these figures to suggest that countries in which child soldiering is an issue are more reluctant to report than those in which it is not.

5.7 Conclusion

This Chapter has shown that, on the whole, State Parties' have a very poor record in submitting their reports according to the timetable set for the CRC. Only a tiny number of States Parties have submitted their reports by the stipulated deadlines. Just over half submitted their initial reports within three years of the deadline, but a quarter submitted over five years late and some had still not reported more than ten years after the deadline. The record of report submissions for second and third periodic reports has been even poorer and submissions for OPAC show a similar pattern. Increasingly the Committee has allowed states to 'consolidate' two or more of their reports as a way of enabling them to make up lost ground.

There is some geographical variation in States Parties' submissions record, with, on average, European and American states performing better than Asians states, and Asian states performing better than African and Oceanic states. High income level states also generally perform better than low income level states, with middle income states falling between the two. Full democracies have, on average, a better record than states with other types of regime. These variables are, of course, overlapping. Correlations between them and submissions are conspicuous but not very strong and perhaps more noteworthy is the number of late submissions in all categories.

CHAPTER SIX

STATES PARTIES' REPORTING PERFORMANCES IN REPORTING ON ARTICLE 38 OF THE CONVENTION ON THE RIGHTS OF THE CHILD

This chapter examines States Parties' reporting on article 38 of the Convention on the Rights of the Child. The data-source used for this research is the same as for the chapters on the effectiveness of the UN's processes for monitoring children rights and the reporting performance for the Optional Protocol on the involvement of children in conflict and war situations: reports submitted by States Parties up to the 44th session of the Committee.

The chapter is divided into four main sections. The first section will look at how adequately the reporting guidelines for the initial and periodic reports have been met by the States Parties and the depth and detail of States Parties' reporting on article 38. Particular attention will be paid to how far States Parties comply with each of the reporting guidelines. For this research all initial, second and third reports submitted to the 44th session have been examined. The second section will examine and evaluate the Committee's List of Issues and Concluding Observations. A selective method was used for this research, a sample amounting to fifty percent of all reports was examined to gain a reliable overview of the Committee's practice. How reporting performance correlates with geographical region, income level and regime type will be examined in the third section. The last section will focus on States Parties that have experienced war or civil conflict during the reporting period and for which there is well-established evidence of the use of child soldiers, either by governments' own militaries or by the militias of non-state groups. Since this is precisely the kind of activity that article 38 is designed to prevent, there is particular reason to examine whether use of child soldiers has been reported by the States Parties concerned.

6.1 The Guidelines for Reporting and States Parties Reporting Performance

As has already been discussed in previous chapters, States Parties are required to submit their initial report to the Committee within two years following entry into force of the Convention and to submit subsequent reports every five years thereafter. To facilitate a more structured discussion, the Committee on the Rights of the Child in its reporting guidelines has grouped the articles of the CRC according to their content and in a logical order. For instance, "General measures of Implementations" section, covers articles 4, 42 and 44.6 of the Convention while articles 28, 29 and 31 are reported in the "Education, Leisure and Cultural Activities" section.

The "Special Protection Measures" section consists of four sub-sections, each of which aims to cover different aspects of children's vulnerability. Article 38 is grouped together with articles 22 and 39 of the Convention, which are to be reported under the 'Children in situations of emergency' subsection. The remaining three subsections are 'Children in conflict with the law' (arts. 40, 37 and 39); 'Children in situations of exploitation, including physical and psychological recovery and social reintegration' (arts.32, 33, 34, 35, 36 and 39); and finally 'Children belonging to a minority or an indigenous group' (art.30).

The general guidelines regarding the form and the content of initial reports to be submitted by States Parties in paragraph 23 state that for articles 22, 38 and 39 "States Parties are requested to provide relevant information, including the principal legislative, judicial, administrative or other measures in force; factors and difficulties encountered and progress achieved in implementing the relevant provisions of the Convention; and implementation priorities and specific goals for the future in respect of each of the articles mentioned in the subsections".[1]

The Committee's reporting guidelines for the structure and content of States Parties' periodic reports are more focused and specific to each article of the convention than its guidelines for the initial reports. In relation to article 38, the guidelines request the States Parties to provide extensive information for each paragraph of the article to ensure its implementation, as well as indicate that the State Party in question ensures respect for the general principles of the Convention, namely non-discrimination, the best interests of the child, respect for the views of the child and the right to life, development and survival to the maximum

[1] UN Doc.CRC/C/5.

extent.[2] For instance, pursuant to article 38, paragraph 2, "States Parties should not only indicate all measures taken to ensure that persons under the age of 15 do not take a direct part in hostilities but also indicate any measures adopted to ensure the protection of the rights of the child during hostilities and mechanisms in place for monitoring such situation".[3] Paragraph 3, provides that States Parties' reports should include the measures adopted to ensure that persons under 15 years of age are not recruited into the armed forces, and to ensure that among those between the ages of 15 and 18, priority is given to those who are oldest. Furthermore, reports should indicate any mechanisms established to monitor this situation, as well as the proportion of children being recruited or voluntarily enlisted into armed forces, categorised by age, gender, social and ethnic origin.[4]

The analysis of States Parties' reports shows, first, a decrease in the numbers of reports submitted by the States Parties for each of the periodic reports. Almost all of the initial reports have been submitted (186 of 195). A substantial number of second periodic reports have been submitted, though this constitutes a little more than half of reports due. Nevertheless, the number of reports submitted is large enough to be indicative of a general pattern to enable comparisons of the sort that will be made in section 3 of this chapter. A very small proportion of the third reports have been submitted. Figures of these have been given in table below, but the proportion is too small to enable a meaningful comment on the pattern of reporting in the third reports.

Of those states that have submitted reports, a significant number have not reported on article 38 at all: 122 states in their initial reports, 54 in their second periodic report and 14 in their third periodic report. States reports in this category either make no reference to article 38 at all, or mention it only in the title of the relevant section and then report only on state policies in relation to articles 22 and 39 of the Convention.

Table 1 shows that two thirds of initial and third periodic reports, and a little more than half of second periodic reports, fail to refer to article 38. Thus only a minority of states' reports for each period actually report on the article 38 of the Convention.

Of those States Parties that do report on article 38, the majority in all three reports report primarily on legislative, administrative and judicial measures in place, but make little or no reference to factors and difficulties they have encountered, the progress they have achieved, and their future

---

[2] Ibid., para.128.
[3] CRC/C/58: para.124.
[4] Ibid. para.125.

goals for the successful implementation of each of the principles of this article.

Table 6.1 Frequency of States Parties' Reporting on Article 38

Reports	Submissions	Reported	%	Not Reported	%
Initial Report	186	64	34.41	122	65.59
Second P.R	102	48	47.06	54	52.94
Third P.R	21	7	33.33	14	66.67

For the initial report, some of the exceptions that do meet the Committee's guidelines more fully are the reports submitted by Austria, Canada, Honduras, Sweden and Swaziland, all of which comment on each paragraph of the article individually. Swaziland's report is divided into three main sections: law and policy, implementations, and constraints, and provides the Committee with a very detailed account of State's policy in implementing the provisions of article 38. Another example is Uruguay, which, despite the fact that it has no compulsory military service, informs the Committee not only about the national and international legislation applicable to the state but also that the minimum age for voluntary conscription is 18.

Analysis of second periodic reports reveals that some States Parties have submitted a much more detailed and structured report than their initial reports. For instance, Germany and Guatemala offer detailed accounts of their national policies and the plans they have in place. Canada, Sweden, Paraguay and Trinidad and Tobago have provided the Committee with very detailed and analytical reports by focusing individually on each of the four paragraphs of the article.

All seven of the third periodic reports that report on article 38 discuss in their reports the national and international documents relating to the article that their states have ratified and national amendments that might take place. Maldives, Russia and Yemen are the only States Parties which in their reports refer to a national strategy to reduce the involvement of children in conflict situations and inform the Committee about the situation in their state or neighbouring states. For instance, Russia's third periodic report describes the situation in Caucasus and in the Chechen Republic and Yemen's reports on mines explosions and how many mines have been cleared at the time of the report.

6.2 The Committee's List of Issues and its Concluding Observations

This section examines the extent to which the Committee's List of Issues and Concluding Observations have addressed States Parties' reports in relation to article 38 of the Convention in each of the three reports submitted by the States Parties.

6.2.1 List of Issues

The Committee uses List of Issues to request additional informational from States Parties. Part IV of the Committee's List of Issues, gives issues that do not require written responses by the State Party in question, but can be addressed by the Committee during the dialogue with the State Party concerned.

Examination of the Committee's List of Issues reveals two main findings. First, when States Parties do not report on article 38, the Committee most frequently does not address this in its List of Issues. For instance, none of the States Parties' third periodic reports that had not reported on article 38, has been addressed by the Committee's List of Issues. Instead the Committee asks them to provide additional information for articles 22 and 39 of the Convention. It does occasionally ask for information relevant to article 38 but that request arises from what States Parties have said about articles 22 and 39, rather than in response to their failure to report on article 38. In general, the Committee asks for additional written information. However, the Committee took up the case of Israel's military actions in the Occupied Palestinian Territories[5] and the issue of child soldiers in Sierra Leone's [6] in Part IV of its List of Issues. Part IV of List of the Issues requires a state to engage in oral dialogue with the Committee rather than provide written responses.

Secondly, the Committee sometimes requests additional information or makes requests from States Parties that have already reported on their national policies and measures in force for the implementation of the article 38. Finland and the Netherlands, for instance, have been very explicit in their initial reports; nevertheless the Committee asked them to

[5] UN Doc. CRC/C/Q/ISR.1 (List of Issues): Israel. 14/06/2002. Israel had reported but not in great detail.

[6] UN Doc. CRC/C/SLE/Q/2: (List of Issues): Sierra Leone. 4/07/2007.

raise their minimum age for military service to 18 years of age.[7] Nepal, Philippines and Rwanda are some of the States Parties that, in relation to their second periodic reports, have been asked to provide additional information regarding children involved in armed conflict.[8] Colombia, despite the fact that it has reported in its third periodic report in great depth on article 38, has been asked to provide the Committee with the exact number of child victims of Human Rights violations and forced recruitment.[9]

Oddly therefore, a State Party that reports on article 38 is liable to be asked for additional information relating to that article, while States Parties that say nothing about article 38 are unlikely to be asked to make good their omission.

6.2.2 Concluding Observations

On January 1993, at Committee's second session it was decided that, once a report by a State Party has been considered, Concluding Observations would be issued to serve as a starting point for the periodic reports to be submitted at a later stage by the States Parties.[10] Concluding Observations would reflect the main points of discussion as well as indicate issues that would require further attention. In fact, the Committee "emphasised the importance of providing the State Party with an authoritative statement that would convey the views of the Committee on the implementation of the Convention by that State Party".[11] It was decided that the structure of the Concluding Observations should comply with the structure of the Concluding Observations issued by the Human Rights Committee.[12] The Committee's Concluding Observations generally start by highlighting positive aspects in the reports, before discussing areas of concern, and making suggestions and recommendations.

Although, all the above mentioned details refer to the Concluding Observations issued to the States Parties of the Convention on the Rights

---

[7] UN Doc. CRC/C.11/WP.6. (List of Issues): Finland. 27/11/95 and UN Doc. CRRC/C/Q/NET.1. (List of Issues): Netherlands. 30/06/99.

[8] UN Doc. CRC/C/Q/NPL/2 (List of Issues): Nepal 04/02/2005: para.10 (i), UN Doc. CRC/C/Q/RWA/2 (List of Issues): Rwanda. 09/02/2004: para.10 (a) and UN Doc. CRC/C/Q/PHL/2 (List of Issues): Philippines. 04/02/2005: para.9 (d).

[9] UN Doc. CRC/C/COL/Q/3 (List of Issues): Colombia. 15/02/2006.

[10] UN. Doc. A/49/41: Report of the Committee on the Rights of the Child: 19/05/1994: 67-8.

[11] Ibid., 68.

[12] Ibid.

of the Child, the same applies to the Concluding Observations regarding the Optional Protocol that will be discussed later on in Chapter 6.

The Concluding Observations are structured according to the following headings: i) introduction; ii) positive aspects; iii) main areas of concern and recommendations; iv) follow-up and dissemination and v) next report.

The Committee's Concluding Observations relating to article 38 can be categorised into three groups of observation. The first group includes all the Concluding Observations addressed to those States Parties who have made no reference to their implementation policies for article 38. In these cases the Committee makes no observation on the states standing in relation to article 38.[13] This can be regarded as a major failing of the Committee.

Secondly, where a State party has reported on article 38 the Committee occasionally uses its Concluding Observations to comment critically on the information it has been given. For instance, in relation to Bahrain's initial periodic report, the Committee in its Concluding Observations note that "*the initial State party report was in accordance with the guidelines, although much of the information related to legal provisions or assertions of guarantees without providing information about how rights are actually enjoyed in practice.*"[14] The Concluding Observations for Iran's initial report state that "*The Committee regrets that the report is essentially legalistic and does not provide a self-critical evaluation of the prevailing*

[13] For instance, the Committee has made no reference in its Concluding Observations for the implementation of article 38 for the following Initial reports UN.Doc. CRC/C/15/Add.168 (Concluding Observations): Cape Verde. 7/11/2001, UN.Doc: CRC/C/15/Add.88 (Concluding Observations): Democratic People's Republic of Korea. 5/06/1998, UN.Doc: CRC/C/15/Add.130 (Concluding Observations): Suriname. 28/06/2000, UN.Doc: CRC/C/15/Add.224 (Concluding Observations): Guyana. 26/02/2004, UN.Doc. CRC/C/15/Add.149 (Concluding Observations): Palau. 21/02/2001, UN.Doc: CRC/C/15/Add.192 (Concluding Observations): Republic of Moldova. 31/10/2002 and UN.Doc: CRC/C/15/Add.214 (Concluding Observations): San Marino. 27/10/2003. Second periodic report of **Kyrgyzstan**, UN.Doc. CRC/C/SLE/CO/2 (Concluding Observations): Sierra Leone. 20/06/2008, UN. Doc. CRC/C/UZB/CO/2 (Concluding Observations): Uzbekistan. 02/06/2006, UN. Doc. CRC/C/15/Add.250 (Concluding Observations): Luxembourg. 31/03/2005, UN. Doc. CRC/C/MUS/CO/2 (Concluding Observations): Mauritius. 17/03/2006, UN.Doc. CRC/C/15/Add.126 (Concluding Observations): Norway. 28/06/2000 and UN.Doc. CRC/C/15/Add.233 (Concluding Observations): Panama. 30/06/2004.

[14] UN. Doc. CRC/C/114 (Report on the Twenty-Ninth Session: Geneva, 14 January – 1 February 2002): Bahrain. para.453.

situation of the exercise of children's rights in the country".[15] The Committees' Concluding Observations on Cyprus' second periodic report mention that "*the Committee regrets that the second periodic report was rather legalistic, did not address practical aspects of implementation and was not prepared in accordance with the general guidelines regarding the form and contents of periodic reports (CRC/C/58).*"[16]

In the third group, while the Committee occasionally makes observations directly related to article 38, it much more frequently makes observations related to articles 22 and 39. For example, New Zealand and Switzerland did in their initial reports provide information related to article 38 but the Committee in its Concluding Observations focused only on articles 22 and 39. China in its second periodic report and Chile, Finland and Denmark in their third periodic report did not provide information related to article 38. Nevertheless the Committee made no observations on that omission but did comment on articles 22 and 39.

Fourthly, the Committee sometimes uses the Concluding Observations to comment on the actual situation of children in the states and to urge states to take practical measures to improve the protection of children from armed conflict. For example, the Concluding Observations on Nepal's second periodic report state "*the Committee is highly alarmed by the number who were killed in armed conflicts in the State party. The Committee notes with grave concern the reports of abduction and forcible conscription of children by the armed groups for political indoctrination and for use as combatants, informants, cooks or porters and as human shield...the Committee is also concerned about the negative impact of the armed conflict on food supplies, education and health acre.*"[17]As a result the Committee recommends that the "*State party develop a comprehensive policy and programme for implementation of the rights of children who have been affected by conflict, and allocate human and financial resources accordingly. In particular, the Committee recommends: Criminalise abduction, recruitment and use of children for military purposes...*".[18]

The Concluding Observations on Philippines' second periodic report express concern "*that the State party is able to provide only the arrested child soldiers with physical and psychological recovery and social*

---

[15] UN. Doc. CRC/C/97 (Report of the Twenty-Forth Session: Geneva, 15 May – 2 June 2000): Iran: para..23.

[16] UN. Doc. CRC/C/132 (Report of the Thirty-Third Session: Geneva, 19 May – 6 June 2003): Cyprus: para.90.

[17] UN. Doc. CRC/C/15/Add.261 (Concluding Observations): Nepal. 21/09/2005: para.81.

[18] Ibid., para. 82.

reintegration services, but the majority of children involved in and affected by armed conflict is never attached...In addition the Committee is concerned at the impact of internal armed conflict on children not involved in hostilities, particularly Muslim children living in the Mindanao."[19]

In relation to Russia's third periodic report the Committee in its Concluding Observations, expressed concern that "*the children living in Chechnya and the Northern Caucasus remain very deeply affected by the conflict, in particular with regard to their rights to education and health*"[20] and recommends that "*the State party strengthen the measures taken to protect children from the consequences of the conflict in Chechnya and in Northern Caucasus, in compliance with article 38, paragraph 1, of the on the Rights of the Child, in particular with regard to their rights to health and education.*"[21]

6.3 Correlations of reporting with Geographical Region, Income Level and Regime Type

This sections looks at how States Parties' reporting performance on Article 38 correlate with geographical region, income level and regime type. Figures for each of the reports are given, but the small number of third periodic reports that have been submitted prevent any meaningful comparisons from being made for that periodic report.

6.3.1 Geographical Region

Tables 2-4 show how the reporting performances of the states from different continents compare with one another.

European States Parties perform better than the States Parties from the other continents, for the initial and second periodic reports, although barely more than half of European states report on article 38. The disparity amongst continents is less marked for the second than for the initial report.

---

[19] UN. Doc. CRC/C/15/Add.259 (Concluding Observations): Philippines. 21/09/2005: para.76.

[20] UN. Doc. CRC/C/RUS/CO/3 (Concluding Observations): Russian Federation. 23/11/2005: para.68.

[21] Ibid., para.69

Table 6.2 Initial Reports: Geographical Analysis of the Frequency of States Parties' reporting on Article 38

Continents	DID REPORT ON ART.38		DID NOT REPORT ON ART.38	
	No of States	%	No of states	%
Africa	13	25.49	38	74.51
America	9	25.00	27	75.00
Asia	16	38.10	26	61.90
Europe	23	51.11	22	48.89
Oceania	3	25.00	9	75.00

Table 6.3 Second Periodic Reports: Geographical Analysis of the Frequency of States Parties' reporting on Article 38

Continents	DID REPORT ON ART.38		DID NOT REPORT ON ART.38	
	No of States	%	No of states	%
Africa	8	40.00	12	60.00
America	9	42.86	12	57.14
Asia	13	48.15	14	51.85
Europe	17	54.84	14	45.16
Oceania	1	33.33	2	66.67

Table 6.4 Third Periodic Report: Geographical Analysis of the Frequency of States Parties' reporting on Article 38

Continents	DID REPORT ON ART.38		DID NOT REPORT ON ART.38	
	No of States	%	No of states	%
Africa	0	0.00	1	100.00
America	2	22.22	7	77.78
Asia	3	60.00	2	40.00
Europe	2	40.00	3	60.00
Oceania	0	0.00	1	100.00

6.3.2 Income Level

Data for the classification of the States Parties according to income level is taken from the World Bank Country Classification, where states are categorised as high income (HI), upper middle income (UMI), lower middle income (LMI) and low income (LI).[22] The percentage given for each type of income level is the percentage of countries falling within that income level that have, or have not, reported on article 38.

Table 6.5 Initial Reports: Income Level Analysis of the Frequency of States Parties' reporting on Article 38

IL	DID REPORT ON ART.38		DID NOT REPORT ON ART.38	
	No of States	%	No of states	%
HI	26	61.90	16	38.10
UMI	11	30.56	25	69.44
LMI	14	25.45	41	75.55
LI	13	25.49	38	74.51

Table 6.6 Second Periodic Reports: Income Level Analysis of the Frequency of States Parties' reporting on Article 38

IL	DID REPORT ON ART.38		DID NOT REPORT ON ART.38	
	No of States	%	No of states	%
HI	15	60.00	10	40.00
UMI	9	42.86	12	57.14
LMI	14	45.16	17	54.84
LI	10	40.00	15	60.00

Table 6.7 Third Periodic Reports: Income Level Analysis of the Frequency of States Parties' reporting on Article 38

IL	DID REPORT ON ART.38		DID NOT REPORT ON ART.38	
	No of States	%	No of states	%
HI	1	20.00	4	80.00
UMI	1	20.00	4	80.00
LMI	4	44.44	5	55.56
LI	1	50.00	1	50.00

HI states have a stronger reporting performance than other states, though less than two-thirds of HI states reported on article 38 in their initial and second reports. Fewer than one-third of UMI, LMI and LI states

[22] 'Country Classifications'.

reported on article 38 in their initial reports. The reporting level of these states is higher for the second periodic reports, though still less than half.. The differences between UMI, LMI and LI states for the initial and second reports are relatively small.

6. 3.3 Regime Type

The percentage given for each regime type is the percentage of countries that did or did not report on article 38 fall within that regime type. The data used for the evaluations is from two independent sources 'The Economist Intelligence Unit's Democracy Index' (EIUDI) and the Freedom House Classifications. The EIUDI divides states into full democracies (FD), flawed democracies (fD), authoritarian regimes (AR) and finally hybrid regimes (HR). Freedom House classifies states as "Free" (F), "Partly Free" (PF), or "Not Free" (NF).[23] States for which no data (ND) are available have been omitted from this analysis.

Table 6.8 Initial Reports: Regime Type (EIUDI) Analysis of the Frequency of States Parties' Reporting on Article 38

REGIME TYPE	DID REPORT ON ART.38		DID NOT REPORT ON ART.38	
	No of States	%	No of states	%
FD	17	62.96	10	37.04
fD	13	27.08	35	72.92
HR	13	43.33	17	56.67
AR	15	28.30	38	71.70
ND	6		22	

Table 6.9 Second Periodic Reports: Regime Type (EIUDI) Analysis of the Frequency of States Parties' Reporting on Article 38

REGIME TYPE	DID REPORT ON ART.38		DID NOT REPORT ON ART.38	
	No of States	%	No of states	%
FD	14	58.33	10	41.67
fD	16	48.48	17	51.52
HR	7	46.67	8	53.33
AR	9	34.62	17	65.38
ND	2		2	

23 'Freedom in the World 2006'.

Table 6.10 Third Periodic Reports: Regime Type (EIUDI) Analysis of the Frequency of States Parties' Reporting on Article 38

REGIME TYPE	DID REPORT ON ART.38		DID NOT REPORT ON ART.38	
	No of States	%	No of states	%
FD	1	16.67	5	83.33
fD	1	16.67	5	83.33
HR	2	40.00	3	60.00
AR	2	66.67	1	33.33
ND	1		0	

EIUDI regime type analysis shows that FD states for the initial and second periodic reports have performed better than the other regimes, though the contrast with other regime types is stronger for the initial reports than for the second reports. HR states do better than fD and AR states in their initial reports, while AR states do significantly worse than fD and HR states in their second report. The reporting rates for these categories of states is better for the second than the initial reports, but, even for the second reports, none of their rates reaches 50%.

Table 6.11 Initial Reports: Regime Type (FH) Analysis of the Frequency of States Parties' Reporting on Article 38

REGIME TYPE	DID REPORT ON ART.38		DID NOT REPORT ON ART.38	
	No of States	%	No of states	%
F	32	38.01	52	61.90
PF	16	29.63	38	70.37
NF	15	34.09	29	65.91
ND	1		3	

Table 6.12 Second Periodic Reports: Regime Type (FH) Analysis of the Frequency of States Parties' Reporting on Article 38

REGIME TYPE	DID REPORT		DID NOT REPORT	
	No of States	%	No of states	%
F	27	50.00	27	50.00
PF	12	48.00	13	52.00
NF	9	39.13	14	60.87

Table 6.13 Third Periodic Reports: Regime Type (FH) Analysis of the Frequency of States Parties' Reporting on Article 38

REGIME TYPE	DID REPORT		DID NOT REPORT	
	No of States	%	No of states	%
F	1	11.11	8	88.89
PF	4	44.44	5	55.56
NF	2	66.67	1	33.34

The obvious point to make about these tables is that they do not show a pattern similar to the EIUDI data. One might have suspected a similar degree of correlation between the EIUDI's FD regimes and Freedom House's F regimes, but the Freedom House data shows a quite small positive difference between the reporting levels of F regimes and those of PF and NF regimes. The main explanation for this is the fact that Freedom House category of F regimes is more inclusive than the EIUDI's FD regimes. A large number of fD states are regarded as F in Freedom House category.

6.4 Child Soldiers and Frequency of States Parties' Reporting on Article 38

This section looks at the States Parties with a long history of use of child soldiers' use in battlefield situations either by governments' own militaries or by the militias of non-state groups, and examines whether their use has been reported by the States Parties concerned. The data-sources used to identify the relevant States Parties are the Global Report on Child Soldiers (2001) issued by the Coalition to Stop the Use of Child Soldiers that covers the period from June 1998 until April 2001, together with the US Department of State's Country Reports on Human Rights Practice[24], the UN Report on Child Soldiers[25], and the recent report from Secretary-General Ban Ki-moon[26] to the Security Council.

---

[24] 'US Military Assistance to Countries Using Child Soldiers: 1990-2007' Centre for Defense Information (http://www.cdi.org/PDFs/CSBillCharts.pdf , 15 February 2008).

[25] Thalif Deen, 'UN Report on Child Soldiers Ignores Worst Offenders' (http://www.commondreams.org/headlines02/1107-05.htm , 10 January 2008).

[26] 'Child Recruitment continues in over one dozen countries, reports Ban Ki-moon' UN News Centre (http://www.un.org/apps/news/story.asp?NewsID=25440&Cr=child&Cr1=soldier, 2 March 2008) and UN. Doc. A/62/609 – S/2007/757 Report of the Secretary-

6. 4.1 Government Militaries

The countries with a systematic use of child soldiers in battlefield situations as members of government forces are: Afghanistan, Burma, Chad, Democratic Republic of Congo, Somalia, Sri Lanka, Sudan and Uganda. Of these states, Burma and Somalia have not signed OPAC while the remaining six states that did sign up have yet to submit their initial reports to the Committee.

Somalia is the only one of these states not to have signed up to CRC, while Afghanistan has not yet submitted any report on the CRC. This leaves six states, none of which none has reported on article 38.

6.4.2 Non-state Groups

The number of States with non-states militia groups recruiting child soldiers is much higher, a total of twenty-one states: Afghanistan, Burma, Burundi, Central African Republic, Chad, Colombia, Democratic Republic of Congo, India, Israel, Iraq, Kenya, Nepal, Niger, Pakistan, Philippines, Rwanda, Somalia, Sri Lanka, Sudan, Thailand and Uganda.[27]

These states include all eight who also have a history of the use of child soldiers in governmental forces and, as we have already seen, the six of these states who have submitted their initial reports on the CRC have made no reference to article 38. Of the other thirteen states[28], all have submitted initial reports on the CRC but only three – Israel, Kenya and Nepal – have reported on article 38 and none of these has made any reference to the use of child soldiers by non-armed groups. Seven of the 21 states have submitted second periodic reports, of which only Uganda has not reported on article 38. However, of the six who have reported on article 38 none has mentioned the use of child soldiers by non-state militias. None of these states has yet submitted its third periodic report.

In short, the analysis of both state and non-state use of child soldiers as active combatants showed that use of child soldiers has not been reported in any of the relevant States Parties reports.

General: Child and Armed Conflict' 21/12/2007 (http://daccess-dds-ny.un.org/doc/UNDOC/GEN/N07/656/04/PDF/N0765604.pdf?OpenElement , 12 March 2008).

[27] 'Child Soldiers Global Report 2004'.

[28] Burundi, Central African Republic, Chad, Democratic Republic of Congo, India, Israel, Iraq, Kenya, Nepal, Niger, Philippines, Thailand, Uganda.

6.5 Conclusion

The most striking finding of this Chapter is the number of States Parties who have failed to report on article 38 at all. Only one third referred to article 38 in their initial reports, almost a half in their second reports, and only one third again for those third reports submitted up to 2007. When States Parties have reported on article 38, some have done so in detail but many have not responded to all elements of the Committee's guidelines for reporting on the article. Although the Committee has introduced the device of Lists of Issues to request additional information from States Parties, it has made little use of these Lists to ask for information relating to article 38 that is missing from States Parties' reports. It also frequently allows non-reporting or inadequate reporting to pass without comment in its Concluding Observations.

Geographically, European states have reported on article 38 in their initial reports more frequently than states in other continents. Europe also heads the table for second periodic reports, but for those reports the differences with other continents is less marked. Even in the case of Europe states, only a little more than half have reported on article 38 in their initial and second reports. The differences amongst states are a little more marked when categorised according to income level and regime type, with high income states and full democracies doing better than others in their categories. Levels of reporting on article 38 are particularly poor for states known to have child soldiers in their own militias or in non-state militias operating in their territories.

CHAPTER SEVEN

STATES PARTIES' PERFORMANCE IN REPORTING ON OPAC

The current analysis examines how States Parties have reported on each of the seven articles of the Optional Protocol. The length of the reports varies from a single page to thirty-three pages. Some states have included a table of contents and have chosen an analytical approach for their reports, while other states present their reports in a slightly different way, and either group certain rights together without actually explaining why they have done so, or group the articles of the OPAC based on their own arrangements. These alterations will not deter us from looking at the actual content of their reports and examining to what extent they have met the Committee's reporting guidelines.

The states that we will be looking at are the twenty-eight states that had submitted their reports up until January 2007, and were part of the forty-fourth session of the Committee on the Rights of the Child. This session serves as a bench mark for our analysis, as it has been used for the reporting performance analysis given in the previous chapter. The 28 reports that had been submitted in the period culminating in the 44th session were examined by the Committee in a number of different sessions stretching from the 34th to the 46th.

The aim of this chapter is to examine the adequacy of the States Parties' reports for the OPAC to the Committee. This will be achieved by using the articles of the OPAC and the Committee's guidelines for reporting as the basis of our analysis. In order to achieve greater precision and objectivity in our judgement, we make extensive use of the Committee's guidelines and regard it as our benchmark in the evaluation of the content and the completeness of the reports.

7.1 The Grading of Reports

The following grading system has been used in assessing States Parties reports.

Grade A.

Reports are awarded this grade if they provide all of the information required by the Committee's guidelines or if they have very minor omissions that are trivial or insignificant. For example, Austria's report on article 1 of the Optional Protocol is the best example for an A report as it reports on: the national legislation that prohibits recruitment and participation of under 18 years-old in military operations; the definition of direct participation and that no one has been taken prisoner.

Grade B.

This grade signifies that a report has minor omissions but ones that are significant rather than trivial. For example, France's report on article 1 has been assessed as B, as it mentions the national legislation regarding the enrolment in the military forces and the minimum age required, as well as the active involvement of French experts in drafting guiding principles in this filed. However, it has not included current measures in force regarding the non-involvement of under 18 years old in areas of conflicts, as well the definition of direct participation.

Grade C.

This grade indicates major omissions from a report, including a failure to provide any of the information the Committee requires on an article. For example, Kazakhstan's report on article 1 falls into this category as it briefly states the existence of Children's Rights Act, without any extensive reference to its role and whether or not there are more acts safeguarding children's rights. Also, the meaning and the role of children's military units is unclear from the report. Finally, there is no reference to any measures taken to prevent under 18 years-old enrolment in the army, nor national definition of the term 'direct participation'.

Grade N.

This grade indicates that the relevant article is not applicable to the State Party. Monaco, Andorra, Iceland and Costa Rica do not have armed forces and are therefore classified as N for article 1 to 3.

Evaluation of States Parties' reports on each of the articles is not always an easy task. But the main purpose of the grading is to convey the general picture of how satisfactory the States Parties' reports are and the way that the Committee has dealt with them in their List of Issues and Concluding Observations, as well as States' response to the list of issues. An overall evaluation of the States Parties' performance will be presented once the evaluation of each article has taken place.

ARTICLE 1

The OPAC states:

"States Parties shall take all feasible measures to ensure that members of the armed forces who have not attained the age of 18 years do not take part in hostilities"

The Committee's guidelines require:

"Please provide information on all measures taken, including of a legislative, administrative or other nature, to ensure that members of the armed forces who have not attained the age of 18 years do not take a direct part in hostilities. In this respect, please provide information notably on:

1. *The meaning of "direct participation" in the legislation and practice of the State concerned;*
2. *The measures taken to avoid that a member of the armed forces who has not attained the age of 18 years is deployed or maintained in an area where hostilities are taking place and the obstacles encountered in applying these measures;*
3. *When relevant, disaggregated data on members of the armed forces below the age of 18 years who were made prisoners, whereas they did not directly participate in hostilities."*

Table 7.1 Article 1

Committee Sessions	STATES	EVALUATION	LoI
46th session	France	B	
	Lithuania	B	
	Luxembourg	B	x
	Qatar	B	
	Spain	A	
	Syrian Arab Republic	C	
45th session	Guatemala	A	
	Monaco	N	
	Norway	A	
	Sweden	C	
44th session	Costa Rica	N	
	Kyrgyzstan	C	x
43rd session	Kazakhstan	C	
	Malta	B	x
	Viet Nam	C	x
42nd session	Belgium	A	
	Canada	B	
	Czech Republic	B	
	El Salvador	B	x
	Iceland	N	
	Italy	B	
41st session	Andorra	N	
	Bangladesh	C	
	Switzerland	A	
40th session	Denmark	C	
	Finland	B	
38th session	Austria	A	
34th session	New Zealand	B	

A States

As has been mentioned in the introduction, States Parties' reports on articles graded A reflect their full compliance with the reporting guidelines set out by the Committee as the States have covered all the relevant aspects required. Regarding article 1 the States Parties had to include in their report information on all legislative and administrative measures taken to prevent persons under the age of 18 from taking part in hostilities as well as, on the three sections mentioned in the guidelines. Some states do not recruit below the age of 18 into their national armed forces but nevertheless still report on their national legislative and administrative measures taken to safeguard children under the age of 18 from taking direct part in hostilities.

B States

States Parties' reports evaluated as B are characterised by minor omissions or in some cases lack of clarity. For instance, the majority of States Parties have not defined the term "direct participation" in their reports. France has not reported on the measures taken to avoid recruits below 18 being deployed or maintained in conflict zones. Luxembourg indicates that its armed forces "participate in peacekeeping operations on a voluntary basis"[1] and that "the Armed Forces Chief of Staff has been given no instructions with regard to participation in military defence operations, just to select only candidates who are at least 18 years old".[2] On the other hand, the terms of direct participation and peacekeeping operations have not been defined, nor it is clear what type of instructions the State is referring to.

The Committee in its List of Issues has requested only three B graded reports to provide additional information. Neither Malta nor El Salvador reported on the definition of the term direct participation, but only Malta has been asked to clarify the term[3] while El Salvador has been asked to inform the Committee on "the rules of engagement with regard to the apprehension of underage prisoners of war, particularly with respect to the Iraq theatre of hostilities"[4].

In the case of Luxembourg the Committee has requested it to define "direct participation on hostilities"[5] and to clarify whether the 'instruction' given to the Chief of Staff is an informal rule or it is actually provided by the law. [6] In short, it seems that the Committee's evaluation, as reflected in its List of Issues, overlooks several failures to comply firmly with its own guidelines.

---

[1] UN.Doc. CRC/C/OPAC/LUX/1 (Initial Reports of States parties due in 2006): Luxembourg. 06/11/2006: paras.8-9.

[2] Ibid.

[3] UN. Doc. CRC/C/OPAC/MLT/Q/1 (List of Issues): Malta. 21/06/2006: para.4.

[4] UN. Doc. CRC/C/OPAC/SLV/Q/1 (List of Issues): El Salvador. 09/02/2006: para.3.

[5] UN. Doc. CRC/C/OPAC/LUX/Q/1 (List of Issues): Luxembourg. 29/06/2007: para.3.

[6] Ibid. para.2.

In their responses, two of the States Parties – El Salvador and Malta – have been vague and have not actually responded to the questions they have been asked. Luxembourg, on the other hand, offers the Committee all the information it has been asked to provide.

C States

The majority of the States Parties' reports in this category have major omissions in their reports relating to the current measures in force, let alone any of the sub-sections. In some cases, reports present information that the State concerned thought to be relevant to this article. For instance, Bangladesh's report states "the recruitment rules of the Bangladesh Army do not permit any person who has not attained the age of 18 to participate in any armed hostilities"[7] with no further reference to any of the Committee's reporting guidelines. Syria's report is the best example of a state report that mentions what it finds convenient rather than what has been asked to. For instance, regarding the meaning of "direct participation" in Syrian practice and law, the State reported that "this issue does not concern Syria, since the minimum age for compulsory or voluntary service is 18 years. Syria closely monitors the age of recruits".[8] In relation to the measures taken to prevent any member of the armed forces below 18 years of age from being transferred to, or kept in, combat zones, the State reports, "In Syria, there are no armed conflicts and minors may not be recruited for compulsory or voluntary military service. The age of recruits is closely monitored".[9]

Only two of the seven C graded States have been asked by the Committee to provide additional information, Kyrgyzstan and Viet Nam. The latter has been asked to clarify the meaning of "direct participation" in hostilities as it appears in the national legislation and on the practical level,[10] while Kyrgyzstan was asked to indicate whether any of its legal provisions prohibit persons below the age of 18 from being involved in hostilities.[11] In its response Kyrgyzstan has presented the Committee with

---

[7] UN. Doc. CRC/C/OPAC/BGD/1 (Initial reports of States parties due in 2005): Bangladesh. 23/12/2005: para.2.

[8] UN. Doc. CRC/C/OPAC/SYR/1 (Initial reports of States parties due in 2005): Syrian Arab Republic. 18/04/2007: 8.

[9] Ibid., 9.

[10] UN.Doc. CRC/C/OPAC/VNM/Q/1 (List of Issues): Viet Nam. 20/06/2006: para.2.

[11] UN. Doc. CRC/C/OPAC/KGZ/Q/1 (List of Issues): Kyrgyzstan. 16/10/2006: para.1.

the relevant article of the national Criminal Code that criminalises use of minors in armed conflicts. Viet Nam has not provided the information requested by the Committee.

N States

The one and only element that Andorra, Iceland and Monaco are Costa Rica have in common is that none of these states has armed forces. Costa Rica, in contrast to the other states, is a less clear case as, although it has no armed forces, it has provided the Committee with information regarding measures taken to protect recruits to the police who are under the legal age of majority.[12] The Costa Rican police preserve public order and are not deployed abroad, so that no member of the national police forces is involved in hostilities abroad[13]. Military forces are not excluded totally, they "may be organised only under a continental agreement or for the national defence; in either case, they shall always be subordinate to the civil power".[14] Furthermore, regarding the definition of direct participation, it says that this is not defined by law since by tradition the State is a "neutral nation devoted to respect of international law".[15] Costa Rica provides a rare example of a state exceeding its reporting obligations.

Overall

The most common elements missing from the reports were definitions of 'direct participation' and information on the number of persons below 18 that have been made prisoners in conflict zones. The Committee in its List of Issues makes clear that the States Parties are requested to explicitly define 'direct participation'. The Committee has addressed the second missing element in only one case in its List of Issues. With the exception of Viet Nam, all the States Parties have provided the Committee with satisfactory responses regarding this article.

---

[12] UN. Doc. CRC/C/OPAC/CRI/1 (Initial reports of States parties due in 2005): Costa Rica. 22/12/2005: para.28.

[13] Ibid., paras. 40-1.

[14] Ibid., para. 26.

[15] Ibid., para. 34.

ARTICLE 2

"States Parties shall ensure that persons who have not attained the age of 18 years are not compulsorily recruited into their armed forces."

The Committee's guidelines require:

"Please indicate all measures taken including of a legislative, administrative or other nature, to ensure that persons who have not attained the age of 18 years are not compulsorily recruited into the armed forces". In this regard, reports should indicate among others:

- *Detailed information on the process of compulsory recruitment indicating the minimum age linked to each step and, at what time in that process, recruits become members of the armed forces;*
- *The reliable documents to verify age, which are required prior to acceptance into compulsory military service (birth certificate, affidavit, etc.);*
- *Any legal provision enabling the age of conscription to be lowered in exceptional circumstances (e.g. state of emergency). In this respect, please provide information on the age it can be lowered to, the process and the conditions for that change.*
- *For States Parties where compulsory military service has been suspended but not abolished, the minimum age of recruitment set up in the previous regime and how, and under what conditions, this previous system can be reinstalled*

Table 7.2 Article 2

Committee Sessions	STATES	EVALUATION	LoI
46th session	France	N	
	Lithuania	B	
	Luxembourg	N	
	Qatar	N	
	Spain	B	
	Syrian Arab Republic	C	x
45th session	Guatemala	A	
	Monaco	N	
	Norway	C	
	Sweden	C	
44th session	Costa Rica	N	x
	Kyrgyzstan	B	
43rd session	Kazakhstan	C	x
	Malta	N	
	Viet Nam	B	x
42nd session	Belgium	A	x
	Canada	N	
	Czech Republic	B	
	El Salvador	A	
	Iceland	N	
	Italy	C	
41st session	Andorra	N	
	Bangladesh	N	
	Switzerland	A	
40th session	Denmark	C	
	Finland	C	
38th session	Austria	A	
34th session	New Zealand	N	

A States

As with evaluation for article 1, all the A States Parties' reports regarding this article provide very detailed and in-depth reports covering all of Committee's guidelines. Concerning the third point of the guidelines, Austria, Guatemala and Switzerland are the only states that have explicitly stated that they do not consider lowering the conscription age even in the most exceptional circumstances. For instance, Switzerland states that, although the government previously had the right to lower the age of conscription to below the age of 18, it was "abolished in 2000 in order to pave the way for ratification of International Labour Organisation (ILO) Convention No. 182".[16] Austria has "no legal provisions enabling the age of conscription to be lowered in exceptional circumstance (e.g. state of emergency)".[17] Belgium, even though it has suspended its compulsory military service since 1992, reports on the special regime applicable to conscripts and makes the Committee aware of the fact that in the event of war "the conscript shall be part of the recruitment reserve from the age of 17".[18]

Although A graded reports are very detailed, the Committee has requested Belgium to be more precise regarding the amendments to the Belgium Anti-Atrocity Law[19] and the contracts concluded between the non-commissioned officer candidates and the officer candidates under the age of 18 and the State Party. In particular, the State Party is asked to clarify whether the candidates have a civilian or a military status.[20]

In its response to the Committee, Belgium responds in great detail on the Anti-Atrocity Law but the status of the candidates' remains vague, for "candidates ...must have reached the age of 16 before they can become a military candidate."[21]

B States

The single element that is missing from all the B states, with the exception of Kyrgyzstan, is information on whether the State Party enables the conscription age to be lowered. Kyrgyzstan is the only B state that does not provide an in-depth account of the procedures and the measures taken to ensure that no one under the age of 18 is compulsory recruited into the national armed forces. On the other hand, it is the only state that explicitly states that it has no laws regarding lowering the conscription age.

The Committee, instead of addressing the States Parties on this matter, has asked Viet Nam to "update the Committee on the amendment to the

[16] UN. Doc. CRC/C/OPAC/CHE/1 (Initial reports of States parties due in 2004): Switzerland. 14/07/2005: para.26.

[17] UN. Doc. CRC/C/OPAC/AUT/1 (Initial reports of States parties due in 2004): Austria. 08/07/2004: para.16.

[18] UN. Doc. CRC/C/OPAC/BEL/1 (Initial reports of States parties due in 2004): Belgium. 15/08/2005: paras. 13-15.

[19] UN. Doc. CRC/C/OPAC/BEL/Q/1 (List of Issues): Belgium. 15/02/2006: para.1

[20] Ibid., para.6

[21] UN. Doc. CRC/C/OPAC/BEL/Q/1/Add.1 (Written replies from the Government of Belgium): Belgium. 03/04/2006: 10.

Law on Military Service,...and other relevant documents mentioned in paragraph 58 of the State Party's report."[22] In its response to the Committee, the State directs the Committee to its initial report where, it claims, the relevant information can be found. In short, it leaves the question unanswered.

C States

The reports in this category are characterised by major omissions. For instance, Syria's report includes the title "minimum age for compulsory service"[23] but reports nothing under that title. Denmark and Kazakhstan in their reports have both specified the documents required for the recruitment. On the other hand, neither mentions anything about the recruitment process or the possibility of lowering the age in crisis situations. Sweden briefly mentions the selection procedure but not in any detail, while there is no reference to the national measures that would be in force or to lower the age of conscription in emergency situations. Bangladesh and Malta both report that "there are no provisions for (conscription) or compulsory recruitment into the armed forces".[24] Malta is a clearer case as it states that, pursuant to article 1 of the Armed Forces Act, recruitment is voluntary.[25] However, it should have informed the Committee whether compulsory recruitment has been abolished and, if so, what is the minimum age set by the previous regime for the compulsory military service. Furthermore, it should have reported on whether or not the State is considering reinstating those conditions and under which conditions.

The Committee has asked Kazakhstan to inform it whether the conscription age can be lowered during states of emergency or armed conflict.[26] Syria has been asked to "indicate whether there is any legal provision criminalising compulsory recruitment or involving in hostilities of a person under 18".[27] Both States Parties have responded to the Committee. The Committee's List of Issues relate to only a small number

---

[22] UN.Doc. CRC/C/OPAC/VNM/Q/1: para.5.

[23] UN. Doc. CRC/C/OPAC/SYR/1.

[24] UN. Doc. CRC/C/OPAC/MLT/1 (Initial reports of States parties due in 2004): Malta. 10/11/2005:para.5 and UN. Doc. CRC/C/OPAC/BGD/1: para.3.

[25] UN. Doc. CRC/C/OPAC/MLT/1: para.5.

[26] UN. Doc. CRC/C/OPAC/KAZ/Q/1 (List of Issues): Kazakhstan. 23/06/2006: para.1.

[27] UN. Doc. CRC/C/OPAC/SYR/Q/1 (List of Issues): Syrian Arab Republic. 29/06/2007: para.1.

of reports that have major omissions and even in these cases the information it requests does not address all the missing elements.

N States

A greater number of states fall into this category than for article 1 since several states have abolished their compulsory recruitment for more than fifty years now. For instance, Canada states that "it has not had compulsory military service since the end of the Second World War[28]". Costa Rica and New Zealand have no legislation regarding compulsory recruitment, but New Zealand explicitly states that "specific legislation will be introduced if the State decides to introduce conscription in any form",[29] while Costa Rica provides the Committee with an in-depth analysis of how its police forces are recruited and what type of documentation is needed to verify their age.[30]

The Committee in its List of Issues addressed to Costa Rica requests further explanation regarding the provisions of the Optional Protocol and whether they would apply under exceptional circumstances.[31] In its response to the Committee, Costa Rica states that the provisions of the Optional Protocol not only take precedence over the national Constitution but also are applicable even in the most exceptional cases. Here, it should be noted that the Committee has addressed a State Party on an issue that is not directly related to the Optional Protocol or to the reporting guidelines.

Overall

Most of the States Parties' reports have either not reported on the first three principles of the reporting guidelines, or are vague and unclear. The guidelines relating to article 2 do not apply to eleven of the 28 states. For those states to which they do apply, only a minority (five) respond adequately to the guidelines. A large number (seven) respond quite inadequately to the first three elements of the guidelines. The Committee in its List of Issues overlooks most of these omissions. Where it does raise

---

[28] UN. Doc. CRC/C/OPAC/CAN/1 (Initial reports of States parties due in 2004): Canada. 29/07/2005: para.5.

[29] UN. Doc. CRC/C/OPAC/NZL/1 (Initial reports of States parties due in 2004): New Zealand. 30/07/2003: paras.12-3.

[30] UN. Doc. CRC/C/OPAC/CRI/1: paras.43-49.

[31] UN. Doc. CRC/C/OPAC/CRI/Q/1 (List of Issues): Costa Rica. 16/10/2006: para.1.

issues, these relate mainly to the third section of the guidelines concerning legal provision for lowering the age of conscription.

ARTICLE 3 (para.1)

"States Parties shall raise in years the minimum age for the voluntary recruitment of persons into their national armed forces from that set out in article 38, para.3, of the Convention on the Rights of the Child, taking account of the principles contained in that article and recognising that under the Convention persons under the age of 18 are entitled to special protection."

The Committee's guidelines require that the reports should indicate:

"i) the minimum age set out for voluntary recruitment into the armed forces, in accordance with the declaration submitted upon ratification or accession or any change thereafter;
ii) when relevant, disaggregated data on children below the age of 18 years voluntarily recruited into the national armed forces (for example, by gender, age, region, rural/urban areas and social and ethnic origin, and military ranks);
iii) when relevant, ..., the measures taken to ensure that in recruiting those persons who have attained the minimum age set out for voluntary recruitment who have not attained the age of 18 years, priority is given to those who are the oldest. In this respect, please provide information on the measures of special protection adopted for the under-18-years-old recruits."

Table 7.3 Article 3, para.1

Committee Sessions	STATES	EVALUATION	LoI
46th session	France	C	
	Lithuania	N	x
	Luxembourg	C	
	Qatar	N	
	Spain	N	
	Syrian Arab Republic	C	
45th session	Guatemala	N	
	Monaco	N	
	Norway	N	x
	Sweden	N	
44th session	Costa Rica	N	
	Kyrgyzstan	N	
43rd session	Kazakhstan	N	x
	Malta	N	x
	Viet Nam	N	
42nd session	Belgium	A	
	Canada	B	x
	Czech Republic	N	
	El Salvador	C	x
	Iceland	N	
	Italy	B	
41st session	Andorra	N	
	Bangladesh	C	x
	Switzerland	N	
40th session	Denmark	N	
	Finland	N	
38th session	Austria	A	
34th session	New Zealand	A	

A States

States Parties' reports in this category have explicitly reported on the minimum age set for voluntary recruitment into the armed forces and provided disaggregated data (when relevant) on children below the age of 18 years in the national armed forces and the measures taken by the State concerned to ensure that priority has been given to those who are the oldest. For example, Belgium's report has produced disaggregated data for 2004 which shows that a total of 64 military candidates have been below the age of 18, of which 38 were aged 17 and 26 were aged 16.[32] The small number of candidates under the age of 18 reflects Belgium's policy to prioritise those who are older; even for those below the age of 18 it appears, that priority has been given to those who are older. Austria in its report states that, as of June 2007, 273 male and 2 female recruits under the age of 18 are enlisted on voluntary basis.[33] Even though it has stated the exact number of those below 18 in the armed forces, Austria's report has not provided the Committee with the exact age of those recruits. The lack of reference to this in the Committee's List of Issues shows that it has not been considered a very important missing element. None of the A-graded states has been requested to provide the Committee with additional information regarding this paragraph, which means that our evaluation is similar to Committee's.

B States

Two States Parties' reports have been graded B because they have not reported on any measures taken for special protection of the under-18-years-old recruits, although they have included disaggregated data on those members of the armed forces below the age of 18. In the case of Italy these data appear as the number of students attending the different classes of the military schools, since, for Italy, voluntary recruitment consists in the admission to a military school where candidates between 15 and 17 years old are accepted.[34] Canada in its report includes data for the ages 16-19 of the recruits[35] and not specifically for those under the age of 18 as currently the Department of Canadian National Defence does not collect statistics for this age group specifically.

There is no List of Issues for Italy. In its List of Issues for Canada, the Committee asks for "information on the number of persons below 18 recruited over the years 2003-2005" and "disaggregated data by ethnic/minority group".[36] Also, the Committee wants to be informed by the State "on the rules and procedures with regard to the apprehension of persons below 18 during hostilities, particularly with respect to the Afghanistan theatre of hostilities".[37] The latter, even though it has no direct reference to this paragraph since it does not refer to voluntary

[32] UN. Doc. CRC/C/OPAC/BEL/1: paras.29-30.
[33] UN. Doc. CRC/C/OPAC/AUT/1: para.22.
[34] UN. Doc. CRC/C/OPAC/CAN/1: para.6 and CRC/C/OPAC/ITA/1 §49-50.
[35] UN. Doc. CRC/C/OPAC/CAN/1: para.8.
[36] UN. Doc. CRC/C/OPAC/CAN/Q/1 (List of Issues): Canada. 16/02/2006: para.1.
[37] Ibid., para.3.

recruitment but to an ongoing conflict, is mentioned here as the Committee requests information for individuals below the age of 18. In its response, Canada provides the information requested by the Committee and discloses that there are no specific provisions for juvenile detainees with respect to the transfer of detainees from the Canadian Forces in Afghanistan to Afghan authorities.[38]

From the above mentioned, it becomes clear that the missing elements reflected in our grading system does not appear to have been of concern for the Committee. Also, the Committee in its List of Issues asks to be informed on matters which, though significant, are not directly related to the Optional Protocol. Finally, even though Italy has produced a very analytical report on this paragraph, it should have been asked by the Committee to provide further information regarding measures taken for special protection for the under-18-years-old recruits, even though these relate to those admitted to the military schools. Canada's response indicates that the protection of under-18 detainees is far from satisfactory.

C States

Of the reports on paragraph 1 of this article that have been graded C, the Czech Republic, Syria, and Denmark make no reference to it at all. The remaining reports all have major omissions. For instance, some states, such as Bangladesh[39] and Luxembourg[40], have only included the age limit for the voluntary recruitment, while making no further reference to any of the other elements of the reporting guidelines. France[41] is one of the States of this category which, while it has included disaggregated data on those under 18, has done so in a very limited way.

Of these states, only El Salvador and Bangladesh have been asked by to provide additional information to the Committee. Both States have been requested "to provide disaggregated data (by gender, age groups, ethnic minority, urban or rural areas) for the period 2002-2005 on the number of children under 18 recruited in the armed forces or in the paramilitary forces, including the number of voluntary recruitment".[42] Bangladesh has

[38] UN. Doc. CRC/C/OPAC/CAN/Q/1/Add.1 (Written replies by the Government of Canada): Canada. 28/04/2006: 3-4.

[39] UN. Doc. CRC/C/OPAC/BGD/1: para.3.

[40] UN.Doc. CRC/C/OPAC/LUX/1: para.13.

[41] UN. Doc. CRC/C/OPAC/FRA/1 (Initial reports of States parties due in 2005): France. 06/11/2006: para.8.

[42] UN. Doc. CRC/C/OPAC/SLV/Q/1: para.1 and UN. Doc. CRC/C/OPAC /BGD/Q/1 (List of Issues): Bangladesh. 02/11/2005: para. §1.

also been asked to provide disaggregated data for the period 2002-2005 on the number and proportion of persons provided to the United Nations Department of Peacekeeping Operations (DPKO) to be deployed in UN peace missions,[43] even though this requested information that has no obvious relevance to any of the OP articles. El Salvador in its response to the List of Issues states that "over the period in question there were no applications from children over 16 but under 18 volunteering".[44] Bangladesh response was that it recruits no one in its Police, Armed Forces and Paramilitary Forces below the age of 18 years.[45]

Once again, it appears to be the case that the Committee through its List of Issues is more concerned about the exact figures of those, if there are any, below the age of 18 who have been recruited. What the Committee has not addressed is the measures taken to ensure that the older are prioritised.

N States

The guidelines require states to report on the minimum age for voluntary recruitment into the armed forces. However, the remainder of the guidelines indicate that the Committee's real concern in relation to this paragraph of article 3 is to elicit information relating to voluntary recruitment below the age of 18. Thus states, who do not allow voluntary recruitment below 18 and who merely report that fact, have been categorised as N rather than A in addition to States with no armed forces.

The Committee has requested four of states graded N to provide additional information. In the case of Lithuania this concerns the role which members of the Riflemen's Union, who have not attained the age of 18, would have in the event of war.[46] This is requested even though the State has already stated that the minimum age for recruitment is 18. In its response, Lithuania clarifies that neither the Law on the Riflemen's Union of the Republic of Lithuania nor other relevant legislation stipulate any functions for members who have not reached the age of 18.[47] Norway, has

---

[43] UN. Doc. CRC/C/OPAC/BGD/Q/1: para.2.

[44] UN. Doc. CRC/C/OPAC/SLV/Q/1/ Add.1 (Written replies from the Government of El Salvador): El Salvador. 12/05/2006: 1.

[45] UN. Doc. CRC/C/OPAC/BGD/Q/1/ Add.1 (Written replies from the Government of Bangladesh): Bangladesh: 1.

[46] UN. Doc. CRC/C/OPAC/LTU/Q/1 (List of Issues): Lithuania. 22/06/2007: para.4.

[47] UN. Doc. CRC/C/OPAC/LTU/Q/1/ Add.1 (Written replies from the Government of Lithuania): Lithuania. 14/09/2007: 5.

been asked regarding volunteers under the age of 18 in the Home Guard Youth and whether their exemption from military disciplinary authority is based on an established practice, as stated in the State Party's initial report in paragraph 7, or embedded in law.[48] In its response, Norway states that it is both an established interpretation of the scope of application of the national Military Disciplinary Authority Act of 1988 and an established practice. Since paragraph 4 of Norway's report stated clearly that the lower age limit for recruitment in the armed forces is 18 years of age, it is not clear why the Committee decided to raise this point.

Kazakhstan has been asked to "advise the Committee of the minimum age for voluntary recruitment and if incentives are used to encourage volunteers to join the armed forces"[49] as in paragraph 11 of its report the State mentions only the minimum age for conscription to be 18 and makes no reference to voluntary recruitment. In its response to the Committee, the State has not offered any clear advice; instead it has reproduced the wording of article 38 of the CRC. This suggests either that the minimum age for voluntary recruitment is 15, pursuant to article 38, or that the State has not answered the question accordingly. Finally, Malta has been asked to provide disaggregated data for the period of 2003-5 on the number and proportion of children under the age of 18 recruited into the armed forces or into the police.[50] Malta in its report in paragraph 6 had already stated that since 1970 there have been no recruits under the age of 18. It repeats this statement in its response to the List of Issues as well as observing that "no recruitment in the police force of persons under the age of 18 has taken place".[51]

Thus, the responses of the four states concerned to the List of Issues are consistent with their being graded as N for this paragraph.

Overall

The evaluation of the States Parties' reports shows that our grading and the missing elements that we have identified in this analysis have not always been shared by the Committee and its List of Issues. The Committee appears to undervalue the significance of the third required element as stated in the Reporting Guidelines, regarding measures taken to

---

[48] UN. Doc. CRC/C/OPAC/NOR/Q/1 (List of Issues): Norway. 08/03/2007: para.3.

[49] UN. Doc. CRC/C/OPAC/KAZ/Q/1: para.3.

[50] UN. Doc. CRC/C/OPAC/MLT/Q/1: para.1.

[51] UN. Doc. CRC/C/OPAC/MLT/Q/1/ Add. 1 (Written replies by the Government of Malta): Malta. 10/08/2006: 2.

ensure that priority is given to those who are the oldest, as it asks none of the States Parties about this requirement. Instead the Committee is more concerned about the disaggregated data. There seems little significance in having a data showing the number of recruits under 18, their origin and their ethnic background if no information is given on measures for their protection. In short, some of the existing guidelines are overlooked by the body that established them at first place.

ARTICLE 3 (paras.2and 4)

"2. Each State Party shall deposit a binding declaration upon ratification of or accession to the present Protocol that sets forth the minimum age at which it will permit voluntary recruitment into its national armed forces and a description of the safeguards it has adopted to ensure that such recruitment is not forced or coerced."

"4. Each State Party may strengthen its declaration at any time by notification to that effect addressed to the Secretary-General of the United Nations, who shall inform all States Parties. Such notification shall take effect on the date on which it is received by the Secretary-General."

The Committee requests:
"Reports should notably provide information on:

- a. *The debate which has taken place in the State concerned prior to the adoption of the binding declaration and the people involved in that debate;*
- b. *When relevant, the national [or regional, local, etc.] debates, initiatives or any campaign aiming at strengthening the declaration if it set out a minimum age lower than 18 year."*

Table 7.4 Article 3, paras 2 and 4

Committee Sessions	STATES	EVALUATION	LoI
46th session	France	C	x
	Lithuania	C	
	Luxembourg	C	
	Qatar	C	x
	Spain	C	
	Syrian Arab Republic	C	
45th session	Guatemala	C	x
	Monaco	N	
	Norway	C	
	Sweden	C	
44th session	Costa Rica	N	
	Kyrgyzstan	C	x
43rd session	Kazakhstan	C	x
	Malta	C	
	Viet Nam	C	
42nd session	Belgium	C	
	Canada	C	
	Czech Republic	C	
	El Salvador	C	x
	Iceland	N	
	Italy	C	
41st session	Andorra	N	
	Bangladesh	C	x
	Switzerland	A	
40th session	Denmark	C	
	Finland	C	
38th session	Austria	A	
34th session	New Zealand	C	

A States

In contrast to the previous paragraph, only Switzerland and Austria have included in their reports all the required elements stated in the reporting guidelines. Austria in its report provides the Committee with the binding declaration as well as comment on the lack of any systematic or comprehensive debate prior to the adoption of the declaration as the existing Austrian legislation "reflected a general consensus on the minimum age".[52] It goes on to report that there are some national children's rights NGOs that advocate the raising of minimum age for voluntary recruitment from 17 to 18 years of age.[53]

B States

No States Parties' report meets the criteria for this category.

C States

The states who fall into this category have either not reported on the guidelines for this paragraph at all, or they have simply mentioned the binding declaration that they entered into at the time of ratification. None provides the information requested in the guidelines. For instance, Spain and Sweden state that upon ratification "the minimum age for voluntary recruitment into armed forces is 18 years"[54], but give no further details. Other reports lack coherence and relevance[55]. Kyrgyzstan, for example, under the heading of these paragraphs mentions the minimum age for military service and data regarding the state-run Military Academy.

N States

Since Andorra, Costa Rica, Iceland and Monaco have no armed forces the request for information on debates concerning the minimum age for military service has been deemed not applicable to them.

Overall

The States Parties were requested to report not only on the binding declaration deposited upon ratification but also on the debate that took place prior to the adoption and the people involved. The analysis showed 25 States' reports made no reference to these debates. There are several possible reasons why this guideline has been so comprehensively ignored. It may be that there was little public debate to report, or if there had been

---

[52] UN. Doc. CRC/C/OPAC/AUT/1: paras.24-5.

[53] Ibid., para.27.

[54] UN. Doc. CRC/C/OPAC/SWE/1 (Initial reports of States parties due in 2005): Sweden. 10/07/2006: para.24 and UN. Doc. CRC/C/OPAC/ESP/1 (Initial reports of States parties due in 2004): Spain. 16/10/2006: para.22.

[55] UN. Doc. CRC/C/OPAC/KGZ/1(Initial reports of States parties due in 2004): Kyrgyzstan: 22/05/2006:3.

public debate, it may not have been recorded or may not have been reportable in a simple coherent fashion. It may also be that states regarded this information request less seriously since it does not relate directly to whether they are compliant with OPAC. Oddly enough there is no reference to these paragraphs in the Committee's List of Issues, which suggests that the Committee itself attaches little importance to the information it requested relating to these paragraphs.

ARTICLE 3 (para.3)

"States Parties that permit voluntary recruitment into their national armed forces under the age of 18 years shall maintain safeguards to ensure, as a minimum, that:

a. *Such recruitment is genuinely voluntary;*
b. *Such recruitment is carried out with the informed consent of the person's parents or legal guardians;*
c. *Such persons are fully informed of the duties involved in such military service;*
d. *Such persons provide reliable proof of age prior to acceptance into national military service."*

The Committee requires:
"With regard to the minimum safeguards that States Parties shall maintain concerning voluntary recruitment, reports should provide information on the implementation of these safeguards and indicate among others:

a. *A detailed description of the procedure used for the recruitment from the expression of intention to volunteer until the physical integration into the armed forces;*
b. *Medical examination foreseen before recruitment of volunteers;*
c. *The reliable documentation used to verify the age of the volunteers (birth certificate, affidavit, etc.);*
d. *Information that is made available to the volunteers and their parent or legal guardian allowing them to formulate their own opinion and to make them aware of the duties involved in the military service. A copy of any materials used for this information to be annexed to the report;*
e. *The effective minimum service time and the conditions for early discharge; the use of military justice or discipline to under-18-years recruits and disaggregated data on the number of such*

recruits under-trial or in detention; the minimum and maximum sanction foreseen in case of desertion;

f. The incentives used by the national armed forces for encouraging volunteers to join the ranks (scholarships, advertising, meetings at school, games, etc.).”

Table 7.5 Article 3, para.3

Committee Sessions	STATES	EVALUATION	LoI
46th session	France	C	
	Lithuania	N	
	Luxembourg	C	
	Qatar	N	
	Spain	N	
	Syrian Arab Republic	C	
45th session	Guatemala	N	
	Monaco	N	
	Norway	N	
	Sweden	N	
44th session	Costa Rica	N	
	Kyrgyzstan	N	
43rd session	Kazakhstan	C	
	Malta	N	
	Viet Nam	N	
42nd session	Belgium	A	
	Canada	B	
	Czech Republic	N	
	El Salvador	C	
	Iceland	N	
	Italy	C	
41st session	Andorra	N	
	Bangladesh	C	
	Switzerland	N	
40th session	Denmark	N	
	Finland	N	
38th session	Austria	A	
34th session	New Zealand	A	

A States

The reports on this paragraph by the States Parties should include a list of detailed information regarding the voluntary recruitment into the national armed forces as well as all the necessary measures preceding their admission. The amount of information requested in the guidelines may explain why only three States achieve grade A.

B States

Canada provides the Committee with substantial information regarding recruitment procedures (including information on verifying proof of age, the mandatory requirement of parental or legal guardian consent, information given to recruits and their parents or guardian on the duties involved in the military service,[56] and the right to withdraw from service at any time). But it has not reported on the medical examination preceding their recruitment or the incentives used to encourage volunteers to join the forces. However, it does indicate that it provides fully subsided university education for those recruits below the age of 18.[57]

C States

States Parties' reports graded C can be categorised in two groups: those that have reported nothing relating to this paragraph, such as Syria and Kazakhstan, and, those which reported but omitted significant information. Bangladesh, El Salvador and Luxembourg have not reported anything that indicates that their recruitment into national armed forces is genuinely voluntary and on the incentives used to attract volunteers, the recruitment procedure and the medical examination needed, nor the information provided to parents or legal guardians. France's report makes no reference to the initiatives used and what type of information, if any, the volunteers have been provided with.

N States

This paragraph applies only to those states that allow voluntary below the age of 18 and therefore is not applicable to the majority of states under examination.

---

[56] UN. Doc. CRC/C/OPAC/CAN/1: paras.9, 11-12.
[57] UN. Doc. CRC/C/OPAC/CAN/1: para.13.

Overall

The grading analysis of this paragraph shows that only three of the States where voluntary recruitment under the age of 18 takes place met the criteria perhaps because of large amount of detailed information required. The majority of the reporting states set 18 as the minimum age for voluntary recruitment and therefore had no reason to report on this guideline. But, for those who do recruit individuals under the age of 18 into their national armed forces, performance is poor. None of the Committee's List of Issues asks States Parties whose reports are graded as C to provide additional information.

ARTICLE 3 (Para.5)

"The requirement to raise the age in paragraph 1 of the present article does not apply to schools operated by or under the control of the armed forces of the States Parties, in keeping with articles 28 and 29 of the Convention on the Rights of the Child."

The Committee states:
"The reports should indicate, among others, information on:

- *a. The minimum age of entry into schools operated by or under the control of the armed forces;*
- *b. Disaggregated data on schools operated by or under the control of the armed forces, including numbers, type of education provided, proportion between academic education and military training in the curricula; length of this education; academic/military personnel involved, educational facilities, etc.;*
- *c. The inclusion in the school curricula of human rights and humanitarian principles, including in areas relevant to the realisation of the rights of the child;*
- *d. Disaggregated data on the students in these schools (for example, by gender, age, region, rural/urban areas and social and ethnic origin); their status (members or not of the armed forces);their military status in the case of a mobilisation or of an armed conflict, a genuine military need or any other emergency situation; their right to leave such schools at any time and not to pursue a military career;*
- *e. All appropriate measures taken, to ensure that school discipline is administrated in a manner consistent with the child's human dignity and any complaint mechanisms available in this regard."*

Table 7.6 Article 3, para.5

Committee Sessions	STATES	EVALUATION	LoI
46th session	France	C	x
	Lithuania	C	
	Luxembourg	C	
	Qatar	C	x
	Spain	C	
	Syrian Arab Republic	C	
45th session	Guatemala	A	x
	Monaco	N	
	Norway	C	
	Sweden	C	
44th session	Costa Rica	N	
	Kyrgyzstan	C	x
43rd session	Kazakhstan	C	x
	Malta	N	
	Viet Nam	C	
42nd session	Belgium	A	x
	Canada	C	
	Czech Republic	A	
	El Salvador	A	
	Iceland	N	
	Italy	A	
41st session	Andorra	N	
	Bangladesh	C	x
	Switzerland	N	
40th session	Denmark	C	
	Finland	N	
38th session	Austria	N	
34th session	New Zealand	N	

A States

All the A States reports on the existence of military schools have made the Committee aware of the existence of such schools and that their character and curricula are designed to enable children to have access to academic education as well as to military training, and to make them aware of human rights and humanitarian principles.

The Committee, though, in its List of Issues has asked two of the states reports graded A to provide the Committee with additional information. These requests do not disqualify these reports from grade A.

The Committee in its List of Issues for Belgium has requested that the State provide information on education, including the presence in the school curricula of courses about human rights and humanitarian law.[58] Guatemala has been asked to report on the status of children attending military schools and to what extent in cases of emergency they can be enlisted in the national armed forces. The Committee also asked about the impartial complaints and investigations mechanisms already in force for the pupils of the military schools and the frequency of their use.[59]

In its response to the Committee, regarding the status of children, Guatemala clarifies that there is only one military school in the State and all of its students are over the age of 18 and under national law they cannot become active members or be enlisted in cases of emergency.[60] With reference to the complaint mechanism, Guatemala's response is vague for it does not clarify whether they are of a different nature since they are directed at children. As for how often they have been used, it states that "no complaints along these lines have been received".[61] Belgium's response is vague as well, as it does not report on what has been asked by the Committee, instead it reports in great depth on the training with some reference to the course on "the Law of Armed Conflict and the Human rules for combatants that are part of the training".[62]

B States

No state falls into this category

C States

Of the 19 States reports not graded N, 14 are C. Once again some States have not reported on whether or not military schools operate in their territory, these States are: Denmark, Norway and Spain. Also we have States Parties' reports in this category that are extremely vague, for instance Lithuania reported on military academy for officer training[63],

[58] UN. Doc. CRC/C/OPAC/BEL/1: para.5.
[59] UN. Doc. CRC/C/OPAC/GTM/Q/1 (List of Issues): Guatemala. 19/02/2007: paras.3,4.
[60] UN. Doc. CRC/C/OPAC/GTM/Q/1/Add.1 (Written replies by the Government of Guatemala): Guatemala. 23/04/2007:2.
[61]Ibid., 3.
[62] UN. Doc. CRC/C/OPAC/BEL/Q/1/Add.1: 6-9.
[63] UN. Doc. CRC/C/OPAC/LTU/1 (Initial reports of States parties due in 2005): Lithuania. 29/06/2006: para.11.

while Sweden reports on the youth activities through courses for young people that are been arranged by the Swedish Armed Forces in order to provide information about the Total Defence and the tasks of the armed forces in general.[64] Kazakhstan refers to educational institutions for children aged 11 and over that operate under the control of the armed forces.[65] Bangladesh, in its report states that the "operation of a special school for the under-18 does not arise as the armed forces do not employ persons under 18".[66] None of these States makes explicit reference to the existence of military schools in their territories. Qatar, finally, in its report makes no clear reference to the curricula in military schools and provides no disaggregated data of the students, although it explicitly mentions the minimum age of entry into military schools.

Of the above mentioned C graded reports, the Committee has asked only two States to provide additional information. Kazakhstan has been asked to provide additional information regarding the exact number of children attending military schools and further details of the school curricula and the percentage of graduates who join the armed forces.[67]In addition to information about the impartial complaints and investigations mechanisms, Qatar has been asked to clarify the status of children enrolled in the annual school children's training programme as well as in the scheme for students removed from day and private schools run by the national armed forces. In order to have an in-depth knowledge on these schemes, the Committee has listed six questions, relating to the status of the students and the programme they take part in as well as the curricula and whether or not the modules taught are in coordination with the Ministry of Education. Finally, the Committee questions the disciplinary measures in place for those children.

Qatar's response clarifies that students of the schools and the participants of the schemes have no military or paramilitary status are therefore not subject to military discipline. It says little about the curricula of these schools apart from commenting that their structure has been set to safeguard CRC and the OP.[68]

---

[64] UN. Doc. CRC/C/OPAC/SWE/1: para.20.

[65] UN. Doc. CRC/C/OPAC/KAZ/1 (Initial reports of States parties due in 2005): Kazakhstan. 21/11/2005: para:13.

[66] UN. Doc. CRC/C/OPAC/BGD/1: para.6.

[67] UN. Doc. CRC/C/OPAC/KAZ/Q/1 (List of Issues): Kazakhstan. 23/06/2004: para:4.

[68]UN. Doc. CRC/C/OPAC/QAT/Q/1/Add.1 (Written replies by the Government of Qatar): Qatar. 06/08/2007:6.

France's and Kyrgyzstan's reports are unique cases of C grade. They might have been graded N based on what they state in their reports. However, once the Committee in its List of Issues had raised questions regarding issues such as military discipline, complaint and investigation mechanisms and the school curricula, it became apparent that both States do have military schools but have not reported on them in compliance with the Committee's reporting guidelines.

N States

None of the States in this category has military schools.

Overall

Half of the States Parties failed to report satisfactory on military schools. The large number of C reports could be due to the demanding nature of this paragraph, as seems to have been the case for paragraph 3. The Committee in its Lists of Issues shows how concerned it is about the complaint and investigations mechanisms in force regarding the school discipline as well as the inclusion of human rights and international law in their curricula.

At times it seems that the Committee looks at minor issues and overlooks the more important ones. Overall though, the Committee has shown that is really concerned about the status of the pupils in these schools, the complaint mechanisms and the disciplinary measures applied.

ARTICLE 4

"1. Armed groups that are distinct from the armed forces of a State should not, under any circumstance, recruit or use in hostilities persons under the age of 18 years.

2. States Parties shall take all feasible measures to prevent such recruitment and use, including the adoption of legal measures necessary to prohibit and criminalise such practices.

3. The application of the present article shall not affect the legal status of any party to an armed conflict."

The Committee requires:
"Please provide information on, inter alia:

a. The armed groups operating on/from the territory of the State concerned or with sanctuary on that territory;
b. Update on the status of the negotiations of the State Party with armed groups;
c. Disaggregated data on children who have been recruited and used in hostilities by the armed groups, and on those who have been arrested by the State concerned (for example, by gender, age, region, rural/urban areas and social and ethnic origin, time spent in the armed groups, and time spent in hostilities);
d. Any written or oral commitment made by armed groups aiming at not recruiting and using children below the age of 18 years in hostilities;
e. Measures adopted by the state concerned aiming at raising awareness amongst armed groups and within the communities of the need to prevent recruitment of children below the age of 18 years and of their legal duties with regard to the minimum age set up in the Optional Protocol for recruitment and use in hostilities;
f. The adoption of legal measures which aim at prohibiting and criminalising the recruitment and use in hostilities of children under the age of 18 by such armed groups and the judicial decisions applying to this issue;
g. The programmes to prevent notably children who are at highest risk of recruitment or use by such armed groups, such as refugee and internally displaced children, street children, orphans (e.g. birth registration campaigns) from being recruited or used by armed groups."

Table 7.7 Article 4

Committee Sessions	STATES	EVALUATION	LoI
46th session	France	B	
	Lithuania	B	
	Luxembourg	C	x
	Qatar	C	
	Spain	C	x
	Syrian Arab Republic	C	
45th session	Guatemala	A	
	Monaco	C	
	Norway	C	x
	Sweden	B	
44th session	Costa Rica	B	x
	Kyrgyzstan	A	
43rd session	Kazakhstan	A	x
	Malta	C	
	Viet Nam	C	x
42nd session	Belgium	B	
	Canada	C	
	Czech Republic	C	x
	El Salvador	B	x
	Iceland	C	x
	Italy	C	
41st session	Andorra	C	
	Bangladesh	A	
	Switzerland	A	x
40th session	Denmark	C	
	Finland	A	
38th session	Austria	A	
34th session	New Zealand	A	

A States

States Parties' reports graded A have made it clear that there are no armed groups operating in their States, but nevertheless they have taken all the necessary legal measures both to prevent and to criminalise such recruitment. Finland's report draws attention to its National Defence

Training Association but this would not normally be regarded as an armed group.[69]

Kazakhstan and Switzerland are the only two A graded reports that have been addressed by the Committee in its List of Issues. Switzerland had been asked to provide information on the amendment of the Military Penal Code of 2003, in particular on the requirement of the "close link to Switzerland".[70] The Committee in the case of Kazakhstan, with reference to the Kazak Criminal Code on recruitment of children, asked how many cases have been investigated since the OP came into force.[71] Kazakhstan responded to the Committee stating that "there have been no cases of children being recruited into military services since the Protocol has come into force".[72] Needless to say, the response given does not answer the question.

B States

Belgium, Sweden and Lithuania have not stated clearly in their reports whether there are any armed groups operating in their territory, while France and Costa Rica state that recruitment is prohibited and the State is keeping a close eye on possible recruitment but have made no reference to the relevant legislation in force. El Salvador's response regarding the measures in force is vague as it stresses that, since there is no internal conflict or involvement in any international conflict, no recruitment takes place. [73] El Salvador, instead, should have considered the option of prohibiting and criminalising such an act, following the example of Austria, New Zealand and all the other A graded reports.

None of the issues identified in our evaluation have been addressed by the Committee.

C States

Reports with major omissions, lack of clarity or no reference to this article have been graded C. For instance, Syria, Norway and Denmark

---

[69] UN. Doc. CRC/C/OPAC/FIN/1 (Initial reports of States parties due in 2004): Finland. 10/03/2005: para:13.

[70] UN. Doc. CRC/C/OPAC/CHE/Q/1 (List of Issues): Switzerland. 02/11/2005.

[71] UN. Doc. CRC/C/OPAC/KAZ/Q/1: para:6.

[72] UN. Doc. CRC/C/OPAC/KAZ/Q/1/Add.1 (Written replies by the Government of Kazakhstan): Kazakhstan. 23/08/2006: 3.

[73] UN. Doc. CRC/C/OPAC/SLV/1 (Initial reports of States parties due in 2004): El Salvador. 15/08/2005: para:30.

make no reference whatsoever to Article 4 of the Protocol. The absence of anything relating to the legal provisions taken by the State Party is the common element of Luxembourg's, Canada's and Monaco's report. Qatar and Spain report that this (article 4) does not apply to them as such cases do not occur in their national territory. Iceland, on the other hand, states that there are "no national forces"[74] and so "no armed groups"[75]

Three of the twelve C graded reports have been approached by the Committee in its List of Issues. Luxembourg and Norway have been both asked to provide information regarding their national legal provisions that criminalise forced recruitment or involvement in hostilities of a person under 18.[76] The Committee has asked Iceland three questions in relation to this article, first, if the State "assumes any extraterritorial jurisdiction for recruitment of children under the age of 15 year"; second, if the State "considers making recruitment of persons under the age of 18 years on its territory a crime"; and finally if the State "considers making recruitment of a citizen under the age of 18 years outside its territory a crime".[77]

In its response Norway makes clear that under its national military code recruitment is punishable, and that a new proposal is in progress for criminalising such acts.[78] Luxembourg's response is less straightforward as it states that, since there is no compulsory military service, "one cannot speak of provisions criminalising compulsory recruitment".[79] Iceland's response, while full of details, fails to respond to the Committee's questions.

In short, only Norway explicitly responded to the question put to it; the other two States Parties' responses were very vague.

N States

No States Parties' reports fall into this category.

---

[74] UN. Doc. CRC/OPAC/ISL/1 (Initial reports of States parties due in 2004): Iceland. 17/07/2005: para:5.

[75] Ibid., 6.

[76] UN. Doc. CRC/C/OPAC/LUX/Q/1:para: 1 and UN. Doc. CRC/C/OPAC/NOR/Q/1: para.2.

[77] UN. Doc. CRC/C/OPAC/ISL/Q/1 (List of Issues): Iceland. 16/02/2006: para.1(a),(b), (c).

[78] UN. Doc. CRC/C/OPAC/NOR/Q/1/Add.1 (Written replies by the Government of Norway): Norway. 14/05/2007:2-3.

[79] UN. Doc. CRC/C/OPAC/LUX/Q/1/Add.1 (Written replies by the Government of Luxembourg): Luxembourg. 22/08/2007:2.

Overall

The analysis of this article is of a special nature as the States Parties had not only to report on whether there are armed groups in the States concerned but also on all feasible measures taken to prevent, prohibit and criminalise such recruitment. Half of the States reported with major omissions, of which the Committee has addressed only six in its List of Issues. But the Committee has also addressed A and B graded reports.

Two of the States Parties (Switzerland and Spain) have not given a written response to the List of Issues while the other States have either explicitly responded or done so vaguely.

ARTICLE 5

"Nothing in the present Protocol shall be construed as precluding provisions in the law of a State Party or in international instruments and international humanitarian law that are more conducive to the realisation of the rights of the child."

The Committee requires:

"Please indicate any provision of the national legislation and of international instruments and international humanitarian law applicable in the State concerned, which are more conducive to the realisation of the rights of the child. Reports should also provide information on the status of ratification by the State concerned of the main international instruments concerning children in armed conflict and on other commitments undertaken by that State concerning this issue."

Table 7.8 Article 5

Committee Sessions	STATES	EVALUATION	LoI
46th session	France	A	
	Lithuania	A	
	Luxembourg	A	
	Qatar	C	
	Spain	A	
	Syrian Arab Republic	C	
45th session	Guatemala	A	
	Monaco	A	
	Norway	C	
	Sweden	A	
44th session	Costa Rica	A	
	Kyrgyzstan	C	
43rd session	Kazakhstan	C	
	Malta	C	
	Viet Nam	C	
42nd session	Belgium	A	
	Canada	C	
	Czech Republic	A	
	El Salvador	A	
	Iceland	A	
	Italy	C	
41st session	Andorra	A	
	Bangladesh	A	
	Switzerland	A	
40th session	Denmark	C	
	Finland	C	
38th session	Austria	A	
34th session	New Zealand	A	

A States

Seventeen of the States Parties' reports have fulfilled all the reporting criteria and indicated the national and international instruments that are more beneficial for the realisation of the rights of the child and are applicable in the States concerned.

B States

No State Parties' reports fall into this category

C States

Seven C graded reports have made reference to Article 5 in their reports. Three States Parties, Finland, Malta and Qatar, are very vague in their reports, while Kazakhstan's reports at great length on a single national provision with no further reference to any international or national legislation applicable in the State

N States

No State Parties' reports fall into this category

Overall

The evaluation of this article showed that the States Parties either reported in great detail or inadequately. The Committee in its List of Issues has not addressed any of the C graded reports.

ARTICLE 6 (Paras 1 and 2)

"1. Each State Party shall take all necessary legal, administrative and other measures to ensure the effective implementation of the provisions of the present Protocol within its jurisdiction

2. States Parties undertake to make the principles and provisions of the present Protocol widely known and promoted by appropriate means, to adults and children alike"

Committee's guidelines require:

"Please indicate the measures adopted to ensure the effective implementation and enforcement of the provisions of the Optional Protocol within the jurisdiction of the State Party, including information on:

a. Any review of domestic legislation and amendments introduced into it;
b. The legal status of the Optional Protocol in national law and its applicability before domestic jurisdictions, as well as, when relevant, the intention of the State Party to withdraws existing reservations made to this Protocol;
c. The competent governmental departments or bodies responsible for the implementation of the Optional Protocol and their coordination with regional and local authorities as well as with civil society;
d. The mechanisms and means used for monitoring and periodically evaluation the implementation of the Optional Protocol;
e. Measures adopted to ensure the relevant training of peacekeeping personnel on the rights of the child, including the provisions of the Optional Protocol;
f. The dissemination in all relevant languages of the Optional Protocol to all children and adults, notably those responsible for military recruitment, and the appropriate training offered to all professional groups working with and for children."

Table 7.9 Article 6, paras 1 and 2

Committee Sessions	STATES	EVALUATION	LoI
46th session	France	C	x
	Lithuania	C	x
	Luxembourg	C	
	Qatar	C	x
	Spain	C	x
	Syrian Arab Republic	C	x
45th session	Guatemala	A	x
	Monaco	B	
	Norway	C	x
	Sweden	A	x
44th session	Costa Rica	A	
	Kyrgyzstan	C	x
43rd session	Kazakhstan	C	x
	Malta	C	x
	Viet Nam	C	x
42nd session	Belgium	C	x
	Canada	C	
	Czech Republic	B	
	El Salvador	C	x
	Iceland	C	
	Italy	A	
41st session	Andorra	C	
	Bangladesh	B	
	Switzerland	A	
40th session	Denmark	C	
	Finland	B	
38th session	Austria	A	
34th session	New Zealand	A	

A States

Seven States Parties' submitted very detailed reports regarding the legal status of the Optional Protocol and all the other relevant information requested by the Committee in its reporting guidelines. However, the Committee has asked Sweden and Guatemala to provide additional information. For Sweden, this concerned the (e) and (f) sections of the guidelines, while Guatemala it concerned only the (e) section. The two States Parties' responses are very detailed. Sweden offers an in-depth account of education and training available to peacekeeping personnel, and

Guatemala specifies that the OP is automatically incorporated in its national law and takes precedence over domestic legislation.

B States

Finland's report, even though it is very analytical, includes little information regarding the monitoring and evaluating bodies of the OP. Bangladesh has not reported on the (e) principle of the reporting guidelines, while, Monaco does not state the legal status of the OP in its national law.

None of these States has been asked by the Committee to provide additional information concerning the elements that we have identified in our grading process.

C States

A large majority of C graded reports have either made no reference to Article 6 in their reports, for instance Denmark, Luxembourg, Syria, or have done so with major omissions, for example Spain, Belgium and Kazakhstan.

The Committee has asked twelve of sixteen C graded reports to provide additional information regarding specific provisions of these paragraphs. Sweden, Guatemala, France and Qatar are amongst the nine States Parties that replied adequately to the Committee's List of Issues, the remaining five States Parties' have replied partially or not at all, such as Spain.

N States

No reports.

Overall

This is the largest number of C graded reports, so far, for which the Committee has requested additional information in its List of Issues. The Committee has also devoted more attention to specific sections of the reporting guidelines for this Article, than for any other.

ARTICLE 6 (Para. 3)

"States Parties shall take all feasible measures to ensure that persons within their jurisdiction recruited or used in hostilities contrary to the present Protocol are demobilised or other wise released from service. States Parties shall, when necessary, accord to such persons all appropriate assistance for their physical and psychological recovery and their social reintegration."

The Committee requires:

"When relevant, please indicate all measures adopted with regard to disarmament, demobilisation (or release from service) and to the provision of appropriate assistance for the physical and psychological recovery and social reintegration of children, taking due account of the specific situation of girls, including information on:

a. Disaggregated data on children involved in that proceeding, on their participation in such programmes, and on their status with regard to the armed forces and armed groups (e.g. when do they stop to be members of the armed forces or groups?)
b. The budget allocated to these programmes, the personnel involved and their training, the organisations concerned, cooperation among them, and participation of civil society, local communities, families, etc;
c. The various measures adopted to ensure the social reintegration of children, e.g. interim care, access to education and vocational training, reintegration in the family and community, relevant judicial measures, while taking into account the specific needs of children concerned depending notably on their age and sex;
d. The measures adopted to ensure confidentiality and protection of children involved in such programmes from media exposure and exploitation;
e. The legal provisions adopted criminalising the recruitment of children and the inclusion of that crime in the competence of any specific justice seeking mechanisms established in the context of conflict (e.g. wart crimes tribunal, truth and reconciliation bodies). The safeguards adopted to ensure that the rights of the child as a victim and as a witness are respected in these mechanism in light of the Convention on the Rights of the Child;
f. The criminal liability of children for crimes they may have committed during their stay with armed forces or groups and the

judicial procedure applicable, as well as safeguards to ensure that the rights of the child are respected;
g. When relevant, the provisions of peace agreements dealing with the disarmament, demobilisation and/or physical and psychological recovery and social reintegration of child combatants."

Table 7.10 Article 6, para.3

Committee Sessions	STATES	EVALUATION	LoI
46th session	France	N	x
	Lithuania	N	x
	Luxembourg	N	x
	Qatar	N	x
	Spain	N	x
	Syrian Arab Republic	N	x
45th session	Guatemala	N	x
	Monaco	N	x
	Norway	N	x
	Sweden	N	x
44th session	Costa Rica	N	x
	Kyrgyzstan	N	x
43rd session	Kazakhstan	N	x
	Malta	N	x
	Viet Nam	N	x
42nd session	Belgium	N	x
	Canada	N	x
	Czech Republic	N	x
	El Salvador	N	x
	Iceland	N	x
	Italy	N	
41st session	Andorra	N	x
	Bangladesh	N	x
	Switzerland	N	
40th session	Denmark	N	
	Finland	N	
38th session	Austria	N	
34th session	New Zealand	N	

A States

No reports.

B States

No reports.

C States

No reports

N States

All States Parties who have reported to OPAC deem this paragraph not applicable to themselves, either expressly or by omission. Reports have been graded N for this paragraph, since the paragraph refers only to those States Parties that are in a state of war or in which war has just finished.

The Committee, however, has not shared this understanding of the paragraph. Only six States Parties have not been asked by the Committee for additional information. The reports of four of these States were examined during the first three sessions of the Committee and those of the remaining two states were examined during the following two sessions. Thus it seems that those six States escaped requests for additional information only because their reports were the first to be examined by the Committee. Thereafter the Committee requested the same additional information from all States.

Article 7

"1. States Parties shall cooperate in the implementation of the present Protocol, including in the prevention of any activity contrary thereto and in the rehabilitation and social reintegration of persons who are victims of acts contrary thereto, including through technical cooperation and financial assistance. Such assistance and cooperation will be undertaken in consultation with the States Parties concerned and the relevant international organisations.

2. States Parties in position to do shall provide such assistance through existing multilateral, bilateral or other programmes or, inter alia, through a voluntary fund established in accordance with the rules of the General Assembly."

The Committee requires that:

"Reports should provide information on cooperation in the implementation of the Optional Protocol, including through technical

cooperation and financial assistance. In this regard, reports should provide information, inter alia, on the extent of the technical cooperation or financial assistance, which the State Party has requested or offered. Please indicate, if the State Party is in a position of providing financial assistance, the existing multilateral, bilateral or other programs that have been undertaken for that assistance."

Table 7.11 Article 7

Committee Sessions	STATES	EVALUATION	LoI
46th session	France	A	
	Lithuania	C	
	Luxembourg	A	
	Qatar	C	x
	Spain	A	
	Syrian Arab Republic	C	
45th session	Guatemala	A	x
	Monaco	A	
	Norway	A	
	Sweden	A	x
44th session	Costa Rica	B	
	Kyrgyzstan	C	
43rd session	Kazakhstan	C	
	Malta	A	
	Viet Nam	C	x
42nd session	Belgium	A	
	Canada	A	
	Czech Republic	B	
	El Salvador	C	
	Iceland	B	x
	Italy	A	
41st session	Andorra	A	
	Bangladesh	C	
	Switzerland	A	
40th session	Denmark	C	
	Finland	A	
38th session	Austria	B	
34th session	New Zealand	A	

A States

Article 7 has the highest number of A graded States Parties' reports; half of the States Parties fulfil the reporting criteria and offer a detailed account of all the technical and financial assistance they offered.

The Committee, nevertheless, has asked two of the A graded States Parties reports to provide some additional information. The fact that the reports are addressed by the Committee does not undermine our grading as the Committee requires information that is not directly linked with the reporting guidelines. For instance, Guatemala has been asked to inform the Committee "regarding the possibilities to provide the Commission [National Commission for the Search of Disappeared Children] with access to relevant military files and documents in order to identify and allow full compensation of all children victims of the armed conflict in the period between 1960 and 1996". [80] The activities of the National Reparations Programme (NRP) that are of specific relevance to the children affected by the armed conflict have attracted the Committee's attention and requires an update.[81] Sweden's findings of the report on "Asylum-seeking Children with Severe Withdrawal Behaviour –Status of Knowledge and Survey" was taken up by the Committee in its List of Issues. In particular, the Committee wanted to know whether the findings of this report have resulted in any follow-up measures in the State concerned.[82]

In its response, Sweden states that the government is monitoring developments and is discussing this matter within the Council framework. Guatemala, also, gives a good account of the number of projects and the number of missing bodies located, but gives no explicit response regarding measures that have been taken to hold people accountable for forced recruitment.

B States

The reports graded B have small irregularities in their reports as the States concerned do mention the priorities and projects they are involved in but not in great detail. Costa Rica, for example, talks about various multinational forums but not in great detail; Iceland reports on various projects but not in great depth.

---

[80] UN. Doc. CRC/C/OPAC/GTM/Q/1: para. 9.

[81] Ibid., 10.

[82] UN. Doc. CRC/C/OPAC/SWE/Q/1 (List of Issues): Sweden. 08/03/2007: para:6.

Iceland has been asked by the Committee to "provide more information on States development assistance with regard to contributions and/or support to programmes abroad specifically concerned with children's rights including children victims of armed conflict".[83] Iceland responds in great detail.

C States

Half of the C graded States Parties' reports (Denmark, Kyrgyzstan, Syria, Qatar, and Viet Nam) have made no reference to this article. El Salvador's response is out of context, while Lithuania is very laconic in its report as it does not reveal the exact level of technical and financial assistance provided. Bangladesh reports on programmes related to the sexual exploitation of children with no reference to children affected by armed conflict. Kazakhstan's report is incomplete.

Viet Nam and Qatar are the only States, whose reports have been addressed by the Committee in its List of Issues. As mentioned above, these states have not reported on this article. Nevertheless, Viet Nam has been asked to provide additional information regarding the rehabilitation and social integration services provided as well as to indicate an engagement in international cooperating activity in this area.[84] Qatar has been asked the same questions. In addition Qatar has been asked whether or not Protocol issues will be taken into consideration in its work plan for 2008-13 and information concerning financial assistance given by the State.[85]

Both States Parties' replies are incomplete. For instance, Qatar lists the type of assistance offered but makes no reference to the finance invested. Viet Nam's response makes no reference to either provisions or activities in this respect.

N States

No reports fit in this category.

---

83 UN. Doc. CRC/C/OPAC/ISL/Q/1: para.2.

84 UN. Doc. CRC/C/OPAC/VNM/Q/: para.6.

85 UN. Doc. CRC/C/OPAC/QAT/Q/1 (List of Issues): Qatar. 22/06/2007: paras.2, 11, 12.

Overall

The grading of reports on this article showed the highest number of A reports, which means the States Parties are involved in implementation policies and offer technical and financial assistance to the States in need. As has been the case with previous articles, here as well, a significant number of States Parties either do not report or do so with major omissions.

The Committee in its List of Issues asked questions of a very specific nature, such as the status of a research project conducted in Sweden, that exceeded the reporting guidelines but were still of some relevance, for instance, the incorporation of Protocol's principles in Qatar's work plan for 2008-13.

7.2 Concluding Observations

Examination of the Concluding Observations shows that, although the Committee's ostensible purpose is to address the overall performance of each of the individual States Parties and to recommend additional measures as necessary, this is not adhered to in practice. In fact, the overall structure of the Concluding Observations prevents the Committee from addressing all the areas of the reports of each State Party.[86] As a result the Committee is 'forced' to address only the selected issues that it regards as more significant.

As it has been already mentioned in section 5.2.2, the structure of Concluding Observations consists of five main sections: i) introduction; ii) positive aspects; iii) main areas of concern and recommendations; iv) follow-up and dissemination and v) next report.

In the introduction, the Committee welcomes the submission of the report and the response by the State concerned to the Committee's List of Issues. It reminds the State Party that these Concluding Observations should be read together with the Concluding Observations issued for the State Party's periodic report for the Convention on the Rights of the Child (CRC). The wording of the introduction is identical for all States Parties, except those that have not been issued with Lists of Issues and Spain that has not provided the Committee with a response to its List of Issues.

---

[86] Ibid., 20ff; UN. Doc. CRC/C/38: Report adopted by the Committee at its 209th session on 27 January 1995. 20/02/1995:10ff and UN. Doc. CRC/C/43: Report adopted by the Committee at its 233rd meeting, on 9 June 1995. 09/06/1995: 10ff. Also see UN. Doc. CRC/C/121: Report on the thirty-first session. 11/12/2002: 8ff.

The positive aspects section of the Concluding Observations focuses on specific aspects of each report and so varies from state to state. For example, Guatemala has been praised for the declaration upon ratification that the minimum age for compulsory recruitment is 18 and for the adoption of the Integral Law for the Protection of Children. [87] Kazakhstan's decision to set the minimum age for voluntary age to 19 and the ratification of the ILO has been highly welcomed by the Committee.[88]

The third part of the Concluding Observations deals with Committee's areas of Concern and Recommendations. The Concluding Observations for the first three (34th, 38th and 40th) sessions have a different character from those for reports considered in later sessions. For these early reports, the Committee produced no List of Issues, but the comments in its Concluding Observations are very like a List of Issues. The explanations for this difference between the character of its early and later Concluding Observations is probably that the Committee was still developing its practice in commenting on reports. It developed a clear distinction between its List of Issues and its Concluding Observations only after the 40th session. However, it is a little surprising that the Committee took several sessions before it developed this practice, since it was already using that practice in relation to CRC.

In reports considered in later sessions the Committee tried to comment on reports more thoroughly. In particular a pattern of specific topics can be identified. Dissemination, Small Arms and Criminal Offences are the three key areas of the Committee's concern. Each of these areas will be examined in greater detail below.

The general areas of concern vary, according to the State concerned. For example, in both Spain's and Norway's Concluding Observations, the Committee has addressed the issue of social reintegration of children that have been recruited or used in hostilities prior to their arrival in these States. In particular, the Committee's main concern is the lack of an adequate identification program for such children and the lack of proper information regarding the asylum process that they have to undergo.[89] Syria, on the hand, is the only State Party where the Committee expresses its concern related to factors and difficulties impeding the implementation

---

[87] UN. Doc. CRC/C/OPAC/GTM/CO/1 (Concluding Observations): Guatemala. 12/06/2007.

[88] UN. Doc. CRC/C/OPAC/KAZ/CO/1 (Concluding Observations): Kazakhstan. 17/10/2006.

[89] UN. Doc. CRC/C/OPAC/ESP/CO/1 (Concluding Observations): Spain. 17/10/2007 and UN. Doc. CRC/C/OPAC/NOR/CO/1 (Concluding Observations): Norway. 06/07/2007.

of the Protocol. For Syria this relates specifically to the occupied Syrian Golan Heights.[90] Although most of the States Parties' Concluding Observations focus on issues that should receive more attention by the States concerned, there are some exceptions. For example, Monaco is encouraged to carry on its International Assistance and Cooperation and Norway is commended for its good financial support to numerous UN agencies. As mentioned above, there is a pattern in some of the issues that the Committee has raised in its Concluding Observations which will be discussed individually.

7.2.1 Dissemination

Dissemination refers to all the measures taken by States Parties to disseminate information on OPAC, including the training of personnel that come in direct contact with asylum-seeking children (accompanied or unaccompanied) and the education in schools, particularly military schools, in subjects like Human Rights, Children Rights and International Humanitarian Law. Each of these is approached as an individual concern by the Committee, however they appear to be interlinked. For instance, in France's Concluding Observations the Committee shows its clear dissatisfaction with the poor dissemination of information and training related to the OP issues has been provided by the State Party.[91] In its recommendations the Committee includes: awareness-raising and training programmes directed at all professional groups that work directly or indirectly with children (asylum-seeking, refugee and migrant children that may have been recruited or used in hostilities), as well as human rights education and in particular peace education to be included in children's education, including that provided by military schools. Once these issues have been addressed, the State Party should in its next report, include information regarding the progress achieved. The Committee comments in similar terms for other States Parties.

7.2.2 Criminal Offences

The Committee's second main concern is the criminalisation of children's compulsory recruitment or any direct or indirect involvement in

---

[90] UN. Doc. CRC/C/OPAC/SYR/CO/1 (Concluding Observations): Syrian Arab Republic. 05/10/2007.

[91] UN. Doc. CRC/C/OPAC/FRA/CO/1 (Concluding Observations): France. 05/10/2007: para.11.

hostilities. The Committee inspects the relevant legislation in force in the States Parties, together with the extraterritorial jurisdiction in place when the above stated acts are committed by or against a person who is a citizen of, or who has other links with, the State Party. If such provisions are non-existent, the State concerned is advised to establish them.

7.2.3 Small Arms

The Committee expresses special concern about small arms and in particular measures taken by States Parties to guarantee that small arms are not shipped to areas in which there is war or conflict. Unlike dissemination and criminal offences, the small arms issue has been addressed to only the nine States Parties who happen to have adopted the EU Code of Conduct on Arms Export.

One of the criteria for Arms Export is the "internal situation in the country of final destination"[92]; "member States will not allow exports which would provoke or prolong armed conflicts or aggravate existing tensions or conflicts in the country of final destination."[93] There is no reference though in the Code of Conduct to the possible recruitment/use of children in hostilities in the country of final destination of the arms that are exported. Very similar wording has been used in the policy recommendations for all States concerned.

From all the above stated, it is apparent that the issues raised in this section of the Concluding Observations are of a very broad spectrum and are not related to specific articles of the Protocol, instead they relate to a combination of principles contained in different articles

The last two sections of the Concluding Observations (follow-up/dissemination and next report) repeat very similar phrases, which differ only when the Committee makes particular reference to the dates by which the periodic report should be submitted to the Committee by the State concerned.

In sum, there is ample reason to conclude that the Committee's Concluding Observations on OPAC reports fall far short of what might reasonably be expected. Too large a proportion of the Observations comment on general issues that bear no particular relation to the state's report on which it is supposed to be commenting. Likewise, too little of the Observations focus on matters to specific to the state's report and, in

---

[92] 'Code of Conduct on Arms Export' (http://ec.europa.eu/external_relations/cfsp/sanctions/codeofconduct.pdf, 10 April 2008).

[93] Ibid.

particular, on the evident inadequacy of much of the information states provide. The Committee's Observations frequently take the form of issues it proposes to take up with the state, rather than serious monitoring of the materials placed before it. In short, rather than policing states' compliance with OPAC, the Committee through its Concluding Observations functions more like a topic initiator.

7.3 Overall Evaluation

Table 7.12 Overall Evaluation in Reporting on OPAC

Reports Grading	Reports Grading		Art.3						Art.6		Art7
	Art 1	Art 2	Par.1	Paras2&4	Par.3	Par.5	Art4	Art5	Paras.1&2	Para.3	
A	6	5	3	2	3	5	8	17	7	0	15
B	11	5	2	0	1	0	6	0	4	0	4
C	7	7	5	22	7	14	14	11	17	0	9
N	7	11	18	4	17	9	0	0	0	28	0

Table 7.12 shows the overall performance of the States Parties in reporting on the Optional Protocol. The full details are given in Table 7.14. Both tables show that the overall performance is poor as the majority of the reports fail to achieve better than a grade C. Some States Parties are better or worse than others in their reporting across all of the Articles. Syria's, Denmark's, Kazakhstan's and Viet Nam's reports have the highest number of C grades as they have major omissions or have not reported at all on the great majority of articles. By contrast, Austria, Switzerland, Belgium and Guatemala are the four States Parties' reports with the highest number of A grades as they have reported fully on almost all of the Articles of the Protocol.

Regarding the performance on the individual articles of the Optional Protocol, Articles 5 and 7 are those on which reporting has been best. Each of these articles provides for two very significant areas of child protection in armed conflict.

On the other hand, reporting performance on Article 3, paras.2 and 4 and Article 6, paras.1 and 2, are very poor. Both articles have been reported on by a majority of the States Parties either with major omissions or with no information at all.

Article 6, paras.1 and 2 of the Protocol refers to the measures adopted by the States Parties to ensure the effective implementation and enforcement of the provisions of the Protocol within the jurisdiction of the State Party concerned, [94] including the dissemination of the Protocol in all relevant languages and training of professional groups working with and for children.[95] Despite its significance, this article has been ignored by seventeen States Parties in their reports.

In short, while failure to report on article 3, paras.2 and 4, might not be thought very significant because those articles are themselves less significant than others in OPAC, the reporting on article 6, paras.1 and 2, is also poor and those paragraphs cannot be dismissed as insignificant.

Table 7. 13 Lists of Issues by Article and Grade

Reports Grading	Reports Grading										
			Art.3						Art.6		Art7
	Art 1	Art 2	Par.1	Paras2&4	Par.3	Par.5	Art4	Art5	Paras.1&2	Para.3	
A	0	1	0	0	0	2	2	0	2	0	2
B	3	1	1	0	0	0	2	0	0	0	1
C	2	2	2	7	0	5	6	0	12	0	2
N	0	1	4	0	0	0	0	0	0	22	0

Table 7.13 shows how the Committee's Lists of Issues for States Parties and particular articles relate to the grading of reports. The information in this table should be compared with that in Table 7.12 Comparison reveals a lack of correspondence between inadequacies in reporting (indicated by report grading) and the matters taken up the Committee in its Lists of Issues. The great majority of inadequacies in reporting are overlooked by the Committee in its Lists of Issues.

For example, in relation to article 3, paras.2 and 4, only 7 of the 22 States Parties who produced C graded reports have been asked by the

[94] UN Doc. CRC/OP/AC/1, 2001.

[95] Ibid.

Committee to provide additional information. The proportion is higher in relation to 6, paras.1 and 2; 12 out of 17 reports. The Committee's indulgent attitude in the way it approaches missing information from the States Parties' reports becomes apparent in relation to Article 3, para.5, for which only 5 of the 14 States Parties' reports graded C in relation to military schools, have been asked to provide additional information.

By contrast, while the Committee's guidelines for article 6, para.3 are not applicable to all 28 States Parties, 22 N graded States Parties have been asked to provide additional information relating to this paragraph. Virtually all States Parties who have reported on OPAC deem this paragraph not relevant to themselves, either expressly or by omission. However, the Committee in its Lists of Issues deemed the Article relevant to children who were now resident in reporting states but who had been members of armed forces or armed groups in other countries. This was an addition to its previous guidelines and explains why the Committee raised this matter in its Lists of Issues, even though the States Parties were not at fault for not dealing with it in their original reports.

In some cases the Committee has raised issues in relation States Parties' reports that have been evaluated A in my research. However, this does not undermine the evaluation as the information requested has been additional to the data required by the Committee's guidelines. In fact, in many cases the missing information identified in my research has been overlooked and the Committee has instead asked States Parties for additional information, not related to its original guidelines or to the Optional Protocol. For example, the Committee has asked whether the State Party concerned has considered becoming a member of the ICC, or if additional measures have been taken regarding periodic reports for the CRC.

Finally, Austria, Denmark, Finland, Italy and New Zealand are the only five States Parties for which the Committee has not produced Lists of Issues. As with Article 6, para.3, here we can identify a pattern in the Committee's approach to the reports at the early stage of its proceedings, for four of the States Parties' reports were examined during the first three sessions. While, Austria and New Zealand have fully reported on each of the articles and therefore not many issues could have been raised, this was not the case for Italy and Denmark. In particular Denmark submitted a report that was only a page and a half in length and that did not meet the reporting guidelines and did not report fully on any of the Articles of the Protocol.

7.4 States Parties' Response to the Lists of Issues

How have States Parties responded to List of Issues presented to them by the Committee? In fact, there is not much to be said about States Parties' Responses to the Lists of Isssues. In fact, only a small number of States approached each of the questions individually and responded in great detail. Almost half of the States Parties responded only vaguely, while the remaining States did not provide any of the information requested by the Committee.

Although Spain and Switzerland have not responded to the Committees' List of Issues, the Committee in its Concluding Observation made no reference to their failure to provide the requested information. This suggests that a failure by a State Party to respond to the List of Issues is not considered a serious violation, despite the fact that in Committee's Reporting Guidelines it had been stressed that the State Party should respond to the List of Issues addressed prior to meeting with the Committee.

Table 7.14 Overall Evaluation of States Parties' Performances in Reporting on OPAC

Com. Sessions	States	Reports Grading										
				Art.3						Art. 6		
		Art.1	Art. 2	Par.1	Paras2&4	Par.3	Par.5	Art. 4	Art. 5	Paras.1&2	Para.3	Art.7
46th	France	B	N	C	C	C	C	B	A	C	N	A
	Lithuania	B	B	N	C	N	C	B	A	C	N	C
	Luxembourg	B	N	C	C	C	C	C	A	C	N	A
	Qatar	B	N	N	C	N	C	C	C	C	N	C
	Spain	A	B	N	C	N	C	C	A	C	N	A
	Syrian Arab Republic	C	C	C	C	C	C	C	C	C	N	C
45th	Guatemala	A	A	N	C	N	A	A	A	A	N	A
	Monaco	N	N	N	N	N	N	C	A	B	N	A
	Norway	A	C	N	C	N	C	C	C	C	N	A
	Sweden	C	C	N	C	N	C	B	A	A	N	A
44th	Costa Rica	N	N	N	N	N	N	B	A	A	N	B
	Kyrgyzstan	C	B	N	C	N	C	A	C	C	N	C
43rd	Kazakhstan	C	C	N	C	C	C	A	C	C	N	C
	Malta	B	N	N	C	N	N	C	C	C	N	A
	Viet Nam	C	B	N	C	N	C	C	C	C	N	C
42nd	Belgium	A	A	A	C	A	A	B	A	C	N	A
	Canada	B	N	B	C	B	C	C	C	C	N	A
	Czech Republic	B	B	N	C	N	A	C	A	B	N	B
	El Salvador	B	A	C	C	C	A	B	A	C	N	C
	Iceland	N	N	N	N	N	N	C	A	C	N	B
	Italy	B	C	B	C	C	A	C	C	A	N	A
41st	Andorra	N	N	N	N	N	N	C	A	C	N	A
	Bangladesh	C	N	C	C	C	C	A	A	B	N	C
	Switzerland	A	A	N	A	N	N	A	A	A	N	A
40th	Denmark	C	C	N	C	N	C	C	C	C	N	C
	Finland	B	C	N	C	N	N	A	C	B	N	A
38th	Austria	A	A	A	A	A	N	A	A	A	N	B
34th	New Zealand	B	N	A	C	A	N	A	A	A	N	A

CHAPTER EIGHT

NGO ANALYSIS

8.1. The Role of NGOs

As mentioned in Chapter 2, the CRC has the closest working relationship with NGOs, and this has been so since the Convention came into force. Pursuant to Article 45 (a) of the Convention,

> the specialised agencies, the United Nations Children's Fund, and other United Nations organs shall be entitled to be represented at the consideration of the implementation of such provisions of the present Convention as fall within the scope of their mandate. The Committee may invite the specialised agencies, the United Nations Children's Fund and other competent bodies as it may consider appropriate to provide expert advice on the implementation of the Convention in areas falling within the scope of their respective mandates. The Committee may invite the specialised agencies, the UNICEF, and other UN organs to submit reports on the implementation of the Convention in areas falling within the scope of their activities.[1]

According to Karp, who was a member of the CRC Committee between 1995-2003, a spirit of partnership has grown, together with formal and informal cooperation between the Committee and the specialised agencies and intergovernmental organisations.[2] This cooperation finds a normative base in the article mentioned above. In fact, NGOs are more or less treated on the same footing as the UN specialised agencies and bodies. The CRC Committee is unique in its cooperation in policy and practice with NGOs.[3] A strong mutually dependent relationship

[1] Convention on the Rights of the Child.

[2] Judith Karp, "Reporting and the Committee on the Rights of the Child" in Anne Bayefsky (ed.) The UN Human Rights Treaty System in the 21st Century (The Hague, Kluwer Law International, 2000): 43.

[3] It is also unique in still in another respect, namely in having the assistance of the NGO Group for the CRC and its Liaison Officer. Judith Karp, "Reporting and the Committee on the Rights of the Child" in Anne Bayefsky (ed.) The UN Human

exists between the CRC Committee and NGOs.[4] The NGO Group[5] has a strong impact on the questions asked and the recommendations made by the Committee.[6] In fact, some of the important functions that the NGO Group performs are: 1) contacts NGOs at the national level to advise them of the requirement upon their government to produce a state report, 2) alerts NGOs to the possibility and importance of preparing a shadow report, 3) encourages NGOs to work together with other NGOs at the national level in the preparation of a report, 4) provides guidelines and other assistance on the preparation of shadow reports, 5) advises NGOs of the forthcoming consideration of reports, and 6) arranges for the participation of small numbers of NGO members from the national level in the pre-sessional working group in Geneva.[7]

NGOs have been invited to participate in the pre-sessional meetings of the Committee since 1995. Their principal role is to provide the Committee with expert advice and information.[8] Further guidelines were adopted in October 1999 in order to facilitate and encourage the process of written submission of NGO reports and participation of NGOs in the pre-sessional Working Group.[9]

There is no doubt that the successful cooperation between the NGO-CRC Group and the Committee would not have been facilitated without the involvement and financial support of UNICEF, and other bodies.[10]

The Convention on the Rights of the Child is the only Human Rights Convention that explicitly allows the involvement of NGOs in the process

---

Rights Treaty System in the 21st Century (The Hague, Kluwer Law International, 2000), 41-42 and The Procedures before the UN Human Rights Treaty Bodies: Divergence or Convergence? By Wouter Vandenhole (2004): 61.

[4] Laura Theytaz-Bergman "State Reporting and the Role of Non-Governmental Organisations" in Anne F. Bayefsky (ed) The UN Human Rights Treaty System in the 21st Century (The Hague, Kluwer Law International, 2000): 48.

[5] The NGO Group for the Convention on the Rights of the Child is based in Geneva and is devoted to liaison with the CRC Committee. Later in this Chapter we will refer extensively to this NGO Coalition.

[6] Laura Theyraz-Bergman, "NGOs Group for the Convention on the Rights of the Child" In Eugeen Verhellen (ed.) Monitoring Children's Rights (The Hague, Martinus Nijhoff, 1996): 539.

[7] Also it Assists in the dissemination of the Committee's list of issues, arranges for small numbers of NGO members from the national level to attend dialogue with the Committee and assists in the dissemination of the Committee's concluding observations. Bayefsky, UN at Crossroads, 48.

[8] UN. Doc. CRC/C/38, paras.262-264.

[9] UN. Doc. CRC/C/90, para. 320.

[10] Bayefsky, UN at Crossroads, 48.

of the examination of the States Parties reports by the Committee on the Rights of the Child

The Committee seeks specific, reliable and objective information from NGOs in order to obtain a serious and independent assessment of the progress and difficulties encountered in the implementation of the Convention and the Optional Protocols. This is to assist the Committee to gain a clear picture of the situation of children in the relevant State; it is well aware of the fact that the reports submitted by the States Parties do not include the implementation process as they are mainly focused on the legislative framework.[11] As is clear from Article 45 of the Convention, UNICEF has a legal obligation to promote and protect children's rights by supporting the work of the Committee on the Rights of the Child. The responsibilities given to UNICEF are: to participate in the consideration of States Parties' reports; to provide expert advice on the implementation of the Convention; to submit reports on implementation to the Committee on the Rights of the Child; and to respond to requests by the Committee for technical advice or assistance to a State Party.[12] On the ground level, UNICEF field officers take part in different stages of the process, from assisting States in organising major consultations prior to the drafting of their reports and participating in the Committee's review of the reports, to working with States and helping them identify implementation strategies in response to the Committee's recommendations.[13]

The Committee on the Rights of the Child has not produced any formal guidelines for the NGO reports analogous to those it provides for States Parties' for initial and periodic reports on the Convention on the Rights of the Child and the two Optional Protocols. Nevertheless the NGO Group for the Convention on the Rights of the Child has provided guidance for other NGOs and in 2006 published the third edition of its Guide.

The NGO Group for the Convention on the Rights of the Child is based in Geneva and has been in existence since 1983 when the drafting of the Convention began. It was then known as the Informal Ad Hoc Group for the Convention on the Rights of the Child and was actively involved in the drafting process. After the Convention came into force in 1990, the

[11] NGO Group for the Convention on the Rights of the Child, 'A Guide for Non-Governmental Organizations Reporting to the Committee on the Rights of the Child (2006 Edition)' CRIN (http://www.crin.org/docs/Reporting%20Guide%202006%20English.pdf, 3 June 2010): 8.

[12] As has been stated by UNICEF. 'UNICEF'S role in the monitoring progress', *UNICEF* (http://www.unicef.org/crc/index_30214.html , 13 May 2010).

[13] Ibid.

Group changed its name to the present one and currently has a membership of more than 70 NGOs. Its mission is to facilitate the promotion, implementation and monitoring of the Convention. Over the years the NGO Group has been a platform for action for members, primarily to influence the UN system but also regional and national forums. One of the significant areas of its work is to assist national NGOs and coalitions in participating in the UN Committee on the Rights of the Child reporting process. Another key area is the development and maintenance of a focal point to monitor global developments on child exploitation issues. [14]

According to the group's guidelines, the aim of an NGO report should be to undertake a systematic analysis of the extent to which law, policy and practice in the State party is in compliance with the principles and standards of the Convention. The report should reflect the experience of children throughout the State Party and apparent discrepancies with the CRC in legislation, administration of services, culture and environment of different jurisdictions need to be incorporated into the report. The report should also draw upon the widest possible sources of knowledge, expertise, and experience and the views and experiences of children should be identified and incorporated into the report.[15]

Major issues should be identified through consultation with key organisations and individuals. The report should seek to analyse the implementation of legislation in order to give an accurate picture of the practice in the country.[16] In fact, "the information provided in the report should be directly linked to an analysis of the implementation of the Convention with clear indication as to which articles are being breached, in what way, and the consequences that this implies. It may be useful to refer to already established interpretation of what constitutes a breach of the Convention".[17]

NGOs may also submit information that complements or supplements the State party report, particularly in areas where the government report

---

[14] NGO Group for the Convention on the Rights of the Child, 'A Guide for Non-Governmental Organizations Reporting to the Committee on the Rights of the Child (2006 Edition)', 10.

[15]NGO Group for the Convention on the Rights of the Child, 'A Guide for Non-Governmental Organisations Reporting to the Committee on the Rights of the Child (1998Edition)', CRIN (http://www.crin.org/docs/resources/publications/NGOCRC/NGOCRC-Guide-en.pdf , 06 May 2010): 6.

[16] Ibid.

[17] Ibid.

lacks information. This information may take the form of recent reports that NGOs have produced on thematic issues, some of which are, street children, working children, children in armed conflict, refugee children, the girl child, and sexually exploited children. Reports that focus on only one issue or on the situation of a particularly vulnerable group may also be useful. [18]

The group's guide encourages NGOs to work together in coalitions. NGO reports prepared by Coalitions of NGOs are much more difficult to disregard and discredit than those of individual NGOs and therefore tend to lend greater legitimacy to information submitted on breaches of rights. The main underlying reasons for this are, first, that a single comprehensive report allows Committee members, who are under intense time pressure, to familiarise themselves with the relevant issues, by studying only one NGO document from, say, 20 organisations – rather than 20 reports from 20 organisations. Second, governments find it more difficult to discredit a report prepared by a group of NGOs, for, States can claim that information submitted by one NGO, should not be taken seriously because that particular NGO is politically motivated, linked to the opposition, not reliable, or is basing its criticism on fantasy rather than fact.[19] However, from the NGO reports submitted so far, it seems that NGOs have not generally responded to the group's recommendation to act as coalitions. A rare exception is the Coalition to Stop the Use of Child Soldiers.

Regarding the format of the NGO reports, it is stated in the guidelines that they should be no longer than thirty pages. An abstract or a summary of the report should help to highlight the key issues and point out principal preoccupations related to the implementation of the Convention. Written information should be supported by facts and should not be worded in a tone that may be considered to be overly political. Subjective opinions should not be included as the aim is for a constructive dialogue rather than conflict. On the other hand, the report should not hesitate to point out problems and suggest concrete measures to be taken. Reports should be submitted in one of the three official languages of the Committee (English, French, Spanish).[20]

NGO reports may be submitted to the NGO Group, to ensure that the information reaches the Committee, or directly to the Office of the High Commissioner for Human Rights.

---

[18] Ibid.

[19] NGO Group for the Convention on the Rights of the Child, 'A Guide for Non-Governmental Organizations Reporting to the Committee on the Rights of the Child (2006 Version)', 10.

[20] Ibid., 7.

This chapter examines the extent to which NGOs have participated in the reporting process; how far they have reported on issues relating to article 38 and OPAC; and the extent to which the Committee appears to have taken account of and responded to NGO reports. As before, the end-point of our analysis is the 44th session. Our analysis will try to establish whether the NGO reports fulfil their purposes in clearly identifying which articles have been breached and the implications of their breach, and in filling the gaps identified in State Parties' reports regarding Article 38 of the CRC and OPAC. The analysis will focus particularly on States Parties with a long history of Child Soldiering in government forces and/ or non-government forces.

For each of the above three cases, we will also look at the role of the Committee on the Rights of the Child and the extent to which it has taken up the issues identified by the NGO reports in its Concluding Observations. Finally, we will look at a specific NGO, the Coalition to Stop the Use of Child Soldiering, and examine whether the issues raised in their reports had been considered by the Committee in its Concluding Observations for the states concerned.

8.2 NGOs' Participation

Table 8.1 shows the number of NGO reports submitted from 1993 to 2007 and how their number compares with the number of State Parties reports examined in each session. An overall increase in the number of NGO reports submitted per session is noticeable, especially from the 30th session onwards. The pattern of increased NGO reporting is not uniform. For instance, there are noticeable dips in 21st and the 33rd sessions, where the number of NGO reports was less than half the number of State Parties reports examined. Furthermore, there have been sessions in which no NGO report has been submitted, such as the 4th and 19th sessions, despite the fact that the number of State Parties reports submitted in those sessions was five and six respectively. On the other hand, in more recent years the number of NGO reports submitted has typically been twice or three times greater than the number of State Parties' reports.

Table 8.1 Numbers of NGO reports to the Committee on the Rights of the Child for the Convention[21]

SESSIONS	Dates	No of State Reports	No of NGO reports
44TH	15-01/2-02/2007	7	21
43rd	11-29/09/2006	10	36
42nd	15-05/2-06/2006	8	20
41st	9-27/01/2006	10	11
40th	12-30/09/2005	8	23
39TH	16-05/3-06-2005	10	22
38th	10/28-01-2005	10	20
37th	13-09/01-10-2004	9	16
36th	17-05/04-06-2004	9	23
35th	12/30-01-2004	9	21
34th	15-09/03-10-2003	9	28
33rd	19-05/06-06-2003	10	4
32nd	13/31-01-2003	8	14
31st	16-09/04-10-2002	9	22
30th	20-05/07-06-2002	10	10
29	14-01/01-02-2002	8	6
28th	24-09/12-10-2001	10	8
27th	21-05/08-06-2001	9	9
26th	8/26-01-2001	10	3
25th	18-09/06-10-2000	10	9
24th	15-05/02-06-2000	9	5
23rd	10/28-01-2000	9	5
22nd	20-09/08-10-1999	6	3
21st	17-05/04-06-1999	6	1
20th	11/29-01-1999	5	3
19TH	21-09/09-10-1998	5	0
18th	19-05/05-06-1998	6	2
17th	05/23-01-1998	3	4
16th	22-09/19-10-1997	6	6
15th	20-05/06-06-1997	6	3
14th	6/24-01-1997	6	5
13th	Sept/ October 1996	6	9
12th	May/June 1996	6	15

[21] All data is taken from 'NGO Alternative Reports submitted to the Committee on the Rights of the Child', Child Rights Information Network (CRIN) (http://www.crin.org/docs/resources/treaties/crc.25/annex-vi-crin.asp , 18 February 2010). For full list see the volume of Supporting Data, p. 141.

11th	January 1996	7	7
10th	October/Nov.1995	6	8
9TH	MAY/JUNE 1995	5	9
8th	January 1995	6	16
7th	Sept/October 1994	6	5
6th	April 1994	6	8
5th	January 1994	5	4
4th	Sept/October 1993	6	0
3rd	January 1993	6	2

Table 8.2 NGO submissions for the Optional Protocols

SESSIONS	Dates	No of States Reports	No of NGO reports (OPAC & OPSC)
44TH	15-01/2-02/2007	2	1 (OPSC)
43rd	11-29/09/2006	5	6 (OPSC)
42nd	15-05/2-06/2006	8	4(1 OPSC &3 OPAC)
41st	9-27/01/2006	5	2 (OPSC)

The Optional Protocols both came into force in 2002, so there are no State Parties' or NGO reports on the Protocols prior to the 41st session. What we see in Table 9.2 is just the first sample of the number of NGO reports regarding the two Optional Protocols. In fact, out of the 13 NGO reports submitted, only 3 related to OPAC even though 13 State Parties submitted reports on OPAC during the same period.

Table 8.3 Summary of NGO Submissions

Sessions	States Reports	NGO Reports For CRC	Optional Protocol States' Reports	NGO Reports For the Optional Protocols
40TH- 44TH	43	98	20	13
30th- 39th	93	180	n/a	n/a
20th- 29th	82	52	n/a	n/a
10th- 19th	57	59	n/a	n/a
3rd- 9th	40	44	n/a	n/a
Total	States Parties' Reports	335	NGO Reports	446

While the overall total of NGO reports is not much greater than the total of State Parties' reports, Table 9.3 also shows the increasing ratio of NGO reports to State Party reporting from the 30th session onwards. The trend in the increase of the number of NGO reports submitted per session has continued beyond the 45th session.

Out of a total of 446 NGO reports that were submitted from the 3rd – 44th session, we have looked at almost half of them based on their relevance to the issue of our concern. Table 9.4 lists those major international NGOs who have reported most frequently. Over 100 national NGOs, have also reported during the period examined.

Table 8.4 The Principal International NGOs Submitting Report on the CRC

No of Reports	International NGOs[22]
28	Child Helpline International(44th -42nd sessions)
28	Coalition to Stop the Use of Child Soldiers (19 during 40th-36th sessions)+(9 all during 34th session)
27	Human Rights Watch(for national reports please consult the Appendix)
17	Global Initiative to End All Corporal Punishment of Children(44th and 43rd sessions)
17	Defence for Children International (for national Reports please look at the Appendix)
12	Save the Children
9	Organisation Mondiale Contre la Torture (began from 28th session)
8	NGO Group for the Convention on the Rights of the Child
6	Children's Rights Alliance

Some NGOs adopt a comprehensive approach by looking at States Parties' performance in relation to the whole Convention on the Rights of the Child, while others adopt a more selective approach, by looking at specific issues; for instance, Child Helpline International limits itself to advocating that a three digit helpline should be available for children so that they can report any abuse that they may suffer. Second, the length of reports varies, from a single page, such as the report submitted by the Coalition to Stop the Use of Child Soldiers on the states of Panama and

22 For a full list of International NGOs, see the volume of Supporting Data, 180.

Dominica[23], to the 287 page report submitted by the Defense for Children International, Israel section, on the state of Israel.[24] The structure of NGO reports also varies. Sometimes, an NGO has recommended that urgent action be taken by the State Party. For instance, in its report on Brunei Darussalam, the Coalition to Stop the Use of Child Soldiers recommended that the state should ratify OPAC and declare its "straight-18 standard" as well as have mechanisms in place to implement OPAC and protect children from recruitment and from their use for military purposes by armed force/group.[25] An analysis of the content of the NGO reports regarding OPAC will be given later in this chapter.

8.3 NGO reporting on Article 38

In this section we examine the overall performance of NGO reports in relation to Article 38 and whether they have identified violations by States Parties in their implementation of that Article. The NGO reports can be categorised into three groups, based on their approach to reporting on article 38. In the first category, we have NGOs that focus on specific parts of the CRC other than article 38, for instance the Global Initiative to End All Corporal Punishment of Children in its report summarises the legal status of corporal punishment in the State concerned, together with any research evidence of the prevalence of corporal punishment in all settings – the home, alternative care and penal systems. One of the key aims of the NGO is to ban all forms of corporal punishment and to develop public education programmes.[26] The Irish Family Planning Association by submitting its reports aims to highlight the constant breach of young people's civil rights and freedoms in Ireland due to lack of access to

---

[23] Coalition to Stop the Use of Child Soldiers, 'Child Soldiers: CRC Country Briefs: Pre-sessional Working Group for 36th session - Dominica', CRIN (http://www.crin.org/docs/resources/treaties/crc.36/Dominica_CSCS_ngo_report.pdf, 1 June 2010).

[24] Defence for Children International, 'NGO Comments on the Initial Israeli Report on Implementing the UN Convention on the Rights of the Child for 31st session – Israel', CRIN (http://www.crin.org/docs/resources/treaties/crc.31/IsraelCoal_ngo_report.pdf, 25 May 2010).

[25] Coalition to Stop the Use of Child Soldiers, 'Child Soldiers: CRC Country Briefs: Pre-sessional Working Group for 34th session – Brunei Darussalam', CRIN (http://www.crin.org/docs/resources/treaties/crc.34/Brunei_CSCS_ngo_report.pdf , 20 May 2010) : 2.

[26] 'Introduction: A Human Rights Issue', Global Initiative to End All Corporal Punishment of Children (http://www.endcorporalpunishment.org/, 10 July 2010).

appropriate information on family planning and sexual health as well as lack of access to dedicated adolescent sexual health services.[27] Further NGOs, among others, that examine specific aspects of the CRC are also: the Centre for Organisation Research and Education (CORE)[28]; the Irish Society for the Prevention of Cruelty to Children and the Child Helpline International.[29] In short, all the above NGOs have one thing in common: they all aim to promote a specific aspect of children's rights other than Article 38 of the Convention.

In the second category we have the NGOs that have as their main goal the protection of children in war and conflicts. The Coalition to Stop the Use of Child Soldiers is the only case of an NGO committed exclusively to ending the use of child soldiers although it is itself a coalition of NGOs.[30] We examine the Coalition later in this chapter.

Finally, we have NGOs that are concerned with the CRC as a whole. The majority of these more often than not make reference in their reports to articles 22 and 39 of the Convention, but only a third of their reports make reference to article 38. Those NGOs that do report on article 38 in general provide very detailed information and indicate the international

---

[27] 'Submission to the UN Committee on the Rights of the Child on Ireland's 2nd Periodic Report on the Rights of the Child', CRIN (http://www.crin.org/resources/infoDetail.asp?ID=10074&flag=legal, 8 July 2010).

[28] CORE (Centre for Organisation Research and Education : Indigenous People's Centre for Policy and Human Rights in India's Eastern Himalayan Territories) is an NGO in Special Consultative Status with the Economic and Social Council of the United Nations. The organisation is working both on local and international level for the promotion and protection of the people in the Northern Eastern Parts of India. 'About us', CORE (http://www.coremanipur.org/about_us.html, 2 July 2010).

[29] The Irish Society for the Prevention of Cruelty to Children (ISPCC) founded in 1889 and aims to facilitate better child parent relationships; facilitate better understanding of children's need for better nurturing of children; eliminate all violence and abuse in the family; improve attitudes towards children and promote equal citizenship of children. 'Who we are and why we exist', ISPCC (http://www.ispcc.ie/About-Us.aspx, 1 July 2010).

[30] Other NGOs such as Human Rights Watch and Amnesty International look at child soldiers as one of their projects of promoting the protection of human rights worldwide. Furthermore, the US Campaign to Ban the Use of Child Soldiers does not provide much information except for the following statement "Keep our children from fighting in war. This site is dedicated to soldiers in the war. We need to keep the soldiers from being killed in an awful war. War is not a place to put our kids. Next time you come to the place where war is happening, you will realize that all the wars in the world should not be fought by soldiers who are just kids". US – Child Soldiers (http://www.us-childsoldiers.org, 15 June 2010).

humanitarian standards that have been violated by the relevant state or militia group.

Human Rights Watch (HRW) in its report on Myanmar is a typical example. It provided the Committee with valuable findings. First, it highlighted the widespread forces recruitment by the National Army, the exact number of which is impossible to ascertain but HRW does suggest that 70,000 or more of the 350,000 soldiers are children. Second, it pointed out that there is a significant number of recruits under 15 and suggested that Myanmar may have the largest number of child soldiers of any country in the world. Third, it reported that children as young as 11 are forcibly recruited from public places (market places, bus, ferry and rail stations, etc).[31] Furthermore, it highlighted the incentives given to recruiters for bringing in new recruits. For instance, soldiers who bring in new recruits are reportedly paid 1,000 to 10,000 kyat, which is equivalent to US $166 to US $1,666 and equates with between one and three months' income for an average person.[32] HRW indicated that another source of recruits is the Ye Nyun (Brave Sprouts) system, whereby Myanmar battalions take in young boys who have been orphaned or displaced, keep them at the battalion base and send them to school. In the past ten years the system has changed, and many young boys are now apparently kidnapped and forced into Ye Nyunt camps. In its report HRW also addressed questions to the government of Myanmar, first, regarding the measures that have been taken to ensure that all recruits into armed forces are at least aged eighteen and are in compliance with national law and second, whether any measures had been taken against members of the armed forces that recruited children in violation of national law and, if so, how many individuals have been sanctioned for recruiting children who are under-age.[33] The Children's Rights Division in its report for the State of Myanmar, mentioned among other recommendations, that the state should develop reliable systems to verify the ages of recruitment into the armed forces as well as develop and impose effective and appropriate sanctions against individuals found to be recruiting children under 18 into the armed forces.[34]

[31] Human Rights Watch, Children's Rights Division 'BURMA (MYANMAR): Right to Education, Recruitment and Use of Child Soldiers', CRIN (http://www.crin.org/docs/resources/treaties/crc.36/Myanmar_HRW_ngo_report.pdf, 21 June 2010).

[32] Ibid., 5.

[33] Ibid., 7.

[34] Ibid.

Another example is provided by Human Rights Watch's report on Uganda.[35] The report touched upon issues such as the abduction of children and the abuses and brutal treatment they receive from the LRA, their life in captivity, training and battle, and the experience of girls as slaves, "wives" and mothers of the members of the LRA. The report divided up its recommendations according to the bodies they were addressed to, for instance the Lord's Resistance Army, the government, the UN Commission on Human Right, UNICEF, Donor Countries to Uganda and the African Committee of Experts on the Rights and Welfare of the Child.

These two cases illustrate how detailed NGO reports can be in their reporting on article 38 and the level of accuracy of their reporting. On the other hand, there are other NGO reports that have used very broad terminology and vague wording when reporting on article 38. For instance, the NGO Forum on the Rights of the Child in its report on Sri Lanka made no reference to the issue of child soldiering and instead referred to child victims of war and conflicts who constitute the vulnerable groups[36]. Le Group de Travail in its report on the Democratic Republic of Congo stated that "child soldiers under 15 years exist not only in the regular army, but in the rebel factions"[37] that "the Working Group notes that the warring parties and allies violate the rights of the civilian populations they are bombing without care. The Working Group invited the belligerents to respect the rights of the civilian population of International Humanitarian Law".[38] As the words indicate, the language used by the NGO was very diplomatic and avoided disclosing too much information on child soldiers, or making any reference to the exact articles that the State in question has breached.

---

[35] Human Rights Watch, 'Stolen Children: Abduction and Recruitment in Northern Uganda March 2003 Vol 15, No 7A', Human Rights Watch (http://www.hrw.org/en/reports/2003/03/28/stolen-children, 20 May 2010).

[36] NGO Forum On the Rights of the Child, 'Supplementary Report to the Initial Report of the State Party of Sri Lanka on the Implementation of the Convention on the Rights of the Child', CRIN (http://www.crin.org/docs/resources/treaties/crc.9/Sri_Lanka_Forum_NGO_Report.pdf, 23 May 2010).

[37] Groupe de Travail des ONGs Pour les Droits de l'enfant, 'Rapport Alternatif et Evaluatif des ONGs sur L'Application de la Convention Relative aux Droits de L'Enfant par la Republique Democrique du Congo', CRIN (http://www.crin.org/docs/resources/treaties/crc.27/Drc.pdf, 22 May 2010): 21 (section 8).

[38] Ibid.

These NGO reports do seem to have an impact on the Committee and its Concluding Observations. In the case of Myanmar, the Committee, on the one hand, welcomed the establishment of the Committee for the Prevention of the Recruitment of Child Soldiers but, on the other hand, was extremely concerned about the use of children below the age of 15 years as soldiers by both the governmental armed forces and the armed groups and about the military training provided to pupils attending the Nyunt Youth Programme.[39] Furthermore, the Committee encouraged the State Party to "continue to take measures to ensure that all military recruits meet the minimum age recruitment of 18 years and that they enter voluntarily".[40] Also, it requests Myanmar to "ensure that all armed groups reintegrated into the national armed forces adhere to the minimum age of recruitment of 18 years".[41] For Uganda, the Committee in its Concluding Observations expressed its concern about all the reports regarding child recruitment by the Local Defence Units (LDUs)[42], the continuous abduction of children and their use as child soldiers, their use as sex slaves by the LRA[43], and the alarming phenomenon of "night commuters" – children who at nights leave their homes and camps in search of greater security and safety from abduction.[44] In its recommendations to Uganda, the Committee first, "urges the State party to seek international assistance to reinforce its support for the work of the Human Rights Desk within the Ministry of Defence to screen potential recruits more systematically, particularly for the LDUs and Uganda's People's Defence Forces (UPDF) 105 Battalion".[45] Second, it "urges the State party to do everything possible to prevent the abduction of children by the LRA and to rescue those who are still being held"[46] and "to address the phenomenon of night commuters and take all necessary measures to protect children against the risk of abduction by the LRA and other armed forces".[47] In its Concluding Observations for the Democratic Republic of Congo, the Committee urged the State Party to "prevent the killing or other forms of harm of children

[39] UN. Doc. CRC/C/15/Add.237 (Concluding Observations): Myanmar. 30/06/2004: para.66.
[40] Ibid. para.67(c).
[41] Ibid. Para67(e).
[42] UN. Doc. CRC/C/UGA/CO/2 (Concluding Observations): Uganda. 23/11/ 2005: para.65.
[43] Ibid. para:67.
[44] Ibid. para:69.
[45] Ibid. para:66.
[46] Ibid. para.68.
[47] Ibid. ara.70.

and to ensure that those persons responsible for committing such acts are prosecuted".[48]

8.4 NGO reports submitted for OPAC

Table 8.5 shows States' Reports on OPAC that have been examined by the Committee on the Rights of the Child up to the 44th sessions and in which cases these have been accompanied by NGO report.

Table 8.5 NGO Reports on OPAC up to 44th session

Sessions	States	NGO Reports	Child Soldiers reported/ not reported
44th	Costa Rica	Child Helpline International (CHI)	Not reported
	Kyrgyzstan	No report	
43rd	Kazakhstan	CHI	Not reported
		Kazakhstan's NGOs' Group on Protection of Children Rights	Not reported
	Malta	No report	
	Vietnam	CHI	Not reported
42nd	Belgium	Coalition Belge contree l'utilisation d'enfants soldats	Reported
	Canada	Canadian Coalition for the Rights of Children	Reported
	Italy	Groupo di Lavoro per la Convezione sui diritti dell'infanzia e dell' adolescenza	Not reported
41st	Andorra	No report	
	Bangladesh	No report	
	Switzerland	No Report	

[48] UN. Doc. CRC/C/15/Add.153 (Concluding Observations): Democratic Republic of Congo. 9/07/2001: para.65.

Table 8.5 shows that 10 State Parties' reports on OPAC have been examined by the Committee on the Rights of the Child up to the 44th session. For five of these, no NGO reports were submitted. For the remaining five, two reports took up the issue of child prostitution; one advocated that a three digit telephone number should be introduced for children and only two, Belgium and Canada, made reference to the issue of child soldiers. The NGO report on Belgium highlighted that, prior to the adoption of the Optional Protocol on Child Soldiers, Belgium had to adopt national legislation (Law of 22 March 2001) that prohibited the participation of children under the age of 18 in military operations. As a result the Belgian Law now prohibits, in an absolute way, any participation of any individual under the age of 18 in any form of armed operational commitment and any peacekeeping operation, in times of both peace or war.[49]

The NGO report on the Canadian State's report was the only NGO report that directly identified practical aspects of the Canadian Forces that go against the purpose of the Protocol. For instance, the report is very critical of the increasing incentives, especially financial incentives, offered to 16 year-olds to join the armed forces.

8.5 NGO reporting on States known to use Child Soldiers

The NGO monitoring process is potentially most important in relation to states that are known to use child soldiers either in government forces or in non-government militias. We have seen that State Parties' own reports do not reveal these violations of Article 38. How far then does the NGO reporting process make good that failing? One might expect NGO concern to be greatest where violations of the CRC are greatest. Does the record to date match that expectation?

---

[49] Coalition Belge Contre L' Utilisation d'enfants soldats, 'Rapprt de la Coalition Belge Contre L' Utilisation d'enfants Soldats dans le cadre du suivi du protocol additionnel a la Convention relative aux droits de l'enfant portant sur les enfants dans les conflits armes', *CRIN* (http://www.crin.org/docs/Belgium_OP_NGO_Report.pdf, 26 May 2010).

Table 8.6 NGO reports Submitted for States Parties that have used Child Soldiers in Government Forces

Sessions	States	Reports	Child Soldiers reported/not reported
	Afghanistan	[No state report]	
14th	Burma	Human Rights Watch/ Asia	Reported
36th		Coalition to Stop the Use of Child Soldiers	Reported
		Human Rights Watch, Children's Rights Division	Reported
		Forum Asia	Not reported
		International Confederation of Free Trade Unions	No access to the report
21st	Chad	No NGO report	
27th	Democratic Republic of Congo	Le Groupe de Travail	Reported
	Somalia	Has not signed CRC	
9th	Sri Lanka	World Organisation Against Torture	Not reported
		NGO Forum on the Rights of the Child	Not reported
33rd		NO NGO report	
4th	Sudan	NO NGO report	
31st		Friends of Children Society (AMAL)	Not reported
16th	Uganda	Human Rights Watch, Children's Rights Project	Reported
		Uganda Child's Rights NGO Network	Not Reported
40th		Human Rights Watch: -Report on HIV/AIDS Programmes	Not relevant
		- Report on Abduction and Recruitment	Reported and is full of details
		-Summary	Not relevant
		Coalition to Stop the Use of Child Soldiers	Reported
		Uganda Child Rights: - NGO Complementary Report to First Periodic Report	Not Reported

		- Addendum	Reported
		Forest Peoples Programme and United Organisation for Batwa Development in	Not Reported

Table 8.6 lists eight countries in which child soldiers are known to have been used in government forces. Of these, Somalia is not a signatory to the CRC, while Afghanistan and Chad have still to submit reports. Table 8.6 lists the NGO reports that have been submitted for the remaining five countries. No NGO reports accompanied Sudan's report considered in the 4th session; one accompanied its report considered in the 31st session but that included no comment on child soldiers. Similarly, no NGO report was submitted in conjunction with Sri Lanka's report considered in the 31st session; one was submitted alongside its report for the 9th session but that made no reference to child soldiers. NGO reports have been submitted for Myanmar (two sessions), Democratic Republic of Congo (one session), and Uganda (two sessions). Some of these NGO reports have taken up the issue of child soldiers, while others have not.

8.5.1 NGO reporting on Non-Governmental militias known to use Child Soldiers

Having looked at the government use of child soldiers, the next stage is to examine the use of child soldiers by militia groups. Table 8.7 lists fourteen countries in which child soldiers are known to have been used in non-government forces. Of these, Afghanistan has still not submitted a report, while for Central African Republic, Chad, Iraq, Thailand and Rwanda (for one of the sessions) no NGO reports have been submitted. So once again, we see an uneven pattern of reporting by NGOs. Of the NGO reports that have been submitted, reports for only nine countries have taken up the issue of child soldiers: Myanmar, Burundi, Colombia, Democratic Republic of Congo, India, Israel, Nepal, Pakistan and Rwanda. In all of these cases, except Israel, the NGO reports have addressed crucial issues such as the percentage of child soldiers that make up the guerrilla groups and the fact that, while paramilitaries maintain an independent command structure, they frequently operate in direct coordination with the national forces, as in the case of Colombia.[50] In the

[50] Human Rights Watch Children's Rights Division, 'Colombia: Children Affected by Armed Conflict', CRIN (http://www.crin.org/docs/resources/treaties/crc.25/colombiaNGOreport1.pdf, 19 June 2010): 4.

case of India, the Asian Centre for Human Rights has been very critical of the situation in that country and states that "India has done very little to implement the Committees' precious Concluding Observations and in fact, India denies the existence of armed conflict despite the fact that India faces intensive internal armed conflicts"[51]. The same critical approach has been used by the National Alliance of Child Rights Organisations for Nepal; it states explicitly in its report that "the government has ignored the truth and has failed to take any steps towards forcing the rebels to stop recruiting child soldiers".[52]

As in the case of government use of child soldiers, where NGOs do report on the use of child soldiers on non-state militias they provide useful and critical information which has often made a difference to Committee's Concluding Observations.

Table 8.7 NGO reports Submitted for the States Parties where Child Soldiers are used in Non-Government Forces

Sessions	States	Reports	Child Soldiers reported/not reported
	Afghanistan	[No state report]	
14th	Myanmar (Burma)	Human Rights Watch/ Asia	Reported
36th		Coalition to Stop the Use of Child Soldiers	Reported
		Human Rights Watch, Children's Rights Division	Reported
		Forum Asia	Not reported
		International Confederation of Free Trade Unions	No access to the report
25th	Burundi	Defense des Enfant International – Burundi	

[51] Asian Centre for Human Rights, 'The Status of Children in India: An Alternative Report to the United Nations Committee on the Rights of the Child in India's first periodic report', CRIN (http://www.crin.org/docs/resources/treaties/crc.35/India_ACHR_ngo_report.pdf , 17 May 2010): 80.

[52] National Alliance of Child Rights Organisations (NACRO), 'CRC Alternative Report' CRIN (http://www.crin.org/docs/resources/treaties/crc.39/Nepal_Nacro_ngo_report.pdf, 19 May 2010): 52.

25th	Central African Republic	No NGO Report	
21st	Chad	No NGO report	
5th	Colombia	OMCT/SOS – Torture	Not Reported
25th		NGO Group for the Convention on the Rights of the Child	Reported
		Human Rights Watch	Reported
42nd		Child Helpline International	Not Reported
		Coalition Contra la vinculacion de ninos	Not Reported
		Observatrio sobre Infancia	Reported
27th	Democratic Republic of Congo	Le Groupe de Travail	Reported
23rd	India	Human Rights Watch/ Asia	Not Reported
		Campaign Against Child Labour	Not Reported
		Centre for Organisation Research and Education (CORE)	Not Reported
35th		Asian Center for Human Rights	Reported
		CORE	Not Reported
		Indian Alliance for Child Rights	No access to the report
		Human Rights Watch – Children's Rights Division	Not Reported
		National Movement of Working Children, India	Not Reported
31st	Israel	Hariri Foundation	Not Reported
		Palestinian Coalition on the Rights of the Child	Not Reported
		Defence for Children International	Reported
		Human Rights Watch, Children's Rights Division	Not Reported
19th	Iraq	No NGO Report	
28th	Kenya	Kenya Alliance Advancement	
		Human Rights Watch	Not Reported
44th		Global Initiative to End All Corporal Punishment	Not Reported
		Child Helpline International	Not Reported
		Kenya Alliance Advancement	Not Reported
		Organisation Mondiale Contre la Torture	Not Reported

12th	Nepal	World Organisation Against Torture	Reported
39th		Child Workers in Nepal	Not Reported
		National Alliance for Child Rights Organisation	Reported
		Asian Center for Human Rights	Reported
30th	Niger	Reseau Nigerian pour L'Enfance	Not Reported
6th	Pakistan	Human Rights Commission of Pakistan	Not Reported
		OMCT/SOS –Torture	Not Reported
34th		Society for the Protection of the Rights of the Child	Not Reported
		Coalition to Stop the Use of Child Soldiers	Reported
8th	Philippines	OMCT/SOS - Torture	Not Reported
		NGO Coalition for Monitoring the CRC	Not Reported
39th		Catholics for a Free Choice	Not Reported
		Children's NGO Network	Not Reported
		3D- Trade – Human Rights	Not Reported
		Philippines NGO Coalition on the CRC	Not Reported
4th	Rwanda	No Report	
36th		Coalition to Stop the Use of Child Soldiers	Reported
19th	Thailand	No Report	
41st		No Report	

How far has the Committee in its Concluding Observations taken account of NGO reports on the use of child soldiers? For all three countries where children have been used by government forces, as we have already seen in section 8.3, the NGOs that have reported on Article 38 have done so in a very detailed and extensive manner and the information they provided was made use of by the Committee in its Concluding Observations to the States Parties.

Regarding the Concluding Observations to the States Parties where children are used by non-governmental forces, we note that the Committee has sometimes taken account of NGO reports but sometimes seems to have disregarded them. For instance, in its Concluding Observations to Pakistan[53] and Nepal in its 12th session[54] the Committee did not make any

---

[53] UN. Doc. CRC/C/15/Add.18 (Concluding Observations): Pakistan. 25/04/1994.

[54] UN. Doc. CRC.C.15/Add.57 (Concluding Observations): Nepal. 7/06/1996.

reference to the breach of Article 38 in either its Concerns or its Recommendations' sections. In contrast, in its 39th session's Concluding Observations for the state of Nepal, the Committee used stronger language in its recommendations; it insisted that, the State should criminalise the abduction, recruitment and use of children for military purposes by any armed forces and armed group.[55]

For the remaining States Parties, the Concluding Observations use almost the same type of language as they do express their concerns and then offer their recommendations without anything further than that. For instance, the Committee welcomes Rwanda's ratification of OPAC and as a recommendation it states that the State should take measures to ensure that under 18s are not recruited in the LDF or in any armed group on the territory of the State Party[56].

8.6. The Coalition to Stop the Use of Child Soldiers

Having looked at general NGOs that have reported on States Parties that are known for their use of child soldiers either in the government or non-government forces, this section will look specifically at one NGO, the Coalition to Stop the Use of Child Soldiers, whose aim is the protection of children from recruitment and involvement in war and conflicts. The Coalition is the only NGO that is devoted specifically to monitoring and reporting on the use of child soldiers. It is therefore worth examining the role it has assumed and the impact it has had on the monitoring process.

The Coalition was formed in May 1998 by leading human rights and humanitarian organisations in order to "promote the adoption and adherence to national, regional and international legal standards – including the OPAC – prohibiting the use in hostilities of any person younger than eighteen years of age; and the recognition and enforcement of this standard by all armed groups, both governmental and non-governmental."[57]

---

[55] UN. Doc. CRC/C/15/Add.261 (Concluding Observations): Nepal. 21/09/2005: Para. 82 (a).

[56] UN. Doc. CRC/C/15/Add.234 (Concluding Observations): Rwanda. 01/07/2004: paras 62-3.

[57] 'The Coalition' *Coalition to Stop the Use of Child Soldiers* (http://www.child-soldiers.org/home, 28 May 2010).

Table 8.8 The Sessions and the States on which the Coalition to Stop the Use of Child Soldiers has reported

Sessions	States	
40th	Uganda	
38th	Bahamas	Iran
37th	Botswana	Equatorial Guinea
	Antigua and Barbuda	Brazil
	Angola	Kyrgyzstan
	Croatia	
36th	Liberia	Dominica
	Sao Tome and Principe	Panama
	Democratic Peoples Republic of Korea	Myanmar
	Rwanda	El Salvador
	France	
34th	Brunei Darussalam	San Marino
	Singapore	Pakistan
	Madagascar	New Zealand
	Canada	Bangladesh
	Georgia	

Table 8.8 shows the States and the Sessions for which the Coalition has submitted reports. It had submitted no report up to and including the 33rd session and no report after the 40th session. In between it reported on all relevant state parties for the 34th and 36th session; on 7 out of 9 state parties for the 37th session; on two out of ten parties for the 38th session, and one out of eight parties for the 40th session. It submitted no reports for the 35th and the 39th sessions. So the Coalition has been an active reporter for the years 2003 – 2005, but has not reported at all either before or after that period. Within that period, it reported comprehensively for some sessions and not at all, or only partially, for others.[58]

The reports submitted by the Coalition varied in length from one page to four pages. In its reports the Coalition made clear whether it was easy or not to obtain information about the total number of under 18s in the armed forces. The issues that they dealt with in their reports were directly related to the protection of under-18s from recruitment into government or non-governmental forces, as well as to the ratification of OPAC. For instance, in the case of Bangladesh, the Coalition reported that around 3% of

[58] I have tried to find out from the Coalition why it was an active participant at some times and not at others, but unfortunately have received no response to my inquiries.

personnel in the armed forces were under 18 years old in 1999[59], while for Liberia, the Coalition reported that the Armed Forces of Liberia had continued to recruit children both forcibly and voluntarily, in Monrovia and in government-controlled areas. Furthermore, non-state armed groups (LURD and MODEL) continued to recruit children.[60] The anti-terrorist Unit of Liberia, according to the Coalition, had taken away children from their parents and shaved their heads and, if parents could not afford to "buy" their freedom, then the children were sent to the front line, often with little or no training. Most importantly though the Coalition addressed questions directly to the State Party in question and offered clear recommendations. For example, for Georgia, Brunei Darussalam and Bangladesh, the NGO reports indicated the urgency of the situation by listing urgent measures that should be taken by the state in order to protect children. These included the ratification of OPAC, the adoption of a "straight-18" standard for recruitment, and the establishment of mechanisms for the implementation of the OPAC. The Coalition also drew attention to cases such as Croatia[61] and Kyrgyzstan[62], where no information was provided or information was unclear.

While the Coalition is the only reporting NGO to have been concerned with child soldiers specifically, other NGOs that have more general purposes have also concerned themselves with child soldiers, as we have already seen in section 3. So it is not the case that the issue of child soldiers received attention from NGOs only during the life of the Coalition. However, it does seem that the Coalition's reports had a significant impact upon the Committee.

---

[59] Coalition to Stop the Use of Child Soldiers, 'Child Soldiers: CRC Country Briefs: Pre-sessional Working Group for 34th session – Bangladesh', *CRIN* (http://www.crin.org/docs/resources/treaties/crc.34/Bangladesh_CSCS_ngo_report.pdf, 26 May 2010): 1.

[60] Coalition to Stop the Use of Child Soldiers, 'Child Soldiers: CRC Country Briefs: Pre-sessional Working Group for 36th Session – Liberia', *CRIN* (http://www.crin.org/docs/resources/treaties/crc.36/liberia_CSCS_ngo_report.pdf, 26 May 2010): 1-3.

[61] Coalition to Stop the Use of Child Soldiers, 'Croatia', *CRIN* (http://www.crin.org/docs/resources/treaties/crc.37/Croatia_CSCS_ngo_report.pdf, 27 May 2010).

[62] Coalition to Stop the Use of Child Soldiers, 'Kyrgyzstan' *CRIN* (http://www.crin.org/docs/resources/treaties/crc.37/Kyrgyzstan_CSCS_ngo_report.pdf, 27 May 2010).

8.7 Conclusion

The record shows that NGOs have made a difference in relation to reporting on article 38, but that difference is not simply described. On the one hand, the reporting of NGOs is irregular in the sense that many states' reports are unaccompanied by any NGO report and, when NGOs do report, they often overlook article 38. This includes cases in which significant front-line use of child soldiers is known to have occurred, either in a government's own forces or in non-governmental militias operating within a state's territory. On the other hand, when NGOs have reported on violations of article 38, they have often done so in considerable detail and in ways that seem to have made a difference to the Committee's observations and recommendations. During the years that it reported to the Committee, the Coalition to Stop the Use of Child Soldiers seems to have had a significant impact and it is unfortunate therefore that the Coalition ceased to report to the Committee after the 40th session, even though it continues to exist as an organisation. We can conclude therefore that the participation of NGOs in the reporting process has had a positive effect, but that the reporting of NGOs has been too patchy and uneven to provide a satisfactory remedy for the failings of States Parties' own reports and of the Committee's responses to those reports. Moreover, even if the contributions of NGOs were more comprehensive, it would be unsatisfactory to rely on the efforts of voluntary groups to correct the inadequacies of the formal monitoring process. NGOs reports can add value to the monitoring process and, since the amount of NGO reporting has gradually increased, they may add even more value in the future. But, whatever the contributions of NGOs, the failings of the monitoring process require reforms to the formal process itself, an issue to which we now turn.

CHAPTER NINE

IMPROVING IMPLEMENTATION: IDEALS AND REALITIES

9.1 Introduction

The research that has been documented in previous chapters on the efficiency of the existing system to monitor States Parties' compliance with the CRC and OPAC has enabled us to identify three types of inadequacies. The first inadequacy concerns the submission rates of the States Parties' reports. Data analysis has shown that only a very small minority of States Parties to the CRC and OPAC submit their reports by the deadline, while several fail to report at all. In fact, the majority of States take between one and ten years to submit their initial reports for the CRC, while a few have exceeded ten years. The OPAC reporting submission rates are no better, as more than half of the States Parties who were due to submit by 2007 have not yet submitted.

Secondly, data on the content of the States Parties reports revealed very variable levels of performance as well as significant and widespread inadequacies in reporting. As documented in Chapters 6 and 7, States Parties' reports on article 38 and the principles of the OPAC, are generally inadequate and often fail to comply with Committee's reporting guidelines.

The Committee's response, and in particular its failure to respond to inadequacies in the reporting process, is a third area of inadequacy. For instance, when States Parties reports have had a poor content, the Committee has failed, either in its List of Issues or in its Concluding Observations, to request or require the State Party to make good its reporting inadequacies. Instead, in its Concluding Observations, the Committee has addressed issues previously raised in its List of Issues regarding the implementation of articles 22 and 39. The Committee's ineffectiveness in relation to the poor content of States Parties' reports on the OPAC has been primarily identified as its failure in its Concluding Observations to address the overall performance of each of the individual States Parties and to recommend specific additional measures. As a result, and due to the structure of the Concluding Observations, the Committee is 'forced' to address only the selected issues that it regards as more significant, such as dissemination, criminal offences and the use of small arms.

In practice the role of the Committee on the Rights of the Child, judged by its Concluding Observations for the CRC and OPAC, is not that of a policeman but of a topic initiator. That is, rather than seeking to make states fully comply with their reporting obligations, it raises topics of special concern with States Parties. The Committee fails to address directly any failings in States Parties' compliance, or to identify ways to improve implementation. Too often there is no reference to any specific laws or practices. Instead, it identifies an area of concern that the relevant state has to report on in its next periodic report.

The aim of this chapter is to address the question of how children's rights can be protected, promoted and secured more effectively. The chapter is divided into three sections. The first section sets the Committee on the Rights of the Child in the context of the general Human Rights Committee system and raises the question of whether the defects found in this research regarding the monitoring of the CRC and OPAC are unique to this Committee or shared by the other Human Rights Committees. The second section examines the broader context of the UN and world politics within which the machinery to implement the CRC and OPAC has to operate, since any proposal for a reform of this machinery has to take into account these political realities. A number of possibilities for reform, modest or radical, together with their pros and cons will be considered in the final section.

9.2 The UN's Human Rights Committees

The Committee on the Rights of the Child is one of the Major International Human Rights Committees, otherwise known as Treaty Bodies, established to assist and monitor States Parties' compliance with the standards of the treaties and their implementation in order to secure the rights provided in the treaties. Given the similarities in the constitution, power and role of these Committees, this section will look at whether the failings identified for the Committee on the Rights of the Child are unique to this Committee or are more general failings of the current system.

Table 9.1 The trend in relation to overdue reports, 1993-1996[1]

Treaty	State Parties		Parties with overdue reports				Total overdue reports	
	1993	1996	1993	% of states parties with overdue reports	1996	% of states parties with overdue reports	1993	1996
ICESCR	119	134	65	54.6%	97	72.4%	65	115
ICCPR	115	134	64	55.7%	84	62.7%	83	114
CERD	132	147	112	84.8%	126	85.7%	342	401
CEDAW	118	153	78	66.1%	115	75.2%	127	189
CAT	71	98	36	50.7%	61	62.2%	38	67
CRC	126	187	59	46.8%	71	38.0%	59	71
Total	**680**	**853**	**414**	**60.9%**	**554**	**64.9%**	**714**	**957**

Although the figures in Table 9.1 are only for the period 1993-96, they do show that for those years the pattern of overdue reports that I have found for the CRC and OPAC is common to all the Human Rights Committees. In fact, in some cases the level of failure to submit reports is worse for other treaties than it is for the CRC. It should be noted here, that these figures show how many reports were overdue in 1993 and 1996; they do not show how many states had failed to meet their deadlines. Also, this table does not take into consideration the different deadlines for different treaties, which might have an impact on the number of overdue reports. Nonetheless, the fact remains that the pattern of overdue reports identified is common to all the Human Rights Committees. Table 9.1 also shows that the number of overdue reports has increased disproportionately with the increase in the number of states due to report, although this is not true for the CRC.

[1] UN. Doc. E/CN.4/1997/74, 1997: Commission on Human Rights: Effective Functoning of Bodies Established pursuant to United Nations Human Rights Instruments: Final Report on enhancing the long-term effectiveness of the United Nations Human Rights Treaty Systems.

Table 9.2 Number of overdue reports as of 1 January 2000[2]

Committee	Number of States Parties	Number of Overdue Reports	Number of Parties with Initial Overdue Reports	% of States Parties with Initial Overdue Reports	Number of States Parties with Overdue Reports[3]	% of States Parties with Overdue Reports
CERD	155	397	20	13%	116	75%
CCPR	144	144	27	19%	91	63%
CESCR	142	164	52	37%	114	80%
CEDAW	165	242	53	32%	129	78%
CAT	118	106	36	31%	74	63%
CRC	191	150	54	28%	130	68%
TOTAL	**915**	**1203**			**654**	**71.5%**
AVERAGE				**27%**		**71%**

As of January 2000 an average of 71% of States Parties to every treaty had overdue reports, and an average of 25% of States had overdue initial reports. For some of the Committees the number of overdue reports is significantly higher than the number of states that have ratified them, which is a result of some States Parties failing to submit more than one of their reports to the Committee. In fact, 71.5% of all States Parties have overdue reports. As with Table 9.1, Table 9.2 does not take account of the fact that different Treaties have different deadlines. Nevertheless, the pattern of overdue reporting remains very clear.

For the CRC, the number of States Parties with overdue reports has almost doubled since 1996, although the number of States Parties has increased by only 4 additional states. This is a dramatic increase, if compared to the period 1993-1996.

In a 2001 report, Anne Bayefsky, suggested that the large number of ratifications reflect the view widely-held by States Parties that no serious consequences are associated with ratification. In fact, in Bayefsky's view, many states ratified precisely because the international scheme was evidently dysfunctional and the lack of democratic institutions at home

[2] Ann, F. Bayefsky 'ANNEX I: Statistical Analysis of the Human Rights Treaty System'(http://www.bayefsky.com/report/annex1g.pdf, 15 September 2009).
[3] 'Overdue' reports include both initial and periodic reports.

made the likelihood of national consequences of failure to comply comfortably remote.[4]

Table 9.3 Overdue Reports as of 2008

Treaty	State Parties	Number of States Parties with Overdue Reports	% of States Parties with Overdue Reports	Number of overdue reports
ICESCR	160	91[5]	57.0 %	197
ICCPR	164	48[6]	29.3 %	107
CERD	173	46[7]	26.6 %	293
CEDAW	186	108[8]	58.1 %	180
CAT	146	120[9]	82.2 %	203
CRC	193	137[10]	71.0 %	223
Total	**1022**	**550**	**53.8 %**	**1203**

Table 9.3 shows clearly that, although the number of States Parties to the treaties has increased, the total number of overdue reports remained overall little better than in 2000. That disguises variations in different treaties, for some the performance has become better and for others it has become worse. In fact, despite the fact that the number of States Parties to all Treaties has increased, the number of States Parties with overdue reports has gone down, except for CAT (an increase of almost 100%) and CRC (an increase of over 60%). As in the case of the previous tables, the exact number of non-submitted periodic reports for each Treaty has not been considered.

---

[4] Bayefsky 'The UN Human Rights Treaty System: Universality at the Crossroads'25-30.

[5] UN. Doc. E/C.12/40/2, 2008: Note by the Secretary-General on the States Parties to the Covenant and the Status of Submission of Reports.

[6] A/63/40: Annual Report of the Human Rights Committee (Volume I): August 2007- July 2008.

[7] A/62/18: Annual Report of the Committee on the Elimination of Racial Discrimination: 01/10/2007.

[8] A/63/38 (SUPP):Annual Report of the Committee on the Elimination of Discrimination against Women: 29/07/2009.

[9] A/63/44: Annual Report of the Committee against Torture (2007-2008).

[10] UN. Doc. CRC/C/49/2: Submission of Reports by States Parties: States Parties to the Convention on the Rights of the Child and its two Optional Protocols and related status of submission of reports. 10/07/2008.

The conclusion that can be drawn from all three tables is that the issue of overdue reports is not unique to the CRC but is common to all the treaties. It should be noted that, over the past seven years, the data shows that the situation for some of the treaties is slightly improving, with minor decreases in the figures, but not for the CRC. Furthermore, over 20 years later, the situation seems to confirm what the then Secretary-General said regarding the large scale of non-reporting, that it "makes a mockery of the system as a whole" and "will lead to a situation in which a diminishing number of States will report very regularly and others will almost never do".[11] Unless the problem of implementation of the CRC and of human rights treaties in general receives the appropriate attention, their effectiveness will remain in question.

It should be noted as well that there is evidence that the quality of States Parties' reports on all Human Rights treaties is poor. In fact, in recent years reports have taken some of the following forms: (a) a mere recitation of the provisions of the constitution or other legislation; (b) three or four page reports; and (c) the inclusion of vague and unspecific claims such as: "there is no problem of minorities...the population being fully integrated socially" [12], "...legislation is based on the principle that persecuted persons and freedom fighters may not be extradited".[13] These, Bayefsky argues, are not isolated phenomena but highlight States Parties' unbridged gulf in understanding and implementing international human rights standards.[14] This suggests that the pattern of reporting for the CRC is not unique to the CRC but has been widely reflected in the reporting for other treaties.

Furthermore, although no data is available for the way that States Parties responded to Committee's List of Issues, there is reason to suspect that they follow the pattern of the CRC as well.

As for the quality of the Concluding Observations, there is evidence that it has been inadequate for other Human Rights Treaties, as well as for the CRC, and the Concluding Observations for the CRC are, on average, twice as long as those of other treaty bodies.

---

[11] Ibid., note 45 and A/51/40, Vol I: Report of the Human Rights Committee: 13/04/1997: para.45.

[12] UN. Doc. CCPR/C/128/Add.1 (Second Periodic reports of States Parties due in 1998): Gabon. 14/06/1999: para.50.

[13] UN. Doc. CAT/C/44/Add.3 (Third Periodic reports of States parties due in 1998): Libyan Arab Jamahiriya. 28/01/1999: para.39.

[14] Bayefsky 'The UN Human Rights Treaty System: Universality at the Crossroads', 22.

In general, CERD has the least developed Concluding Observations, while the CAT's Concluding Observations are the briefest, as it focuses on the narrowest range of issues, with recommendations not exceeding six sentences. [15]

Overall, Committees' Concluding Observations are often extremely general, thereby frustrating all participants who are interested in using them to advocate, or plan, or implement reforms at the national level. The following examples reflect the general nature of the Concluding Observations: "The Committee requests the States Party to provide more data in its second periodic report on the problem of poverty...and urges the Government to take all remedial measures in order to combat poverty" [16] and "...The Committee recommends that the State party monitor all tendencies which may give rise to racial or ethnic segregation and counter the negative consequences of such tendencies." [17] As in the case of the CRC, the above examples show that Concluding Observations do not identify specific laws or practical ways that will be of great use for the State concerned in dealing with the areas they have identified.

According to Bayefsky, Concluding Observations have integrated political biases in everything from their opening remarks to the identification of so-called "positive aspects", the language used, and the substance of specific recommendations. To some extent, she says, the quality of Concluding Observations depends on the committee members assigned as country rapporteur, while the extent or detail of the consideration of state reports is also affected by the political biases of other members.[18] The selection of the treaty body members is solely States Parties' responsibility; therefore, if Bayefsky is right in suggesting that States Parties fail to elect truly independent experts, States Parties themselves are indirectly responsible for the quality of Concluding Observations.

9.3 Reform and the Political Realities of the UN

At the founding of the UN meeting in San Francisco, the drafters of the UN Charter never imagined that they were putting in place the foundations

[15] Ibid., 67.

[16] UN. Doc. E/C.12/1/Add.35 (Concluding Observations of the Committee on Economic, Social and Cultural Rights): Ireland. 14/05/99: para.26.

[17] UN. Doc. CERD/C/304/Add.91 (Concluding Observations by the Committee on the Elimination of Racial Discrimination): France. 19/04/2000: para.10.

[18] Bayefsky 'The UN Human Rights Treaty System: Universality at the Crossroads', 67-69.

for an international system of human rights, nor that the various human rights provisions in the Charter would serve as a system of human rights protection.[19] The Preamble of the UN Charter clearly states that one of the aims of the United Nations is "to establish conditions under which justice and respect for the obligations arising from treaties and other sources of international law can be maintained" and in order to achieve this will "employ international machinery for the protection of the economic and social advancement of all peoples."[20] Pursuant to article 55, member states of the United Nations undertake to promote: (i) higher standards of living, full employment, and conditions of economic and social progress and development; (ii) solutions to international economic, social, health, and related problems, and international cultural and educational cooperation; and (iii) universal respect for, and observance of, human rights and fundamental freedoms for all without distinction as to race, sex, language, or religion.[21] And by agreeing to the Charter, "All Member pledged themselves to take joint and separate action in cooperation with the Organisation for the achievement of the purposes set forth in Article 55."[22]

However, in order to achieve the above mentioned aims, as stated in Article 2 of the Charter, the Organisation and its Members shall act in accordance with its principles, some of which are: "(1) The Organisation is based on the principle of the sovereignty and equality of all its Members; and (2) All Members, in order to ensure to all of them the rights and benefits resulting from membership, shall fulfil in good faith the obligations assumed by them in accordance with the present Charter."

The six main bodies into which the UN is divided into are: the General Assembly, the Security Council, the Economic and Social Council, Trusteeship Council, the International Court of Justice and the Secretariat.[23] It is worth noting that these bodies are: i) of unequal size, as some possess many subsidiary bodies and committees, while others have very few; ii) of different status, with some being quite powerful, while others have become almost obsolete; and iii) of varying relevance to human rights, some of these bodies focus more extensively on the issue while others have little or no relevance for the protection and promotion of human rights.[24]

---

[19] Mertus, *The United Nations and Human Rights: A guide for a New Era*, 37.
[20] 'Charter of the United Nations'.
[21] Ibid.
[22] Ibid., art. 56.
[23] Ibid., art.7.
[24] 'The United Nations Human Rights System' *Human Rights Education Association* (http://www.hrea.org/index.php?doc_id=437 , 10 May 2008).

The UN mechanism in place regarding human rights issues are either Charter-based or treaty-based. Charter-based mechanisms are those based on the UN Charter and include: the Universal Declaration of Human Rights; the Commission on Human Rights; and the Sub-Commission on the Promotion and Protection of Human Rights.

The treaty-based mechanisms run on a parallel track to the Charter-based mechanisms and involve international law taking precedence over the domestic law of the state. A large number of multilateral treaties currently exist and cover a wide range of topics, from racial discrimination to the rights of migrant workers. There is no central oversight body for all the treaties; instead, each treaty has its own compliance and oversight bodies embedded within its structure.[25] The key difference between the Charter-based bodies and treaty-based bodies is that the latter are legally binding while the former at times are either not legally binding or require permission to be executed.[26] Furthermore, while the treaty bodies are independent of governments as their members are independent experts, the various charter-based bodies have strong governmental influence: at high levels, the bodies are composed of governments and therefore are highly politicised.[27]

From the above mentioned, and in particular Article 2 of the Charter, it becomes clear that the 'real' powers of the Organisation are limited, especially if we consider that it has to rely on the 'good faith' of its member states. In fact, the UN treaty system lacks coercive powers and treaty body findings are not legally binding. 'Treaty body findings' here refers to a committee's Concluding Observations, in which the committee will note the negative and positive aspects of the performance of a state in relation to its treaty obligations and make specific recommendations to the state. The non-binding status of these recommendations provides reason to doubt the effectiveness of the committees as treaty monitoring bodies.[28] This leads us to question its effectiveness and efficiency overall and in particular of the Treaty Monitoring Bodies.

---

[25] Mertus, '*The United Nations and Human Rights: A guide for a New Era*', 64.

[26] Ibid., and 'The United Nations Human Rights System'.

[27] 'Leaflet No. 3: UN Charter Based Bodies and Indigenous Peoples' (http://www.ohchr.org/Documents/Publications/GuideIPleaflet3en.pdf, 10 February 2008).

[28] Michael O'Flaherty and Claire O'Brien 'Reform of UN Human Rights Treaty Monitoring Bodies: A Critique of the Concept Paper on the High Commissioner's Proposal for a Unified Standing Treaty Body' Human Rights Law Review 7(1) (2007): 164.

According to the Law of International Institutions, the United Nations does not impair the sovereignty of Member States but only imposes some restrictions on their freedom.[29] Could that explain the increasing number of states who decide to sign up to treaties, especially if we consider that as recently as 1969 there was not a single human rights treaty body in existence? States were extremely reluctant to subject their human rights record to any sort of scrutiny, and the terms agreed in the text of the several treaties that had been adopted then set out a minimalist approach to monitoring.[30]

Now, forty years later, one of the main problems that the Human Rights treaty supervisory system has to overcome is the reluctance of all governments to facilitate the emergence of a truly effective international human rights monitoring regime, and the lack of resources available to the UN for such activities.[31]

Furthermore, it is very difficult to achieve flexible institutional and substantive changes in the context of a regime which has its foundations in a range of treaties, each of which was to some extent drafted so as to limit the possibilities of dramatic change from within, by process of interpretation and application as distinct from amendment.[32]

9.4 Proposals and Possibilities of Committees

The possibility of improving the system so that it achieves its objectives to the maximum is not a new topic. The issue was put on the table for the first time soon after the establishment of the first treaty body, the Committee on the Elimination of Racial Discrimination, in 1970.[33]

[29] Magdalena M. Martin Martinez, *National Sovereignty and International Organisations* (London: Kluwer Law International, 1996): 71.

[30] The system established in 1956 and disbanded in 1981 called upon states to report to the Commission on Human Rights, on the basis of the UDHR. The reports were expected to describe 'developments and the progress achieved during the preceding three years in the field of human rights, and measures taken to safeguard human liberty'. CHR Res.I (XII) (1956), para.1. See Philip Alston, The United Nations and Human Rights: A Critical Appraisal (USA: Oxford University Press, 1999): 183-4 and Philip Alston and James Crawford, The Future of UN Human Rights Treaty Monitoring (Cambridge: Cambridge University Press, 2000): 522.

[31] Alston and James Crawford, The Future of UN Human Rights Treaty Monitoring , 522.

[32] Ibid.

[33] HRI/MC/2006/2: Concept Paper on the High Commissioner's Proposal for a Unified Standing Treaty: 22/03/2006: para.5.

Over the last forty years a number of reports have been submitted led by UN, NGOs[34] and academics. This chapter, apart from making extensive use of the existing academic literature, will make particular use of the following sources:

- "Long-Term effectiveness of the UN Human Rights Treaty System" (1989) a report conducted by an independent expert, Philip Alston[35]
- "The UN Human Rights Treaty System: Universality at the Crossroads" (2001), a report written by Prof. Anne F. Bayefsky in collaboration with the Office of the UN High Commissioner (OHCHR) for Human Rights[36]
- "Strengthening the United Nations: An Agenda for Further Change" (2002)[37]
- "Report of a Brainstorming Meeting on Reform of the Human Rights Treaty Body System" (2003)[38]
- "Methods of work relating to the State reporting Process" (2003)[39]
- "In Larger Freedom: Towards the Development, Security and Human Rights for all", a report of the Secretary-General (2005)[40]
- "Plan of Action" submitted by the United Nations High Commissioner for Human Rights (2005)[41]

---

[34] For a full list of reports in relation to the Reform of the UN Human Rights Treaty System, see: Bayefsky 'The UN Human Rights Treaty System: Universality at the Crossroads'.

[35] Alston prepared three reports. The first A/44/668: Effective Implementation of International Instruments on Human Rights, Including Reporting Obligations Under International Instruments on Human Rights: 08/11/1989 , an interim report A/CONF.157/PC/62/Ass.11/Rev.1: World Conference on Human Rights: 22/04/1993 and a final updated report E/.CN.4/1997/74: Effective Functioning of Bodies Established Pursuant to United Nations Human Rights Instruments: Final Report on enhancing the ling-term effectiveness of the United Nations human rights treaty system: 27/03/1997.

[36] Bayefsky 'The UN Human Rights Treaty System: Universality at the Crossroads'.

[37] A/57/387: Strengthening of the United Nations: an agenda for further change: 09/09/2002: paras: 52-4.

[38] HRI/ICM/2003/4: Report of a Brainstorming Meeting on reform of the Human Rights Treaty Body System, 4-7 May, 2003: 10 June 2003.

[39] HRI/ICM/2003/3/Add.1: Methods of work relating to the State Reporting Process: 10/06/2003.

[40] A/59/2005: In Larger Freedom: Towards development, security and Human Rights for all: Report of the Secretary-General: 21/03/2005.

- "Concept Paper on the High Commissioner's Proposal for a Unified Standing Treaty Body" (2006)[42]

Even though the issue was brought up in 1970s, the first call for reform came after the appointment of Philip Alston, as an independent expert, by the Secretary-General, to carry out research on the long-term effectiveness of the UN Human Rights Treaty System. Alston identified that "setting standards cannot protect human rights if the standards laid down are then blatantly disregarded…Ratification is not enough. Implementation is the essential task for us".[43] Therefore, in order for the different treaty bodies to fulfil their vital role of giving substance to the concept of international accountability, well developed and well applied effective monitoring procedures should be in place.[44] The way to do this, according to Alston, was by consolidating the treaty bodies into one (possibly two) treaty bodies.[45]

Bayefsky's report was conducted in collaboration with the Office of the High Commissioner for Human Rights and supported by the Ford Foundation, in order to present recommendations for the enhancement of the operations of the human rights treaty system.[46] Bayefsky, in her report, gives a very detailed account of all the areas of concern and provides principal recommendations for the Treaty Bodies, but also the OHCHR, NGOs, UN Agencies and States Parties.

The Secretary-General's second reform report, "Strengthening the United Nations: An Agenda for Further Change", called for the international human rights treaties to "craft a more coordinated approach to their activities and standardise their varied reporting guidelines" and suggested that "each State should be allowed to produce a single report summarising its adherence to the full range of international human rights treaties to which it is a party."[47]

Three years later, in 2005, the Secretary-General in his report, "In Larger Freedom", re-addressed the need for strengthening the treaty body

---

[41] A/59/2005/Add.3: Plan for Action: Submitted by the High Commissioner for Human Rights: 26/05/2005.

[42] HRI/MC/2006/CRP.1: Concept Paper on the High Commissioner's Proposal for a Unified Standing Treaty Body: 14/03/2006.

[43] A/44/668: para. 110.

[44] Ibid.

[45] Ibid., para.179.

[46] Bayefsky 'The UN Human Rights Treaty System: Universality at the Crossroads', 1.

[47] A/57/387: para.54.

system, and called for the implementation of harmonised guidelines on reporting to all treaty bodies, so that the treaty bodies could operate as a unified system.[48] In addition, the report invited the High Commissioner to devise more far-reaching measures to make the treaty system more effective and responsive.[49]

The High Commissioner reiterated the Secretary-General's call in her "Plan of Action" (2005) and proposed a unified standing treaty body that would not only strengthen and make more effective the existing monitoring system but also, would increase, on the national level, the impact of the human rights treaty system.[50]

Meanwhile, the outcomes of Malbun's 'brainstorming session' on Treaty Body reform reflected not only the lack of firm reform leadership from the Treaty monitoring bodies themselves, but also, the range of divergent views within the committees as well as some uncertainty regarding the best route forward.[51] At the session, representatives of all treaty bodies and others participated and differing opinions were ventured across the spectrum of reform issues, with positive consensus on only a few, very broadly defined, areas. These included: the need to improve the effectiveness of monitoring, dialogue and follow up; to improve coordination and to ensure the coherence of the overall system;[52]and for sustained efforts on capacity building.[53] Here, efforts towards harmonised reporting received greater support, while the idea of a single state report was rejected.[54]

Finally, the Concept Paper, although it recapitulates the current system's contribution to the promotion and protection of human rights,

---

[48] A/59/2005: para.147.

[49] O'Flaherty and O'Brien 'Reform of UN Human Rights Treaty Monitoring Bodies: A Critique of the Concept Paper on the High Commissioner's Proposal for a Unified Standing Treaty Body', 155.

[50] A/59/2005/Add.3: paras.99-100.

[51] O'Flaherty and O'Brien 'Reform of UN Human Rights Treaty Monitoring Bodies: A Critique of the Concept Paper on the High Commissioner's Proposal for a Unified Standing Treaty Body', 156.

[52] A/ 58/123: Letter dated 13 June 2003 from the Permanent Representative of Liechtenstein to the United Nations addressed to the Secretary-General: 08/07/2003: para.12. See also, HRI/ICM/2003/3: Methods of Work Relating to the State Reporting Process, Background document prepared by the Secretariat: 11/04/2003.

[53] A/ 58/123: para. 66 and O'Flaherty and O'Brien 'Reform of UN Human Rights Treaty Monitoring Bodies: A Critique of the Concept Paper on the High Commissioner's Proposal for a Unified Standing Treaty Body', 156.

[54] A/ 58/123: paras.16, 20.

clearly shows its strong preference for the unification of Treaty Bodies. In fact, the Paper suggests that, as a set of disparate bodies rather than an as integrated one, the treaty body system is ill-matched to its overall goals, as "the multiplicity of recommendations emerging from each treaty monitoring body makes it difficult for States Parties and other national stakeholders to gain a comprehensive picture of the key human rights concepts and recommendations vis-à-vis the human rights situations in States, which may diminish the possibility that States Parties will translate this output into integrated cross-sectoral national planning and programming."[55]

Having provided background information on each of the existing reports giving reform proposals, the following section will examine the reform proposals contained in these documents regarding: monitoring committees, the powers of the committees, the submission and the content of the reports, and implementation policies.

9.4.1 Monitoring Committees

9.4.1.1 Nature of the Committees

Before considering solutions for the better functioning of the existing Committees, it is worth reiterating that the root of the existing problems lies in the rapid expansion of the treaty system and in the fact that the existing implementation schemes were drafted during "a period of time when effective international monitoring was neither intended nor achievable"[56].

The majority of the treaty bodies were established on a case-by-case basis, without any relationship to each other. Furthermore, the lack of coordination and cooperation between the government bodies concerned makes the establishment of better coordination between the various government departments and state human rights institutions participating in the preparation of reports an absolute necessity. It would certainly be of help if governments developed and implemented concrete mechanisms to prepare their reports.[57] Alston and Bayefsky believe that a possible solution lies in the better coordination of work between the provision of the treaties and improved cooperation and coordination between treaty

---

[55] HRI/MC/2006/CRP.1:para.23.

[56] Bayefsky 'The UN Human Rights Treaty System: Universality at the Crossroads', 2.

[57] Christof Heyns and Frans Viljoen, *Impact Study of the United Nations Human Rights Treaties in Twenty UN Member States* (Pretoria: Pretoria Law Press 2000): 447.

bodies and national and international NGOs, UN agencies, bodies and programmes.[58] The fundamental reasons for these proposals lie, first, in the substantial overlap of the treaty rights and freedoms, which ultimately result in overlaps of reporting and dialogue.[59] Children's rights, for instance, are extensively covered by the CRC but are also provided for by CEDAW, CERD, CAT, ICESCR and ICCPR. CEDAW is concerned with the wellbeing of a girl child and CERD with the discrimination faced by children belonging to different groups or minorities. The CAT Committee focuses on the cases of ill-treatment of minors and the ICESCR Committee on the impact of economic and social difficulties on the situation of children and their access to education. Finally the ICCPR deals with children's rights and forced labour, corporal punishment and juvenile justice.[60] According to Eric Tistounet, there are other examples that could be multiplied, including women's rights, cases of discrimination and ill-treatment of the person.[61]

Second, Treaty Bodies meetings currently take place in either Geneva or New York, which limits their impact and the chances of cooperation with international NGOs and other nationally focused programs. If, instead, the meetings become more regional, they would make a difference as they would be more accessible to national governments, UN agencies and NGOs.[62]

The most radical option that has been put forward for resolving many of the problems currently being experienced by the existing treaty bodies is to consolidate them all into one or perhaps two new treaty bodies.[63] The initial attraction of such a proposal is considerable. The existing regime is "untidy" in virtually every respect. It is therefore appealing to contemplate its replacement by a system that would, inter alia, standardise the various procedures to be followed; reduce the overall volume of documentation; eliminate the need for multiple reports and accordingly reduce the overall

---

[58] A/44/668 and Bayefsky 'The UN Human Rights Treaty System: Universality at the Crossroads'.

[59] Bayefsky 'The UN Human Rights Treaty System: Universality at the Crossroads', xiv.

[60] Alston and Crawford, *The Future of UN Human Rights Treaty Monitoring,* 388. Also worth looking at HRI/MC/2006/2: para.17.

[61] Ibid. p.388.

[62] Heyns and Viljoen, *Impact Study of the United Nations Human Rights Treaties in Twenty UN Member States*, .327.

[63] Michael Bowman, ' Towards a Unified Treaty Body for Monitoring Compliance with UN Human Rights Conventions? Legal Mechanisms for Treaty Reform' *Human Rights Law Review* 7.1 (2007):225-249.

reporting burden imposed on States; and facilitate the emergence of an extremely competent supervisory committee potentially enjoying both considerable credibility and high visibility.[64]

Bayefsky argues that the "six different working methods, documents, practices, rules of procedure, and reporting guidelines do not serve users" [65] and agrees with Heyns and Vilijoen who believe that the consolidation of the treaty bodies or of the reporting system would, among other things, reduce the duplication in reporting requirements, while at the same time emphasising the indivisibility of human rights and minimising duplication in the reporting requirements. [66] Therefore, consolidation of the treaty bodies into one or two bodies might be seen as a solution to the existing problems. Nevertheless, it has to be said that consolidated reports or consolidation of treaty bodies would require formal amendments to the treaties – a procedure which could be time-consuming and cumbersome.[67]

On the other hand, Craig Scott maintains that one of the benefits of the current pluralistic structure – six treaty bodies for six treaties – is the diversity of knowledge it brings to the scrutiny of any State's human rights performance.[68]

Regarding the impact of either of these proposals on the CRC and OPAC, maintaining the status quo has its disadvantages but also can have its advantages for the monitoring Committees and their efficiency. The radical measures proposed, though, might result in bringing the existing machinery to a halt. In addition it would not only narrow the level of expertise but it might also result in the prioritisation of some of the treaties over others. In fact, the Chairperson of the Committee on the Rights of the Child clearly stated that "a single report might marginalise the specific issues covered by the Convention", though "cooperation across treaty

---

[64] A/44/668: para. 179.

[65] Bayefsky 'The UN Human Rights Treaty System: Universality at the Crossroads', xiv.

[66] Heli Niemi and Martin Scheinin, *Reform of the United Nations Human Rights Treaty Body System Seen from the Developing Country Perspective* (Institute for Human Rights: Abo Akademi University 2002).pp.26-7.

[67] Bayefsky 'The UN Human Rights Treaty System: Universality at the Crossroads', Heyns and Frans Viljoen, *Impact Study of the United Nations Human Rights Treaties in Twenty UN Member States.*

[68] Scott Craig, 'Bodies of knowledge: A diversity promotion role for the UN High Commissioner for Human Rights' in Philip Alston and James Crawford (ed) *The Future of UN Human Rights Treaty Monitoring* (Cambridge: Cambridge University Press, 2000): 403-437.

bodies should also be strengthened…and the possibility of adopting joint general comments explored."[69]

9.4.1.2 Membership of the Committees

The quality of membership of the treaty bodies can be critical to the performance and perception of their work. It is determined by the States Parties who nominate and elect the experts.[70] Despite a recommendation from the treaty body chairpersons calling on states parties to "refrain from nominating or electing to the treaty bodies persons performing political functions or occupying positions which were not readily reconcilable with the obligations of independent experts under the given treaty", states have continued to put forward candidates who fail to meet the basic criteria of independence, impartiality and expertise.[71]

A study prepared three years ago, which reviewed all the curricula vitae of individuals both nominated and elected to treaty bodies over the history of the treaty system, found that nearly half of those elected to serve on the treaty bodies were individuals holding government positions. It also found that elected experts had neither the time nor incentive to study the information contained in the government and non-government reports sent to them, prior to examinations.[72] This contravenes the principle that it is not acceptable for an individual holding a government position to act, or be seen to act, concurrently as an independent member of a body which is itself holding governments to account for their actions.[73]

The process of nominating treaty body members is one which is often not well publicised at the national level. Yet a transparent process with

---

[69] HRI/ICM/2003/3/Add.1 .

[70] The treaties broadly define the experts as persons of "high moral character" possessing "recognised competence in the field of human rights". in the case of the CAT and ICCPR, some experts should have "legal expertise", and in relation to the CERD, "acknowledged impartiality". Amnesty International, 'United Nations Proposals to Strengthen the Human Rights Treaty Bodies' *Amnesty International* (http://asiapacific.amnesty.org/library/pdf/IOR400182003ENGLISH/$File/IOR400 1803.pdf, 15 December 2008): 14.

[71] A/52/507: Human Rights Questions: Implementation of Human Rights Instruments: 21/10/1997.

[72] Bayefsky 'The UN Human Rights Treaty System: Universality at the Crossroads'. The study found that 51% of those nominated and 48% of those elected, had previously been employed in some capacity by their government.

[73] Amnesty International, 'United Nations Proposals to Strengthen the Human Rights Treaty Bodies', 15.

broad consultation with civil society could ensure that an effective method is devised to attract the best possible candidates, including women. States Parties can advertise treaty body vacancies, based on the profiles and criteria, through their own press office, in national newspapers, and in professional and other relevant journals, and request all relevant sectors of civil society to encourage applications from qualified persons. Once nominations have been received, states should ensure that the list of applicants is also made publicly available, including information about their skills and experience. Mechanisms should be put in place whereby civil society and others can provide substantive comments and information about an applicant and their application.

In the final stages of selection, States Parties should be rigorous in opposing candidates who do not fulfil the criteria of independence, impartiality and expertise in order to ensure the highest calibre of members on each treaty body.[74]

According to the current arrangements, although several members of the treaty bodies can be considered real experts in the field in question, there is hardly any examination of the actual 'expertise' of the experts by the states parties at the time of their election, which is the result of a number of problems in this context. First, some candidates do not have the relevant background to qualify as an expert, or a potential expert, on the obligations contained in the treaty in question. Second, their elections are simply part of the bigger set of elections that take place in and around the UN. Votes for a member of the Committee on the Rights of the Child are traded, for example, for votes for a member of the Tribunal on the Law of the Sea.[75] Vote trading between unrelated UN bodies is so common as to be unremarked. This is of course part of a broader problem. UN electoral processes are no doubt irreducibly political, but there has been no effort to distinguish between the political property so-called and the purely venal. Some form of scrutiny of candidates for minimum qualifications could bring great dividends in terms of the quality of membership, but there is for the time being no prospect that the electorate of state party representatives will adopt such a step.[76]

---

[74] Ibid., 16.

[75] NGOs have so far failed to acquire the curriculum vitae of the candidates and to expose those who are unqualified to serve as 'impartial' experts 'in a personal capacity'. Philip Alston and James Crawford, *The Future of UN Human Rights Treaty Monitoring* (Cambridge, CUP, 2000):188-9.

[76] One of the difficulties is that major reform is extremely difficult to achieve, and tinkering is unlikely to help. Still, there are steps in the right direction in other bodies, which may provide precedents in terms of any long-term restricting. For

It should also be noted that, based on the recommendation and requests of the Committee on the Rights of the Child made in the first five years of activity, two types of support will be necessary to strengthen the operation of the Committee in order to maximise the Committee's impact on the effective enjoyment by children of their rights. "First, the substantive support for the Committee's work with States parties reports should be significantly strengthened. Second, follow-up mechanisms will be devised to transform recommendations into reality. This will necessitate resources and coordination."[77]

The implementation of these plans, according to the Plan of Action, would be a result of voluntary financial contributions from states parties to a treaty body that will finance the activities of additional staff – consultants, experts, etc – assigned specifically to that treaty body's activities.[78] The reality has shown that the actual implementation is indeed costly – the CRC Committee estimated the resources required from voluntary contributions, on an annual basis, to be approximately US $1.25 million which excludes 13 percent of UN programme support costs.[79]

9.4.2 Powers of the Committees

The issue of increasing the powers of the Committees has not been mentioned in any of the existing proposals for reform. This might imply that the powers of the existing Committees are thought adequate and there is no need for further development, or that increasing the powers of the existing machinery is politically and practically unrealistic.

The growth in the number of treaties and ratifications has resulted in a steep increase in the workload of the treaty bodies and the Secretariat, backlogs in the consideration of reports and individual complaints, and increasing resource requirements. At the same time, the treaty bodies have

---

example, the new electoral process for judges of the European Court of Human Rights requires governments to nominate several candidates who are then subject to a form of scrutiny; cf. Also the prohibition of re-election of judges, under the Rome Statute of the International Criminal Court, 17 July 1998 (A/CONF.183/9) article 36 (9)(a) (which, if extended to the treaty bodies, would require longer and staggered terms of office) in Alston and Crawford, *The Future of UN Human Rights Treaty Monitoring*, 9.

[77] UNHCHR, Revised Plan of Action to Strengthen the Implementation of the Convention on the Rights of the Child, Geneva, 1996. HRI/MC/1997/2: Improving the Effectiveness of the Human Rights Treaty Bodies: 29/07/1997: para.3.

[78] Alston and Crawford, *The Future of UN Human Rights Treaty Monitoring*, 484.

[79] Ibid., 485.

been under-resourced, and their meeting time has been insufficient to handle their workload. Individual complaints procedures are underutilised, but the time between submission of a complaint and pronouncement of a final decision currently averages 30 to 33 months, which severely challenges the system's ability to provide redress for serious violations of the rights of individuals. An increase in petitions would further delay the processing of individual complaints.[80]

Treaty bodies' lack of resources, both financial and professional staff, is not a new issue, although in some treaties it is stated that 'the Secretary-General of the United Nations shall provide the necessary staff and facilities for the effective performance of the functions of the Committee'[81] In fact, too few professional staff have been assigned to treaty body work, and even those who have been assigned to this work have sometimes been seconded to other work. As a result, meetings have been cancelled, interpreting has sometimes been restricted and summary records are sometimes not prepared.[82]

For instance, the workload of the Human Rights Committee until recently has been added due to secretariat's lack of capacity to read different languages (particularly Russian), or due to the volume of incoming correspondence. At the moment the Committee registers about 60 cases per year, an average which has not substantially varied in the past five years.[83] For this reason the Human Rights Committee in 1989 created the position of the Special Rapporteur on New Communications, in order to assist the secretariat in dealing with cases at preliminary stages.[84]

One of the roles that the Secretariat has to fulfil is gathering information, organising it and presenting it in a manageable form.[85] This approach has been favoured by the CRC, which obviously makes more demands on its Secretariat. The CRC has more staff members than other treaty bodies (with respect to state reports). It is assisted by an NGO

---

[80] HRI/MC/2006/2: Concept Paper on the High Commissioner's Proposal for a Unified Standing Treaty: 22/03/2006: para.18.

[81] Article 36 (ICCPR), article 17.9 (CEDAW), CAT 18.3, CRC 43.11. Different arrangements apply to the ICESCR and CERD. Elizabeth Evatt,'Ensuring Effective supervisory procedures: the need for resources' in Philip Alston and Kames Crawford (ed) *The Future of UN Human Rights Treaty Monitoring* (Cambridge: Cambridge University Press, 200): 461.

[82] Ibid., 462.

[83] Bayefsky 'The UN Human Rights Treaty System: Universality at the Crossroads', 27 and note 73.

[84] Ibid., 30.

[85] Ibid., 41.

network dedicated to the Committee's work. It is also assisted by UNICEF, which has made the implementation of the Convention and cooperation with the Committee a fundamental part of its operations. If the resources were provided to other treaty bodies, it seems clear that some filtering of the large quantity of information and organising of source material in relation to the specific provisions of the treaty would benefit all treaty bodies. At the moment, different staff members often prepare background information on the same state for different treaty bodies.[86]

In short, although the professional staff of the Secretariat is highly competent, they are unable to respond effectively to the growing needs of the treaty bodies. Thus, if all the States Parties had reported on time, the Secretariat would have been overloaded and unable to respond to such a vast amount of information. According to Evatt, a possible solution lies in the consolidation of the treaty bodies and the creation of a single monitoring body that would ultimately call for a unified Secretariat, with a significant responsibility to work with an essentially full-time independent treaty body.[87]

The Committees have no real power to compel States to comply with the procedures, but at the same time, with their current working methods, they could not accommodate full compliance by States parties with reporting obligations.[88] The Committees' lack of 'real power' is a possible reason for the absence of effective, comprehensive follow-up mechanisms that would ensure that the current system has a sustained and systematic impact on the enjoyment of human rights at the national level.[89]

Providing Treaty Bodies with 'real' power may require legal as well as non-legal changes. In principle, providing the Bodies with greater legal powers could render them more effective but, in practice, this could be a difficult and unrealistic route to take. If the treaties were re-written, they would have to be agreed to afresh by each of the states who are parties to the existing treaties. In addition, states are unlikely to be willing to subordinate themselves to a Committee with increased legal powers. Hence, the consequence of an increase in the legal powers of the Committee might be a great reduction in the number of states who sign up to the revised treaties and who are subject to the Committee's powers.

[86] Ibid., 42.

[87] Evatt, 'Ensuring Effective supervisory procedures: the need for resources',465, 470. For a complete list of the Secretariat functions look at p.471.

[88] HRI/MC/2006/2: para.15.

[89] Ibid., para.26.

9.4.3 Submission of the Reports

The late or non submission of periodic reports by States Parties is not a new phenomenon. It has been a prominent issue for over two decades, despite the fact that various reform proposals have been placed on the table. It is worth noting that the analysis of the data has shown that this is not an issue for developing countries only but one that arises in relation to all types of state.

Reform proposals include the following: a degree of cooperation between various government agencies; the participation of national human rights institutions or use of consultants (if they exist) in the reporting process; the creation of inter-departmental institutions that coordinate report writing[90]; taking reporting more seriously and committing adequate resources to the reporting exercise; implementing concrete mechanisms to prepare reports, e.g. by setting up an effective inter-ministerial team to coordinate the reporting process (this may initially increase the delay in the submission of reports, since new expertise would have to be created); and training officials in report writing and trying to find ways to combat the frequent turnover of persons so trained.[91]

All the above mentioned measures, if implemented, could significantly improve the currently poor submission rates of the States Parties' reports.

9.4.4 Content of the Reports

Currently States Parties' reports tend to be descriptive, formalistic and legalistic, rather than critical, frank, reflective and focused on practical realities and problems encountered.[92] As was the case with overdue reports, this is by no means a problem that concerns developing countries only. More consultation with civil society could improve the quality of reports, as evidenced by the UNICEF-funded consultations in India and Zambia during the preparation of their initial CRC reports. Facilitating wide consultations between government and civil society would constitute one form of UN assistance to developing countries.[93]

---

[90] Niemi and Scheinin, *Reform of the United Nations Human Rights Treaty Body System Seen from the Developing Country Perspective,* 3-4. The first treaty body first met in January 1970 and the UNHCHR was established in 1994. Ibid., 8.

[91] Ibid.,51.

[92] Ibid., 28 and Heyns and Viljoen, *Impact Study of the United Nations Human Rights Treaties in Twenty UN Member States,* 24.

[93] Niemi and Scheinin, *Reform of the United Nations Human Rights Treaty Body System Seen from the Developing Country Perspective,* 28.

The second proposal, more radical than the previous one, was first introduced by the then Secretary-General in 2002 in a document entitled *Strengthening of the United Nations: an agenda for further change* according to which, "each state should be allowed to produce a single report summarising its adherence to the full range of international human rights treaties to which it is a party".[94] Furthermore, there is a consensus among the treaty bodies for a new reporting model which would require States Parties to present an "expanded core" document together with a "focused" report for each relevant treaty body.[95] The purpose of the core document would be to avoid duplication by allowing states to include this general information in one document rather than in several, while the aim of the focused State Party report would be to focus on a specific range of issues, after consideration of a comprehensive initial report. The "focus" would be identified in advance, and would be based on the concluding observations of the previous review of the state party report, together with new and significant developments.[96] This model might yield a reporting process which, over time, could become so slim that critical issues would fall off the agenda. Its success would also be largely dependent on a preparatory process into which a breadth of reliable information from knowledgeable sources could flow, and on concluding observations which were comprehensive, specific, and accurately reflected the concerns expressed during the review of the state party report.

Regarding measures dealing with inadequate reports submitted by States Parties, four of the six treaty bodies currently allow the secretariat, usually in consultation with a member(s) of the treaty body, to work with states parties and to encourage revision of those reports that do not meet the reporting guidelines to a significant extent. The experience has sometimes been the re-submission of a much improved report.[97] Bayefsky

---

[94] A/57/387.

[95] HRI/ICM/2003/5: Report of the Second Inter-Committee Meeting of the Human Rights Treaty Bodies: 27/06/2003. This records the agreement of all treaty body participants with these models.

[96] A/53/125: Effective Implementation of International Instruments on Human Rights Including reporting Obligations under International Instruments on Human Rights: 14/05/1998. As conceived by the chairpersons "the principal criteria in determining the appropriate focus of more limited reports should include the recommendations contained in the previous concluding observations relating to the State in question, significant new measures of a legislative, judicial, administrative or policy nature adopted since the examination of the last report, and any issues identified by a pre-sessional working groups as requiring a sustained focus".

[97] Bayefsky 'The UN Human Rights Treaty System: Universality at the Crossroads', 23.

in her report recommends the Treaty Bodies to encourage the OHCHR secretariat to identify those reports that fail to follow the reporting guidelines and to suggest informally to States Parties ways and means to resubmit an improved report prior to its consideration by the monitoring Committee.[98]

9.4.5 Concluding Observations

The content of the concluding observations should be the benchmark for measuring present compliance and future progress not only for the treaty party, but also for civil society as well as different UN actors that are seeking to integrate the concluding observations' remarks into country-based initiatives. Therefore, they should accurately identify the failures of states to comply with the treaty and contain specific recommendations to improve implementation. Currently their content varies between treaty bodies.[99]

According to Bayefsky, the success of concluding observations depends on two elements: "(a) their accuracy, as rigorous assessments of human rights conditions, and (b) their functionality, as perceptive evaluations of needs and priorities".[100] It has been maintained that the treaty bodies' recommendations are often too broad, too vague or too farfetched to enable effective implementation.[101] These characteristics also make it difficult to determine whether the appropriate steps toward implementation are being carried out, and whether compliance with convention obligations is being achieved.[102] Heyns and Viljoen emphasise that concluding observations should offer "yardsticks" to assess government compliance and performance, not only for the UN human rights bodies themselves but for governments and NGOs as well.[103] Moreover, these yardsticks should be supported by substantive reasoning to explain clearly why the treaty body arrived at its conclusions.[104] Heyns and Viljoen would also prefer

---

[98] Ibid., 23.
[99] Amnesty International, 'United Nations Proposals to Strengthen the Human Rights Treaty Bodies', 24.
[100] Bayefsky 'The UN Human Rights Treaty System: Universality at the Crossroads', 62. Also Niemi, and Scheinin, Reform of the United Nations Human Rights Treaty Body System Seen from the Developing Country Perspective, 34
[101] Heyns and Viljoen, Impact Study of the United Nations Human Rights Treaties in Twenty UN Member States, 197.
[102] Ibid.
[103] Ibid., 574.
[104] Ibid., 448.

comments to be as specific and as action-oriented as possible, rather than verdicts on governments' general performance in the field of human rights.[105] In their view, concluding observations should contain more recommendations on what the State should do in order to improve the promotion and protection of human rights, including realistic advice on how to deal with urgent questions, as well as target dates by which the State Parties must take the recommended measures.[106] The Committees could also provide proposals and ideas for implementation based on the achievements and experience of other countries. Here one can take the HRC as an example of "best practice": each paragraph in its concluding observations includes brief legal reasoning as to the interpretation of the CCPR provision, in most cases including an explicit reference to a specific provision. Thereafter, a recommendation follows combining a legal treaty obligation with a policy recommendation.[107]

Heys and Viljoen argue that concluding observations should contain more detailed analysis of the state reports[108], including divergences between the government's obligations arising from the relevant treaty and the process that has been achieved and the difficulties encountered.[109] The Committees could also include in their general observations and recommendations a point-by-point listing of the observations stated in previous reports with which there has not been compliance.[110] On the other hand, Tistoutnet observes: "...overly-detailed observations may be criticised if they fail to emphasise important issues. Additionally, they run the risk of containing technical or legal considerations which may not accurately reflect the legal or practical situation in the state concerned, thus providing the government with grounds for attacking the report."[111]

---

[105] Ibid., 248.

[106] Ibid., 197, 331, 541, 639, 248 and Niemi, and Scheinin, *Reform of the United Nations Human Rights Treaty Body System Seen from the Developing Country Perspective*, 35.

[107] Niemi, and Scheinin, *Reform of the United Nations Human Rights Treaty Body System Seen from the Developing Country Perspective*, 35.

[108] Heyns and Viljoen, Impact Study of the United Nations Human Rights Treaties in Twenty UN Member States, .639.

[109] Ibid., 350&248.

[110] Ibid., 448.

[111] Eric Tistounet, 'The problem of Overlapping Among Different Treaty Bodies' in Philip Alston and James Crawford (ed.) *The Future of UN Human Rights Treaty Monitoring* (Cambridge: Cambridge University Press, 2000): 393.

9.4.6 States Parties

All the above mentioned recommendations are directed at improving Committees' efficiency, which goes hand in hand with States Parties' compliance with the principles of the Treaties that they have signed up to. In this section, therefore, we look at some of the recommendations directed at States Parties.

The basis for a steady long term improvement lies in States Parties' acknowledgement of the following key principles:

- They have ultimate responsibility for the successful implementation of the human rights treaties
- The voluntary nature of their participation and the self-assumed character of their obligations
- The universality of the standards and the goal, namely, the common human interest in ameliorating the suffering of human rights victims everywhere.[112]

The above principles can be implemented at the national level by each of the States Parties securing consistency between their domestic legislation and practices and the provisions of International Human Rights Treaties and by submitting reports that meet the reporting guidelines and that are submitted on time.[113]

However, even when reports are submitted on time, some States Parties either are not present when their report is considered or their representatives are not qualified to respond to the questions addressed to them by the Committee members. In such cases, States should be clearly informed of the importance of sending qualified representatives to the dialogue and should be directly contacted by the secretariat to reinforce the matter. Failures to do so should be subject of commentary in concluding observations. Names of the delegates should appear in annual reports.[114]

Following what has already been discussed in a previous section regarding Committee members, it is worth recalling that it is solely States Parties' responsibility to ensure that they nominate and elect individuals to

---

[112] Bayefsky 'The UN Human Rights Treaty System: Universality at the Crossroads', 190.

[113] Amnesty International, 'United Nations Proposals to Strengthen the Human Rights Treaty Bodies', 25-6.

[114] Bayefsky 'The UN Human Rights Treaty System: Universality at the Crossroads', 166.

the treaty bodies who fulfil the basic criteria of independence, impartiality and expertise, while candidates holding government positions should be automatically disqualified.[115]

Finally, once a constructive dialogue with the Committee members has taken place and the Committee has produced its Concluding Observations, it is States Parties' responsibility both to disseminate and implement them through direct engagement with the relevant Treaty Bodies. [116]

In Chapter 2 a number of factors were identified that affected states' compliance or non-compliance with the obligations they have assumed in committing themselves to human rights treaties. How do those factors affect the prospects for reform and the likelihood that reform will make a difference to states' compliance with treaty obligations?

Insofar as a substantial number of states are 'sincere ratifiers' and are genuinely committed both to human rights and to their implementation, there is reason to be optimistic about the possibility of reform. That is, the sorts and reforms we have considered in this Chapter are not in simple conflict with the political reality of states' behaviour and what drives their behaviour. There is also reason to think that many states would genuinely endeavour to comply with a reformed and more effective reporting process. We have seen that compliance with the current process is mixed but a reformed process could itself contribute to a greater degree of compliance. After all, strategic ratifiers as well as sincere ratifiers would have an incentive to be seen as compliant with the process. However, we also identified in Chapter 2 a number of factors that might encourage non-compliance. Perhaps, the most important of these was the lack of an enforcement mechanism that could make non-compliant or incompletely compliant states fall into line. Given states' reluctance to subordinate themselves to any such mechanism, reforms are likely to fall short of enforcement for the foreseeable future. How far should that lead us to conclude that improvements in the submission and content of states' reports are really in the hands of states themselves? Can changes to the reporting system make any difference to states' compliance or will compliance continue to be determined by factors other than the reporting system, so that reforms the UN makes to its monitoring systems will make little difference to states' behaviour? In other words, will it really be the type of state, as set out in Beth Simmon's typology of ratifiers, that remains the dominant factor and one that the UN can do little to change?

---

[115] Amnesty International, 'United Nations Proposals to Strengthen the Human Rights Treaty Bodies', 25-6.
[116] Ibid.

Beth Simmons' typology might suggest that the states' compliance is entirely a matter of how states, or their governments, are predisposed to behave.[117] Sincere ratifiers will comply with the reporting obligations. Strategic ratifiers will do so insofar as it serves their interests. False positive simply will not comply. Thus the fate of the CRC is entirely in the hands of the states. If we cannot alter states and their governments, we cannot do anything that will affect states' compliance with their obligations under the CRC. Changes to the UN's monitoring process will make no difference. However, the findings of this thesis do not correlate entirely with Simmons' typology regarding commitment. This gives me an opportunity to make some interesting and significant observations.

It is often not easy to know which states belong to which categories in Simmons's typology. There is also a danger of circularity: if a state performs well in the reporting process we might conclude that it must have been a sincere ratifier and, if it performs poorly, we might suppose that it must have been a strategic ratifier or a false positive. However, we do not have to fall into that circularity. Simmons's typology applies to states at the point of ratification rather than to their subsequent behaviour. So it is consistent with some strategic ratifiers and false positives actually going on to perform relatively well in the reporting process and with some sincere ratifiers going on to perform relatively poorly.

Perhaps the indicator used in this thesis that is closest to Simmons's typology is regime type. In section 5.5 of Chapter 5, we examined how the submission performances of states correlated with regime type for both the initial reports and the second and third periodic reports. The figures did show a degree of positive correlation between regimes that the EIU classified as 'full democracies' and those that Freedom House classified as 'free'. The correlations were more marked for the figures based on the EIU's categories than for those based on Freedom House's categories, reflecting the greater degree of refinement of the EIU's classification. However, the correlation was far from perfect, with some full democracies

[117] For another attempt to give a typology of states that correlates with the quality of states' reporting performances and one that focuses specifically on the CRC, see Charlotte Friedner Parrat, 'The Politics of Reporting: a Study of States' Strategies for Reporting to the UN Committee on the Rights of the Child' *Political Studies* 58.3(2010): 472-496. The links Parrat makes between types of state and reporting performances are highly speculative. She uses a game theory approach and the claims she makes about types of state are supported in each case only by a single example. The evidence presented in this thesis indicates that an accurate matching of state type to reporting performance would involve a more complicated and qualified story than the one that Parrat proposes.

performing more poorly than states that possessed other sorts of regime (see Tables 5.22-5.37). In section 6.3.3 of Chapter 6, we examined how far reporting on Article 38 correlated with regime type. A similar pattern emerged. There was a degree of positive correlation between the EIU's 'full democracies', and Freedom House's 'free' regimes. But again the correlation was far from perfect with a significant number of full democracies or free regimes not reporting on Article 38 and a significant number of other sorts of regime reporting on the Article (see Tables 6.8-6.13). Our findings for correlation with income level, showed a somewhat weaker correlation between high income levels and good reporting performances (see Tables 5.14-5.21 and 6.5-6.7). What is significant about these findings in the present context is that they indicate that a state's reporting performance is not a simple function of the kind of state it is. Rather states' conduct in the reporting process has proved more flexible and variable than that. The fate of the reporting process is not therefore wholly dependent on the character of states' regimes, which in turn suggests that there is significant scope for reforms in the UN's reporting process to make a difference to the quality of states' reporting.

Two qualifications need to be added to this optimistic conclusion. First, my findings on the content of reports relate only to article 38 and OPAC, although the analysis of the punctuality or lateness of report submissions relates to the CRC as a whole. It is possible therefore that some states that perform badly in reporting on article 38, perform well on other parts of the CRC, and vice versa. Secondly, my assessment relates only to the reporting process and does not investigate states' actual conduct in relation to children's rights. It is possible therefore that those of Simmons's sincere ratifiers, who perform poorly in the reporting process, will perform well in actually maintaining and promoting children's rights, and similarly that strategic ratifiers and false positives who report relatively well do much less well in actually providing for children's rights.

We have not yet mentioned here Simmons's fourth category – false negatives. Since all but two states have ratified the CRC, there are only two candidates for that category: the US and Somalia. In its own eyes, the US would no doubt rank as a false negative; its failure to ratify the CRC is not symptomatic of its failure to be concerned about and to respect children's rights. In general terms that is probably a fair assessment and we should note that the US has ratified OPAC. Somalia, on the other hand, is a failed state caught up in a civil war and should almost certainly be categorised as a 'true negative'.

A comprehensive assessment of the effectiveness of the UN's efforts to protect and promote children's rights would have to take account of the wider impact of the CRC and its Optional Protocols. The very existence of the CRC and OPAC, along with the reporting process, has helped to promote people's awareness of children's rights. The same is true of NGOs that have come into existence because of the CRC and who have adopted the promotion of the CRC as their goal. All of these developments have helped establish in people's minds, especially in the minds of those who are most concerned with the welfare of children, norms of acceptable conduct in relation to children. That can certainly be claimed for awareness of the rights of children in war and armed conflict. In particular, the recruitment of children for military purposes, especially for active fighting, is now very widely regarded as wrong and intolerable. The 'child soldier' has become an unacceptable phenomenon. Of course, that does not mean that child soldiering no longer occurs. But it creates a strong moral disincentive for governments not to recruit child soldiers. We might say, more cynically, that it creates a strong disincentive for governments not to be *known* to recruit child soldiers. But it is not easy for a government that recruits and uses child soldiers to hide that fact, or to escape the opprobrium of the international community. Perhaps that is why the use of child soldiers seems nowadays to be, proportionately, greater amongst non-government militias than amongst government militias.

So, even though this thesis has focused upon the reporting process and how adequately it works, it would be incorrect to judge the success of the CRC and OPAC solely in terms of that process. It should also be judged by its larger role in promoting global norms concerning children's rights.

9.5 Conclusion

While this thesis is concerned with the provision for children in war and armed conflict in the CRC and OPAC, the machinery for monitoring those treaties and that for monitoring compliance with other human rights treaties is very similar. The inadequacies in the monitoring of different human rights treaties are also very similar. For those reasons, it is difficult to consider how the machinery for monitoring compliance with the CRC and OPAC might be improved without simultaneously considering how the equivalent machinery might be improved for monitoring all human rights treaties. Indeed, all of the major UN reports considering possible reforms have addressed the monitoring system in general rather than only that for a specific treaty. Consequently, this chapter has examined possible reforms to the UN's system for monitoring compliance with human rights in general rather than reforms that might be made to the monitoring of the CRC and OPAC in particular. Indeed, the reality is that improvements in the monitoring of the CRC and OPAC are likely to come about only as part of more general reforms in the monitoring of human rights treaties as a whole. Even if those general reforms are made, very much will still depend upon the behaviour of states themselves and how far they are inclined to take their reporting obligations seriously. However, we have seen that there is reason to believe that reform in the UN's processes would make a difference to states' behaviour. Finally, we have to remember that reporting is not an end in itself, but a means of securing respect for children's rights as these are recognised in the CRC. States could improve their reporting while making no improvement in their actual respect for children's rights. But again, there is reason to be optimistic that these two factors would not be entirely separate and that more rigorous reporting processes would give states an incentive to avoid major differences between what they do and what they report themselves as doing, particularly since they will be subject to the scrutiny of NGOs.

CHAPTER TEN

CONCLUSION

10.1 Findings

This thesis has investigated the effectiveness of the process that the UN has established to monitor and promote states' compliance with the CRC and OPAC. It has done so by focusing on three aspects of that process: the extent to which states comply with their obligation to submit reports at regular intervals to the Committee on the Rights of the Child, the adequacy of the content of their reports, and the response of the Committee to those reports.

In Chapter 2 we looked at the historical development of human rights thinking from the idea of natural rights in order to understand the general background to the CRC. Having briefly examined Locke's understanding of natural rights, we looked at the 20th century understanding of natural rights and the change to the language of human rights. The shift from a "metaphysical" to a "political" idea of rights was clear during the 20th century. The most vivid example of that shift was provided by the UN, which, through the UDHR, managed to establish human rights as international norms. Building on the foundation provided by the UDHR, the UN has gone on to establish several Human Rights Covenants and Conventions, the CRC being one of them. Finally, Chapter 2 examined the role of the states in this process and, in particular, their motives for commitment and compliance with the various human rights treaties to which they are parties.

We saw in Chapter 3 how international recognition of children's rights in general, and of their rights in situations of war and armed conflict in particular, developed during the twentieth century from two sources: human rights law and international humanitarian law. These developments led eventually to the 1959 Declaration of the Rights of the Child, which in turn provided the basis for the drafting of the UN's Convention on the Rights of the Child in 1979. The UN General Assembly formally adopted the Convention in 1989 and it came into force in 1990. 192 countries have now ratified the Convention, making it the most widely ratified international treaty. Article 38 of the CRC provides specifically for the rights of children affected by armed conflict. It has been supplemented by the Optional Protocol on the Involvement of Children in Armed Conflict, which the General Assembly adopted in 2000 and which came into force in 2002. 110 states have ratified OPAC. In recent years, there have been other international developments affecting children's rights, especially the establishment of the International Criminal Court, but the CRC and its two Protocols remain the principal international instruments providing for the rights of the child.

Chapter 4 examined the debates that arose about the content of article 38 during its drafting and the significance of the formulation it eventually received. While there are reasons to welcome article 38, there are also reasons to regret its modest ambitions and some of the vagueness of its terminology. Several states were dissatisfied with the limited demands of the article, especially its setting the age-limit for recruitment into the military at 15 rather than 18. That dissatisfaction led to the drafting and adoption of OPAC, which provides more detailed protection for children in the context of armed conflict, including setting the age-limit for recruitment into the military at 18, though still with some exceptions. OPAC constitutes a considerable advance upon article 38, yet Chapter 4 identified reasons to be less than fully satisfied with the Protocol, particularly its failure to define some of its key terms precisely.

However, the principal critical focus of the research conducted in this thesis has been not on the content of article 38 and OPAC, but on the machinery for ensuring that states that have ratified the CRC and OPAC comply with the treaty obligations they have assumed. In other words, the main issue the thesis has investigated is not the adequacy of article 38 and OPAC, but the adequacy of the machinery and the processes the UN has established to ensure that states comply with article 38 and OPAC. Chapter 4 therefore gave close attention to the make-up and procedures of the Committee on the Rights of the Child and to the obligations of States Parties in relation to the Committee.

The conclusion of Chapter 4 marked the shift from formalities to practicalities. How does the process established to monitor compliance with the CRC and its Optional Protocols work in reality? In answering that question, this thesis has focused on three aspects of that process: the extent to which states comply with their obligation to submit reports at regular intervals to the Committee on the Rights of the Child, the adequacy of the content of their reports, and the response of the Committee to those reports.

Chapter 5 provided statistical data on the performance of states in submitting reports at the intervals required for the CRC and OPAC. It revealed that, for initial reports and second and third periodic reports relating to the CRC, only a very small number of states submitted their reports by the deadline, amounting to roughly 1% or 2% of all State Parties. Just over half had submitted their initial reports within three years of the deadline, but a quarter had still not submitted their reports five years after the deadline and ten states (5.13%) had not submitted reports more than 10 years after the deadline. Examination of states' performance rates in submitting second and third periodic reports disclosed an even poorer level of performance. Roughly a third of states submitted their second report within three years of the deadline, while more than half failed to submit within five years of the deadline. As at 2007, almost a third had still to submit their reports. Because the third reports have more recent deadlines, there was a shorter time-period over which states' performances could be assessed, but the available data did not suggest any improvement in states' submission rates. One symptom of states' poor performance is the increasing number of states that the Committee has permitted to submit 'consolidated' reports, that is, reports that consolidate two or three periodic reports in a single report.

OPAC was not instituted until 2002, so there is a much shorter time period than for the CRC over which to assess the performance of states that have ratified the Protocol. But once again, only a miniscule proportion of states (1.8%) submitted their reports by the required deadline and over half had not submitted more than three years after the deadline. That proportion is potentially worsened by the fact that 20% of states had submission dates after 2007 and we can expect several of those states eventually to report more than three years late. For purposes of comparison, submission rates for the CRC's other Optional Protocol (on the Sale of Children, Child Prostitution and Child Pornography) were also examined. These revealed an even poorer record of submissions.

Chapter 5 also investigated how states' performances in submitting reports correlated with three variables: geography, income level and regime type. For geography, there was no entirely consistent pattern across the initial, second and third reports, but overall European and American states performed better than African and Oceanian states, with Asian states falling between these two categories. The relative income levels of states was a potentially more significant variable. In general the figures do reveal a positive correlation between reporting performance and higher income level. States with high income levels had, on average, the best performance rates and those with low income levels the worst performance rates, while upper and lower middle income states fell between the two and were not very different from one another.

Regime type also promised to be a more significant variable than mere geography. One might expect regimes rated as 'freer' and as possessing a better human rights record to be more punctilious in performing their obligations in respect of a human rights treaty. There was indeed a positive correlation between submission rates and those states that the EIU's Democracy Index ranked as 'full democracies' and that Freedom House ranked as 'free'. However, there was no clear correlation with the EIUDI's other regime types (flawed democracies, authoritarian regimes, and hydrid regimes) or with the regimes that Freedom House ranked as 'partially free' and 'not free'.

None of these correlations was very strong. If we take the best performers, a significant minority of European and high income and 'fully democratic' or 'free' performed relatively poorly in their submission rates, and a significant minority of African and Oceanian and low income and less than 'fully democratic' or 'free' performed relatively well ('relatively' here meaning by comparison with other states). In other words, if the income levels of states improved and if more states came to have democratic or 'free' regimes, we might expect some improvement, but not a dramatic improvement, in submission rates.

Chapter 6 investigated how far States Parties to the CRC fulfilled their obligation to report on article 38 of the Convention. The Committee on the Rights of the Child has provided guidelines for the structure and content of initial and periodic reports, so States Parties need be in no doubt about the issues their reports should address. The most remarkable finding revealed by the examination of reports was that a majority of States Parties fail to report on article 38 at all: 122 states (66%) in their initial reports, 102 states (53%) in their second periodic reports, and 21 states (67%) in their third reports. (At the time the research was conducted only a relatively small proportion of states had submitted their third reports.) Of those states who do report on article 38, some do so in considerable detail and in ways that meet the Committee's guidelines, but many fail to respond to all elements of the guidelines.

How has the Committee responded to this state of affairs? It uses the device of 'Lists of Issues' to request information from States Parties additional to the information provided in their reports. Yet it has not used these Lists to ask for information from states who fail to report on article 38. Oddly, it has sometimes asked for additional information from States Parties who have reported on article 38. It has also used Lists of Issues to request additional information on articles 22 and 39, which are grouped with article 38 for reporting purposes and on which States Parties report more frequently.

The Committee also frequently makes no mention of states' failure to report on article 38 in its Concluding Observations on reports. When the Committee does make Observations on article 38, these are most commonly addressed to states who have reported on the article, though its Observations relating to article 38 often arise from its comments on articles 22 and 39. The Committee does sometimes use its Concluding Observations to raise issues and to make recommendations relating directly to article 38, but the overall picture is one of patchy and unsystematic comment.

Examination of how states' reporting, or failing to report, on article 38 correlated with geography revealed some variation amongst continents. For initial reports, European states reported most frequently (51%) followed by Asian states (28%), with African, American and Oceanic states reporting with virtually identical frequencies (25%). The pattern was somewhat different for second periodic reports, the order of merit being: Europe (55%), Asia (48%), America (43%), Africa (40%) and Oceania (33%). Given that these figures relate to whether states reported on article 38 at all, rather than to how well they reported, their most striking feature is how relatively poorly states perform across all continents.

Reporting on article 38 did correlate positively with higher income levels. For initial reports, 62% of high income states reported on article 38, compared with 31% of upper middle income states and 25% of lower middle income and low income states. For second periodic reports, 60% of high income states reported on article 38, compared with 43% of upper middle income states, 45% of lower middle income states, and 40% of low income states.

A similar, though by no means identical or even, pattern of correlation emerged in relation to regime types. For initial reports, using the EIU's Democracy Index, regimes reported on article 38 as follows: full democracies 63%, flawed democracies, 27%, hybrid regimes 43%, authoritarian regimes 28%. For second reports, the pattern was: full democracies 58%, flawed democracies, 48%, hybrid regimes 46%, authoritarian regimes 35%. Using Freedom House classifications, the correlations with regime type were, for initial reports: free 38%, partially free 30%, not free 34%. For second reports, the pattern was free 50%, partially free 48%, not free 39%. The less discriminating nature of the Freedom House classifications yields a more 'flattened' pattern of correlation than does the EIU Democracy Index.

Article 38 relates particularly to the child soldiers and it matters most that those States Parties should report on this part of the article for whom child soldiering has been a real issue. Chapter 5 therefore investigated reporting on article 38 by States Parties that had a history of the use of child soldiers either by their own governments or by non-state militias. Eight states were identified that had a history of use of child soldiers in government forces. Of these, Somalia was not a signatory to the CRC and Afghanistan had yet to submit a report. Of the six states who had submitted initial reports, none had reported on article 38. Twenty one states were identified who had in their territories non-state militia groups that recruited child soldiers, and these included all eight states who had a history of use of child soldiers in government forces. Of the nineteen of these states who had submitted initial reports, only three had reported on article 38 and none of these had made any mention of the use of child soldiers. Seven states had submitted second periodic reports and six of these had reported on article 38; yet none of these had reported on the use of child soldiers by non-state militias. The reporting process on article 38 therefore seems to be signally ineffective just at those points where it matters most.

Chapter 7 examined the adequacy of states' performance in reporting on their compliance with OPAC. OPAC includes many more provisions for the protection of children in armed conflict than article 38 of the CRC and therefore requires fuller reporting by states that are parties to the Protocol. The Committee on the Rights of the Child has laid down detailed guidelines for the content of States Parties' reports, and these make it very easy for those Parties to know what their reports should contain. The guidelines also greatly facilitate an assessment of how adequately states have fulfilled their reporting obligations. To enable an overall assessment of states' reporting performances, a system was constructed for grading the adequacy of reporting. Grade A indicated a report that provided all the required information with only trivial or insignificant omissions; grade B indicated minor but significant omissions; grade C indicated major omissions, including cases in which a state failed to provide any of the required information. Grade N (standing for 'not applicable') was used to provide for cases in which a particular clause of OPAC did not apply to a state, so that no reporting on that clause was required. During the period on which research was conducted, 28 states had reported on OPAC. These states could not claim to be an entirely representative sample of the 110 states who are Parties to the Protocol; in particular, 16 out of the 28 are European states. Nevertheless, they constitute a sufficiently large and diverse sample, to make possible a meaningful assessment of how adequately the reporting process on OPAC has been working.

The grading of reporting on the different articles and paragraphs of OPAC revealed a very mixed picture. A small number of states – Austria, Guatemala, New Zealand and Switzerland – performed well with reasonable consistency. A larger number – notably Denmark, Syria and Viet Nam – performed consistently poorly. Kazakhstan, Kyrgyzstan, Norway and Qatar did little better. Most states' reports earned a mixture of grades. Overall, grade A occurred with twice the frequency of grade B, but grade C occurred more frequently than grades A and B taken together. Setting aside grade N, grade C appeared more frequently than grades A+B in the reporting profiles of 12 countries, and with a frequency equal to grades A+B in the reporting profiles of 7 countries. Thus only 9 countries had reporting profiles in which A+B appeared more frequently than C.

Reporting performances were also uneven across different articles and subsections of articles of OPAC. The general level of reporting was conspicuously better for articles 5 and 7 than for other articles. It was conspicuously worse for paragraphs 2, 4 and 5 of article 2 and paragraphs 1 and 2 of article 6.

After the 40th session, the Committee in monitoring OPAC made use of 'Lists of Issues' to request information from states additional to that given in the reports they had submitted. The Committee has sometimes used these Lists to request missing information. However, my research shows that the great majority of omissions passed unnoticed by the Committee; that is, in most cases the Committee made no formal request of states to make good their failure to comply with the reporting guidelines. For example, 22 States Parties produced reports on paragraphs 2 and 4 of article 3 that warranted a C grade, but the Committee asked only seven of these to provide additional information. When the Committee has asked for more information through its Lists of Issues, this has often been for information that is additional to that required by its own guidelines.

The Committee has been more willing to comment critically on states and their reports in its Concluding Observations. Yet, even here, it has been far less critical than it might have been. It has still overlooked most of the failings in States Parties' reports and, rather than addressing the merits and demerits of each state, most of its recommendations have been of a generic kind, so that the same concerns are expressed repeatedly in its Concluding Observations on different states' reports.

Chapter 8 investigated the role played by NGOs in the CRC's monitoring process. It found that, since 1990, NGOs' contributions have increased significantly. A large number of the NGOs making these contributions have been international in character and have reported on a variety of states, but an even larger number have been national NGOs who have reported only on their own state. Reporting by NGOs has been very uneven, both with respect to the parts of the CRC with which they have been concerned and with respect to the States Parties on which they have reported. That observation applies to NGO reporting on article 38; only roughly one third of NGO reports that aim to address the CRC as a whole have included comment on article 38. Because OPAC has come into effect much more recently, there is a much shorter period over which the contribution of NGOs can be assessed; but NGO reporting on OPAC during that period displays the same selective and uneven character. On the other hand, when NGOs have reported on article 38, they have frequently done so in some detail and in ways that have identified clear breaches of the article. In so far as it is possible to judge, it also seems that the information they have made available to the Committee has had an impact on its Concluding Observations. NGOs therefore have been making a positive contribution to the monitoring process, but one that has been too sporadic and uneven to correct for the failings in States Parties' reports and for the failings in the Committee's response to those reports.

The inadequacies in the reporting process on article 33 of the CRC and OPAC, identified by this research, form part of a larger picture of inadequacy affecting all of the UN's Human Rights treaties. Drawing on the research of others, Chapter 8 showed that the failings identified by this thesis are part of a pattern of failure that is common to the monitoring of all of the UN's Human Rights treaties. Authorities at the UN have shown some awareness of the unsatisfactory nature of the current situation and have commissioned various reports on how the system might be improved. Chapter 9 examined a number of reforms that have been proposed in these reports, particularly those most relevant to improving states' compliance with, and reporting on, article 38 and OPAC.

The most radical proposal concerning the nature of the monitoring Committees themselves is that they should be consolidated into a single Committee. This, in turn, would entail each State Party's submitting a single report on all of its human rights treaties obligations rather a separate report for each treaty. This reform would avoid some of the duplications in reporting and monitoring that characterise the current system. It might, however, make for an even more cumbersome process, a loss of expertise on specific treaties, and the uneven monitoring of treaties. In itself, replacing the current monitoring committees with a single grand monitoring committee promises to do little to rectify the failings identified in this thesis. More might be achieved by ensuring that the membership of committees, including membership of the Committee on the Rights of the Child, is fully independent of the governments they monitor. If members feel beholden to governments, they will be inhibited in their criticisms – especially in their public criticisms – of the performance of governments.

Turning to the performance of committees themselves, this would certainly be enhanced by increasing the resources available to them. Ironically, the failure of states to submit their reports as required has been a blessing in disguise for committees since, had states met their obligations in full, the committees would have been unable to cope with the consequent workload. No report has proposed increasing the powers of monitoring committees. While this may seem surprising, it may reflect the legal and political realities that provide the context for reform. Changes in committees' powers would require changes to treaties, which would then have to be agreed to by all existing parties to those treaties. Proposals for increased powers would also face resistance from states who are generally reluctant to subordinate themselves to increased international policing.

Various reforms that might result in punctual, or less unpunctual, submission of reports were identified in Chapter 9, as were reforms that might improve the quality of reports. However, while these mainly piecemeal reforms might result in some improvement, they are unlikely to remedy all of the current defects. Something that is more under the control of monitoring committees is their Concluding Observations on reports. There is certainly scope for these Observations to be more rigorous, specific, detailed and action-oriented. There is no very obvious excuse for the failure of the Committee on the Rights of the Child to be more publicly critical of states that fail adequately to meet their reporting obligations.

Nevertheless, it would be a mistake to suppose that rectifying the failings of the existing system is solely a matter of reforming the UN's monitoring machinery and processes. The UN is the creature of its member states and it has limited powers over those states. In significant measure, improving states' performances in relation to their human rights obligations depends upon states' own sense of international responsibility and their willingness to comply fully with their treaty obligations. In Chapters 2 and 9 we identified reasons to be optimistic as well as pessimistic about the possibility of improvements in states' behaviour, including improvements that might be effected by a reformed monitoring system. Even if it would be utopian to aim for a system that worked perfectly, there is certainly scope for the machinery implementing the CRC and OPAC to work less imperfectly than it does at present and also reason to believe that a reformed system would significantly improve the performance of states in meeting their treaty obligations.

10.2 Strengths, Limits and Proposals for Future Research

My research has provided firm and unambiguous data on the operation of each of the major components of UN's implementation machinery for the CRC and OPAC. It has also enabled me to reach informed judgements on the effectiveness of its working. This would have not been the case if I had not made use of primary sources – States Parties reports on the CRC and OPAC, the CRC Committee's responses to those reports, and the effectiveness of the NGO reports – to analyse and evaluate the working of the UN's machinery for implementing the CRC and OPAC. The use of primary sources – which I believe is one of the major strengths of this research – has also allowed me to assess the UN machinery by the UN's own standards, since the criteria I have used to access that machinery are based on those specified by the process itself. Even though the area of my research has been the rights of the child in war and armed conflict, there is good reason to suppose that its findings are not unique to those parts of the CRC. In fact, my findings are similar in nature to those of researchers who have worked on the machinery relating to other human rights conventions. Consequently, this research contributes to a larger picture that encompasses the whole of the UN's efforts to secure compliance with human rights.

Nevertheless, I recognise that there are clear limits to the scope of my research, which relate not only to the scope of its subject-matter but also to the way in which it has investigated the workings and effectiveness of the UN's efforts to secure the rights of children in war and armed conflict. In the following paragraphs I provide an acknowledgement of those limits with proposals for further research.

First, as already mentioned above, my research has been based on primary sources – written documentation generated by the reporting process on the CRC and OPAC. It has not been possible for me to witness at first hand the activities of the various personnel involved in the process. It is a common feature in real life institutional processes that they actually operate in ways that are not fully captured by their formal institutions. It would therefore be useful to research the way in which States Parties go about compiling their reports, how their representatives interact with the CRC's Committee, how the Committee deliberates on the reports and how it decides on the content of its Concluding Obligations. This research could also include interviews of the various actors in the process to discover what their own conceptions of the process are, how they assess it, and what they expect of it. Doubtless that research would capture features of the process that are not fully apparent from the written documentation I have used. It would, however, depend upon the researcher's being able to witness various stages of the machinery at first hand, to interview major players in the process and to secure frank and honest comment from those interviewees. That degree of access may be difficult to achieve.

Secondly, the influence of the reporting process on the actual behaviour of governments and governing officials and, in particular, how far they actually respond to Committee's recommendations has not been examined in my research. This could be researched in detail, by examining the actual histories of governments over the last twenty years in relation to their policies and actions on the rights of the child. It would need to cover a range of states of different types and would ideally include interviews with the most relevant politicians and officials as well as inspection of written materials. In reality therefore, it would have to comprise several research projects rather than only one. It would also have to overcome governments' desire to keep sensitive information confidential.

Thirdly, my research has not made any estimation of the impact of the CRC and OPAC on the actual use of child soldiers by governments and non-government militias in front-line conflicts during the last twenty years. Clearly the prevention of that sort of military use of children must be the prime concern of any effort to protect their rights in relation to war and armed conflict. What my research has shown is that, in those states in which we know that child soldiers have been used by governments or by non-government forces, that usage appears nowhere in the relevant States Parties' reports. Thus, if the CRC and OPAC have had any impact on the use of child soldiers in armed conflicts, that impact cannot be gauged by examining States Parties' reports. It would have to examine what has happened 'on the ground' in the relevant states. However, there are at least three reasons why this research would be difficult to conduct. First, it is very difficult to access or to compile reliable data on the number and use of child soldiers in the relevant conflicts. Secondly, any effort to conduct fieldwork on the front-line use of child soldiers would obviously be extremely hazardous and might be impossible. Thirdly, as I mentioned in my note on method in the Introduction, it would be very difficult to establish the impact of the CRC and OPAC on the ground even if we had complete and reliable data on the use of child soldiers. If, for example, the use of child soldiers had declined over the last twenty years, we could not automatically credit that to the CRC and OPAC; equally, if the use of child soldiers had increased during the last twenty years, we could not infer that the CRC and OPAC had entirely failed, since usage might have been even greater had they not existed. Thus, while the impact of the CRC and OPAC on the actual use of child soldiers in front-line roles is perhaps the most important test for the efficacy of Article 38 and OPAC, it is a test that is extremely difficult to carry out.

Fourthly, my research has not investigated the wider impact of the CRC and OPAC, in particular their impact upon thinking across the world on what is acceptable conduct for governments. It might be, for example, that those conventions have played a significant role in establishing as a global norm the unacceptability of using children for military purposes, especially in front-line conflicts. If they have played that role, that might be every bit as significant as anything achieved through the formal reporting process. A full assessment of the success of the CRC and OPAC would have to include an assessment of that wider sort of impact. Clearly, however, that wider impact would not be easy to investigate or to assess in any very precise way.

Finally, the kind of research I have conducted in this thesis could be repeated in the future for a time period following the period up to 2007 that I have investigated. That research could assess whether the performance of States Parties and the Committee had improved, stayed the same, or worsened. It would have additional value if the UN's machinery were reformed in ways that I have indicated it could be, so that we would be able to assess the success of a reformed process.

BIBLIOGRAPHY

Alston, Philip, *The United Nations and Human Rights: A Critical Appraisal* (USA: Oxford University Press, 1999).

Alston, Philip and James Crawford, *The Future of UN Human Rights Treaty Monitoring* (Cambridge: Cambridge University Press, 2000).

Amnesty International, 'Children in South Asia – securing their rights' AI Index ASA 04/001/1998, 22 April 1998 (http://www-secure.amnesty.org/en/library/asset/ASA04/001/1998/en/d6b07591-e827-11dd-9deb-2b812946e43c/asa040011998en.pdf, 18 February 2008).

Ang, Fiona, *A Commentary on the United Nations Convention on the Rights of the Child: Article 38 Children* in Armed Conflict (Leiden [The Netherlands]: Martinus Nijhoff, 2005).

Amnesty International, 'UGANDA: Child "night commuters" fear abduction' AI Index: AFR 59/016/2005, 18 November 2005 (http://asiapacific.amnesty.org/library/Index/ENGAFR590162005?open&of=ENG-UGA , 15 June 2008).

Asian Centre for Human Rights, 'The Status of Children in India: An Alternative Report to the United Nations Committee on the Rights of the Child in India's first periodic report', *CRIN* (http://www.crin.org/docs/resources/treaties/crc.35/India_ACHR_ngo_report.pdf , 17 May 2010).

Baldwin, Simeon E., 'The International Congress and Conferences of the Last Century as Forces Working Toward the Solidarity of the World' *AJIL* 1.3 (1907): 565-578.

Bayefsky, F. Ann, 'ANNEX I: Statistical Analysis of the Human Rights Treaty System' (http://www.bayefsky.com/report/annex1g.pdf, 15 September 2009).

—. 'The UN Human Rights Treaty System: Universality at the Crossroads' (http://www.bayefsky.com/report/finalreport.pdf, 15 September 2009).

Bollen, Kenneth A., 'Political Rights and Political Liberties in Nations: An Evaluation of Human Rights Measures, 1950 to 1984' *Human Right Quarterly* 8.4 (1986): 567-591.

Brett, Rachel, 'Child Soldiers: law and practice' *International Journal of Children's Rights* 4(2) (1996): 115-128.

Brett, Rachel and Margaret McCallin, *Children: The Invisible Soldiers* (Stockholm: Radda Barnen [Swedish Save the Children], 1996).

Brett, Rachel and Irma Specht, *Young Soldiers: Why they choose to fight* (London: Lynne Rienner, 2004).

Bowman, Michael, 'Towards a Unified Treaty Body for Monitoring Compliance with UN Human Rights Conventions? Legal Mechanisms for Treaty Reform' *Human Rights Law Review* 7.1 (2007):225-249.

Cape Town, South Africa, 27-30 April 1997: The Cape Town Principles and Best Practices: Adopted at the Symposium on the Prevention of Recruitment of Children into the Armed Forces and on Demobilisation and Social Reintegration of Child Soldiers in Africa. (http://www.unicef.org/emerg/files/Cape_Town_Principles(1).pdf , 15 May 2009).

Centre for Humanitarian Dialogue, 'Briefing Paper, Small Arms and Human Security: A snapshot of the humanitarian Impacts' November 2003 (http://www.hdcentre.org/files/RXbriefing.pdf, 15 March 2007.

Charnovitz, Steve, 'Non-governmental Organisations and International Law' *The American Journal of International Law* 100.2 (2006): 348-372.

Chayes, Abram and Antonia H. Chayes, *The New Sovereignty: Compliance with International Regulatory Agreements* (United States of America: Library of Congress, 1995).

Coalition Belge Contre L' Utilisation d'enfants soldats, 'Rapprt de la Coalition Belge Contre L' Utilisation d'enfants Soldats dans le cadre du suivi du protocol additionnel a la Convention relative aux droits de l'enfant portant sur les enfants dans les conflits armes', *CRIN* (http://www.crin.org/docs/Belgium_OP_NGO_Report.pdf, 26 May 2010).

Cohen, C. P., 'The Role of Nongovernmental Organisations in Drafting of the Convention on the Rights of the Child', *Human Rights Quarterly* 12 (1990):137-47.

'Convention on the Rights of the Child' *Population and Development Review* 15 (1989): 779-783.

Craig, Scott, 'Bodies of knowledge: A diversity promotion role for the UN High Commissioner for Human Rights' in Philip Alston and James Crawford (ed) *The Future of UN Human Rights Treaty Monitoring* (Cambridge: Cambridge University Press, 2000): 403-437.

Deflem, Mathieu, *Habermas, Modernity and Law* (London: Sage, 1996).

Detrick, Charon and Jaap Doek, The United Nations Convention on the Rights of the Child: A Guide to the "Travaux Preparatoires" (London: Martinus Nijhoff, 1992).

Evatt, Elizabeth, 'Ensuring Effective supervisory procedures: the need for resources' in Philip Alston and Kames Crawford (ed) *The Future of UN Human Rights Treaty Monitoring* (Cambridge: Cambridge University Press, 200): 461-480.

Donin, Antonio, 'The Bureaucracy and the Free Spirits: Stagnation and Innovation in the Relationship Between the UN and NGOs' *Third Wold Quarterly* 16.3 (1995): 421-439.

Downs, George W. and Michael A. Jones, 'Reputation, Compliance and International Law' *Journal of Legal Studies* XXXI (2002): 95-114.

Flowers, Nancy, 'Human Rights Here and Now: Celebrating the Universal Declaration of Human Rights' (http://www1.umn.edu/humanrts/edumat/hreduseries/hereandnow/Part-5/6_glossary.htm, 10 July 2009).

Forsythe, David P., *Human Rights in International Relations* (Cambridge: Cambridge University Press, 2004).

—. *Human Rights and World Politics* (Lincoln: University of Nebraska Press, 1989).

Freeman, Michael, *The Ideologies of Children's Rights* (London; Martinus Nijhoff Publishers, 1992).

Gamba, Virginia, 'Small Arms Foster Social Turmoil: Illegal Trafficking Disrupts African Communities, Spreads Crime'(http://www.un.org/ecosocdev/geninfo/afrec/subjindx/121weaps.htm , 10 January 2008).

Goodman, Ryan and Jinks, Derek, Measuring the Effects of Human Rights Treaties *EJIL* 14 (2003): 171-183.

Graça Machel report "Promotion and Protection of the Rights of Children: Impact of Armed Conflict on Children" A/51/306 (26 August 1996) submitted to 51st session of the General Assembly (http://www.unicef.org/graca/a51-306_en.pdf , 15 February 2009).

Greenwood, Christopher, 'Scope of Application of Humanitarian Law' in Dieter Flack (ed.), *The Handbook of Humanitarian Law in Armed Conflicts* (Oxford: OUP, 1995): 39-64.

Groupe de Travail des ONGs Pour les Droits de l'enfant, 'Rapport Alternatif et Evaluatif des ONGs sur L'Application de la Convention Relative aux Droits de L'Enfant par la Republique Democrique du Congo', CRIN (http://www.crin.org/docs/resources/treaties/crc.27/Drc.pdf, 22 May 2010).

Hafner-Burton, Emilie M., 'Human Rights in a Globalising Word: The Paradox of Empty Promises' *American Journal of Sociology* 110.5 (2005): 1373-1411.

Happold, Matthew, *Child Soldiers in International Law* (Manchester: Manchester University Press, 2005).

Harvey, Rachel, *Children and Armed Conflict: A guide to International Humanitarian and Human Rights Law* (Essex: Children and Armed Conflict Unit and International Bureau for Children's Rights, 2003).

—. 'Children and Armed Conflict: A guide to International Humanitarian and Human Rights Law' *Children and Armed Conflict Uni*t (http://www.essex.ac.uk/armedcon/story_id/000044.pdf, 10 July 2009).

Hathaway, Oona, 'Why do countries commit to human rights treaties?' *Conflict Resolution* 51.4 (2007): 588-621.

—. 'Do Human Rights Treaties Make a Difference?' 112 *Yale L.J* (2002):1935-2042.

Henkin Louis, *The International Bill of Rights: the Covenant on Civil and Political Rights* (New York: Columbia Press, 1981).

Heyns, Christof and Frans Viljoen, *Impact Study of the United Nations Human Rights Treaties in Twenty UN Member States* (Pretoria: Pretoria Law Press 2000).

—. The Impact of the United Nations Human Rights Treaties on the Domestic Level *Human Rights Quarterly* 23.3 (2001): 483-535.

Hodgson, D, 'The Historical Development and 'internationalisation' of the Children's Rights Movement' *Australian Journal of Family Law* 6 (1992): 252-279.

Hogg, Charu Lata, "Child Recruitment In South Asian Conflicts: A Comparative Analysis of Sri Lanka, Nepal and Bangladesh" (Coalition to Stop the Use of Child Soldiers: Chatman House, 2006): 1-52. (http://www.reliefweb.int/rw/lib.nsf/db900sid/PANA-794KLM/$file/chatham-nov2006.pdf?openelement , 15 January 2008).

International Committee of the Red Cross, 'Optional Protocol to the Convention on the Rights of the Child concerning the Involvement of children in armed conflicts: position of the international committee of the red cross Geneva, 27 October 1997*, International Review of the Red Cross* 322 (1998): 107-125.

International Relations and Security Network, 'Child Soldiers: The Use of Child Soldiers': 2. (http://www.isn.ethz.ch/isn/content/download/8067/80345/file/01%20 Use%20of%20Children.pdf, 15 May 2009).

Jones, Peter, *Rights* (Basingstoke: Macmillam, 1994).

Kaplan, Eben, 'Child Soldiers Around the World' *Council on Foreign Relations* (http://www.cfr.org/publication/9331/, 12 January 2009).

Keck, Margaret E. and Kathryn Sikkink, *Activities beyond Borders: Advocacy Networks in International Politics* (Ithaca: Cornell University Press, 1998).

Kekic, Laza, 'The Economist Intelligence Unit Index of Democracy" *The Economist* (http://www.economist.com/media/pdf/DEMOCRACY_INDEX_2007_v3.pdf, 15 March 2007).

Kleffner, J.K, (ed.), *Yearbook of International Humanitarian Law* (Universiteit van Amsterdam: Cambridge University Press, 2006).

Krill, Francois, 'The Protection of Children in Armed Conflict', in Michael Freeman and Philip Veerman (ed.), *The Ideologies of Children's Rights* (London: Martinus Nijhoff, 1992): 347-357.

Kuper, Jenny, *Military Training and Children in Armed Conflict: Law, Policy and Practice* (Netherlands: Martinus Nijhoff Publishers, 2005).

Laslett, Peter, *John Locke: Two Treatises of Government: A critical Edition with an introduction and Apparatus Criticus* (Cambridge: Cambridge University Press, 1967):

Lauterpacht, Hersch, *International Law and Human Rights* (London: Longmans, 1950):

Leaflet No. 3: UN Charter Based Bodies and Indigenous Peoples' (http://www.ohchr.org/Documents/Publications/GuideIPleaflet3en.pdf, 10 February 2008).

Lieber, Francis, *On Civil Liberty and Self-Government* (http://files.libertyfund.org/files/1943/Lieber_1382_EBk_v5.pdf129, 10/11/2010).

Lloyd, Thomas D. A , *Locke on Government* (London: Rutledge, 1995).

Loquer, Walter and B. Rubin (eds.), *The Human Rights Reader* (Philadelphia: Temple University Press, 1979.

Lorey, Mark, 'Child Soldiers: Care & Protection of Children in Emergencies: A Field Guide', *Save the Children* (http://www.savethechildren.org/publications/technical-resources/emergencies-protection/ChildSoldiersFieldGuide.pdf, 10 June 2009).

Mamalakis, Pappas A., *Law and the Status of the Child* (New York: The United Nations Institute for Training and Research, 1983).

Manoharan, N, 'Child Soldiers III: 'Baby Brigades' of the LTTE', Article No. 1184, 21 October 2003, *Institute of Peace and Conflict Studies (IPCS (*http://www.ipcs.org/article_details.php?articleNo=1184, 6 June 2009).

Martinez, Magdalena M. Martin, *National Sovereignty and International Organisations* (London: Kluwer Law International, 1996).

Meron, Theodor, 'The Humanisation of Humanitarian Law' *American Journal of International Law* 94 (2) (2000): 239-278.

Merry, Sally Engle, *Human Rights and Gender Violence: translating international law into local justice* (Chicago: The University of Chicago Press, 2006).

Mertus, A. Julie, *The United Nations and Human Rights: A Guide for a New Era* (London: Routledge, 2005).

Miller, Lynn H., *Global Order: Values and Power in International Relations* (Boulder, CO: Westview Press, 1994).

Moravcsik, Andrew, 'The Origins of Human Rights Regimes' *International Organisation* 54 (2000): 217-252.

Mwakasungura, Undule, 'Firearms Proliferation: a real threat to Malawi's economy' (http://www.chrr.org.mw/press%20releases/April%202008/Small%20 Arms%20Proliferation%20article.doc, 15 July 2009).

Neumayer, Eric, 'Do International Human Rights Treaties improve respect for human rights?' Journal of Conflict resolution 49.6 (2005): 925-53.

Niemi, Heli and Scheinin, Martin, Reform of the United Nations Human Rights Treaty Body System Seen from the Developing Country Perspective (Institute for Human Rights: Abo Akademi University 2002).

Nickel W. James, *Making Sense of Human Rights* (London: University of California Press, 1987).

Obote-Odora, Alex, 'Legal Problems with Protection of Children in Armed Conflict' *Murdoch University Electronic Journal of Law* 6 (1999) (http://www.murdoch.edu.au/elaw/issues/v6n2/obote-odora62_text.html#t34, 15 August 2008).

O'Byrne, Daren J., *Human Rights: An Introduction* (London: Pearson Educations LTD, 2003).

O'Flaherty, Michael, and Claire O'Brien 'Reform of UN Human Rights Treaty Monitoring Bodies: A Critique of the Concept Paper on the High Commissioner's Proposal for a Unified Standing Treaty Body' *Human Rights Law Review* 7(1) (2007): 141-172.

Oppenheim Lassa and Sir Ronald Roxburgh, *International Law* (New Jersey: The Lawbook Exchange Ltd, 2006).

Parrat, Charlotte Friedner, 'The Politics of Reporting: a Study of States' Strategies for Reporting to the UN Committee on the Rights of the Child' *Political Studies* 58.3(2010): 472-496.

Pictet, Jean, *Development and Principles of International Humanitarian Law* (Lancaster: Martinus Nijhoff, 1985).

Ramcharan, B.G., *Human Rights: Thirty Years after the Universal Declaration* (Dordrecht: Martinus Nijhoff, 1979).

Reich, Simon and Scott Gates, 'Think again: child soldiers' *Foreign Policy* May 2009 (http://www.foreignpolicy.com/story/cms.php?story_id=4944 , 10 June 2009).

Sheppard, A, 'Child soldiers: Is the Optional Protocol evidence of an emerging "straight-18" consensus?' *The International Journal of Children's Rights* 8 (2000): 37-70.

Simmons, Beth A., *Mobilising for Human Rights: International Law in Domestic Politics* (NY: Cambridge University Press, 2009.

Smith, Jackie, Ron Pagnucco and George A. Lopez, 'Globalizing Human Rights: the work of Transnational Human Rights NGOs in the 1990s' *Human Rights Quarterly* 20. 2 (1998): 379-412

Sohn, Louis B., 'The Improvement of the UN Machinery Human Rights', *International Studies Quarterly* 23 (2) (1979): 186-215.

Syse, Henrik, 'From Natural law to Human Rights – some reflections on Thomas Pogge and Global Justice' in A. Follesdal and T. Pogge (ed.), *Real World Justice* (Netherlnads: Springer, 2005): 229-237.

Tabatha Abu El-Haj and Carolyn Hamilton, 'Armed Conflict: The Protection of Children under International Law', *The International Journal of Children's Rights* 5 (1997): 1-46.

Thalif Deen, 'UN Report on Child Soldiers Ignores Worst Offenders' (http://www.commondreams.org/headlines02/1107-05.htm, 10 January 2008).

Tistounet, Eric, 'The problem of Overlapping Among Different Treaty Bodies' in Philip Alston and James Crawford (ed.) *The Future of UN Human Rights Treaty Monitoring* (Cambridge: Cambridge University Press, 2000): 383-402.

Tomuschat, Christian, *Human Rights: Idealism and Realism* (Oxford: OUP, 2008),

UNICEF, Coalition to Stop the Use of Child Soldiers, *Guide to the Optional Protocol on the involvement of children in armed conflict* (New York: UNICEF and Coalition to Stop the Use of Child Soldiers, 2003).

Van Bueren, Geraldine, 'The International Legal Protection of Children in Armed Conflict' *International Comparative Law Quarterly* 43 (1994): 809-826.

Vandewiele, Tiny, *Optional Protocol: The Involvement of Children in Armed Conflicts* (Leiden: Martinus Nijhoff Publishers, 2006).

Veerman, Philip E. *The Rights of the Child and the Changing Image of Childhood* (Netherlands: Martinus Nijhoff, 1992).

Von Bernstorff, Jochen, 'The Changing Fortunes of the UDHR: Genesis and Symbolic Dimensions of the Turn to Rights in International Law' *EJIL* VOL19 (5) (2008): 903-924.

Wessells, G. Michael, *Child Soldiers: From Violence to Protection* (Cambridge, London: Harvard University Press, 2006).

Zacher, Mark W., 'The Decaying Pillars of the Westphalian Temple: Implications for International Order and Governance' in James N. Rosenau and Ernst-Otto Czempiel, eds., *Governance without Government: Order and Changes in World Politics* (Cambridge: Cambridge University Press, 1992): 58-101.

UN Documents

A/44/668: Effective Implementation of International Instruments on Human Rights, Including Reporting Obligations Under International Instruments on Human Rights: 08/11/1989.

A/51/40, Vol I: Report of the Human Rights Committee: 13/04/1997.

A/52/507: Human Rights Questions: Implementation of Human Rights Instruments: 21/10/1997.

A/ 58/123: Letter dated 13 June 2003 from the Permanent Representative of Liechtenstein to the United Nations addressed to the Secretary-General: 08/07/2003.

A/53/125: Effective Implementation of International Instruments on Human Rights Including reporting Obligations under International Instruments on Human Rights: 14/05/1998.

A/57/387: Strengthening of the United Nations: an agenda for further change: 09/09/2002.

A/59/2005: In Larger Freedom: Towards development, security and Human Rights for all: Report of the Secretary-General: 21/03/2005.

A/59/2005/Add.3: Plan for Action: Submitted by the High Commissioner for Human Rights: 26/05/2005.

A/62/18: Annual Report of the Committee on the Elimination of Racial Discrimination: 01/10/2007.

A/62/609 – S/2007/757 Report of the Secretary-General: Child and Armed Conflict' 21/12/2007 (http://daccess-dds-ny.un.org/doc/UNDOC/GEN/N07/656/04/PDF/N0765604.pdf?OpenElement , 12 March 2008).

A/63/38 (SUPP): Annual Report of the Committee on the Elimination of Discrimination against Women: 29/07/2009.

A/63/40: Annual Report of the Human Rights Committee (Volume I): August 2007- July 2008.
A/63/44: Annual Report of the Committee against Torture (2007-2008).
A/CONF.157/23: "World Conference on Human Rights: 12/07/1993 (http://www.unhchr.ch/huridocda/huridoca.nsf/(symbol)/a.conf.157.23.en, 10 April 2011)
A/CONF.157/PC/62/Ass.11/Rev.1: World Conference on Human Rights: 22/04/1993
Charter of the United Nations, 'Preamble of the Charter of the United Nations' *The United Nations* (http://www.hrweb.org/legal/unchartr.html , 19 August 2009).
Convention on the Rights of the Child. Adopted and opened for signature, ratification and accession by General Assembly Resolution 44/25 in November 1989. Entry into force 2 September 1990, in accordance with article 49.
Convention II for the Amelioration of the Condition of Wounded, Sick and Shipwrecked Members of the Armed Forces at Sea. Adopted on 12 August 1949. by the Diplomatic Conference for the Establishment of International Conventions for the Protection of Victims of War, held in Geneva from 21 April to 12 August 1949. Entry into force 21 October 1950. (http://www.icrc.org/ihl.nsf/7c4d08d9b287a42141256739003e636b/44072487ec4c2131c125641e004a9977 , 15 May 2009).
Convention III relative to the Treatment of Prisoners of War. Adopted on 12 August 1949. by the Diplomatic Conference for the Establishment of International Conventions for the Protection of Victims of War, held in Geneva from 21 April to 12 August 1949. Entry into force 21 October 1950. (http://www.icrc.org/ihl.nsf/7c4d08d9b287a42141256739003e636b/6fef854a3517b75ac125641e004a9e68, 15 May 2009).
Convention IV relative to the Protection of Civilian Persons in Time of War. Adopted on 12 August 1949. by the Diplomatic Conference for the Establishment of International Conventions for the Protection of Victims of War, held in Geneva from 21 April to 12 August 1949. Entry into force 21 October 1950. (http://www.icrc.org/ihl.nsf/7c4d08d9b287a42141256739003e636b/6756482d86146898c125641e004aa3c5 , 15 May 2009).
Defence for Children International, 'NGO Comments on the Initial Israeli Report on Implementing the UN Convention on the Rights of the Child for 31st session – Israel' *CRIN*

(http://www.crin.org/docs/resources/treaties/crc.31/IsraelCoal_ngo_report.pdf, 25 May 2010).

'Diplomatic Conference on the Reaffirmation and Development of International Humanitarian Law applicable in Armed Conflicts, Geneva, 1974-1977' Human Rights Library (http://www1.umn.edu/humanrts/instree/1977d.htm , 12 May 2009).

E/C.12/40/2, 2008: Note by the Secretary-General on the States Parties to the Covenant and the Status of Submission of Reports.

E/CN.94/RES/1994/91: Office of the High Commissioner for Human Rights on the Implementation of the Convention on the Rights of the Child.

E/.CN.4/1997/74: Effective Functioning of Bodies Established Pursuant to United Nations Human Rights Instruments: Final Report on enhancing the ling-term effectiveness of the United Nations human rights treaty system: 27/03/1997.

E/CN.4/2000/74, 2000: Report of the Working group on a draft optional protocol to the Convention on the Rights of the Child on involvement of children in armed conflicts on its sixth session.

General Assembly Resolution (A/RES/51/77) "The Rights of the child" adopted by the General Assembly [on the report of the Third Committee (A/51/615) (20 February 1997) without a vote at 82nd plenary meeting on December 12, 1996. (http://www.un.org/documents/ga/res/51/ares51-77.htm, 10 March 2009).

General Assembly Resolution (A/RES/55/2) "55/2 United Nations Millennium Declaration" adopted by the General Assembly [without reference to a Main Committee (A/55/L.2) (8 September 2000). (http://www.un.org/millennium/declaration/ares552e.pdf, 10 April 2011).

General Assembly Resolution 60/1. "2005 World Summit Outcome" (24 October 2005) [adopted by the General Assembly without reference to a Main Committee] 1 (http://unpan1.un.org/intradoc/groups/public/documents/un/unpan021752.pdf, 2 March 2011).

General Assembly Resolution 60/231. "Rights of the Child" (23 December 2005) [adopted by the General Assembly on the report of the Third Committee] (http://www.endcorporalpunishment.org/pages/pdfs/GA-Res_Dec2005.pdf , 10 March 2009).

Geneva Convention I for the Amelioration of the Condition of the Wounded and Sick people in Armed Forces in the Field. Adopted pn 12 August 1949 by the Diplomatic Conference for the Establishment of International Conventions for the Protection of Victims of War, held

in Geneva from 21 April to 12 August 1949. Entry into force 21 October 1950. .
(http://www.icrc.org/ihl.nsf/7c4d08d9b287a42141256739003e636b/fe20c3d903ce27e3c125641e004a92f3, 15 May 2009).

HRI/ICM/2003/3: Methods of Work Relating to the State Reporting Process, Background document prepared by the Secretariat: 11/04/2003.

HRI/ICM/2003/3/Add.1: Methods of work relating to the State Reporting Process: 10/06/2003.

HRI/ICM/2003/4: Report of a Brainstorming Meeting on reform of the Human Rights Treaty Body System, 4-7 May, 2003: 10 June 2003.

HRI/ICM/2003/5: Report of the Second Inter-Committee Meeting of the Human Rights Treaty Bodies: 27/06/2003.

HRI/MC/2006/CRP.1: Concept Paper on the High Commissioner's Proposal for a Unified Standing Treaty Body: 14/03/2006.

HRI/MC/2006/2: Concept Paper on the High Commissioner's Proposal for a Unified Standing Treaty: 22/03/2006.

HRI/MC/1997/2: Improving the Effectiveness of the Human Rights Treaty Bodies: 29/07/1997.

International Covenant on Civil and Political Rights (ICCPR). Adopted and opened for signature, ratification and accession by General Assembly resolution 2200A (XXI) of 16 December 1966. Entered into force 3 January 1976, in accordance with article 49

International Covenant on Economic, Social and Cultural Rights (ICESCR). Adopted and opened for signature, ratification and accession by General Assembly resolution 2200A (XXI) of 16 December 1966. Entered into force 3 January 1976, in accordance with article 27.

'International Human Rights Law Group: Guidelines on preparing shadow reports for the CERD'
http://docs.google.com/viewer?a=v&q=cache:kwMIJ8gtNiAJ:action.web.ca/home/narcc/attach/USA%2520-%2520CERD%2520shadow%2520report%2520guide%2520-%2520IHRMG%2520-%25202001.pdf+Human+Rights+Law+Group+GUIDELINES+FOR+PREPARING+A+SHADOW+REPORT+FOR+THE+CERD&hl=en&gl=uk&sig=AHIEtbQe-JzOp6gEst4LI21jqDcKHBB9og , 20 August 2007).

Office of the United Nations: High Commissioner for Human Rights, 'Fact Sheet No.30. The United Nations Human Rights Treaty System: An Introduction to the core human rights treaties and the treaty bodies': 29-31.
(http://www2.ohchr.org/english/bodies/docs/OHCHR-FactSheet30.pdf, 15 September 2008).

Optional Protocol to the Convention on the Rights of the Child on the Involvement of children in armed conflict. (OPAC). Adopted and opened for signature, ratification and accession by the General Assembly resolution A/RES/54/263 of 25 May 2000. entered into force on 12 February 2002.

'Optional Protocol on the Sale of Children, Child Prostitution and Child Pornography. Adopted and opened for signature, ratification and accession by General Assembly resolution A/54/RES/263 of 25 May 2000, entered into force on 18 January 2002' *Child Rights Information Network* (http://www.crin.org/law/Instrument.asp?InstID=1002 , 10 April 2009).

Protocol Additional to the Geneva Convention of 12 August 1949, relating to the Protection of Victims of International Armed Conflicts (Protocol I), 8 June 1977 (http://www.icrc.org/ihl.nsf/7c4d08d9b287a42141256739003e636b/f6c8b9fee14a77fdc125641e0052b079, 15 May 2009).

Protocol Additional to the Geneva Conventions of 12 August 1949, and relating to the Protection of Victims of Non-International Armed Conflicts (Protocol II), 8 June 1977. (http://www.icrc.org/ihl.nsf/7c4d08d9b287a42141256739003e636b/d67c3971bcff1c10c125641e0052b545, 15 May 2009).

Security Council Resolution 1071[S/RES/1071] 'On the Situation in Liberia' adopted by the Security Council at its 3694th meeting on 30 August 1996.

Security Council Resolution 1083[S/RES/1083] 'On the Situation in Liberia' adopted by the Security Council at its 3717th meeting on 27 November 1996.

Security Council Resolution 1181 [S/RES/1181] 'On the Situation in Sierra Leone' adopted by the Security Council at its 3902nd meeting, on 13 July 1998.

Security Council Resolution 1231[S/RES/1231] 'On the Situation in Sierra Leone' adopted by the Security Council at its 3986th meeting, on 11 March 1999.

Security Council Resolution 1261 [S/RES/1261] 'On the Children in armed conflict, adopted by the Security Council at it 4037th meeting, on 25 August 1999.

Security Council Resolution 1314 [S/RES/1314] 'On the Children and armed conflict' adopted by the Security Council at its 4185th meeting, on 11August 2000.

Security Council Resolution 1378 [S/RES/1379] 'On the Children and armed conflict' adopted by the Security Council at its 4423rd meeting, on 20 November 2001.

Security Council Resolution 1460 [S/RES/1460] ' On the Children and armed conflict' adopted by the Security Council at its 4695th meeting, on 30 January 2003.

'The Geneva Conventions of 1949' *ICRC* (http://www.icrc.org/Web/eng/siteeng0.nsf/htmlall/genevaconventions #a1, 15 May 2009).

'The International Convention for the Suppression of the Traffic in Women and Children' articles 2-3 (http://www.vilp.de/Enpdf/e158.pdf , 10 October 2009).

'The Rome Statute of the International Criminal Court' (http://untreaty.un.org/cod/icc/statute/english/rome_statute(e).pdf, 18 May 2009).

The Universal Declaration of Human Rights (UDHR) 1948

UN. Doc. A/49/41: Report of the Committee on the Rights of the Child: 19/05/1994.

UN Doc. A/53/482 (12 October 1999) "Protection of Children Affected by Armed Conflict" paras.13, 14-17, 40 (http://daccess-dds-ny.un.org /doc/UNDOC/GEN/N98/301/73/PDF/N9830173.pdf?OpenElement, 8 August 2009).

UN Doc. A/CONF.157/24 (Part I): World Conference on Human Rights Report of the World Conference on Human Rights, Report of the Secretary-General, Vienna, 14-25 June 1993.

UN. Doc. CAT/C/44/Add.3 (Third Periodic reports of States parties due in 1998): Libyan Arab Jamahiriya. 28/01/1999.

UN. Doc. CCPR/C/128/Add.1 (Second Periodic reports of States Parties due in 1998): Gabon. 14/06/1999.

UN. Doc. CERD/C/304/Add.91 (Concluding Observations by the Committee on the Elimination of Racial Discrimination): France. 19/04/2000.

UN Doc. CRC/C/4/REV.1, 2005: Committee on the Rights of the Child, Provisional Rules of Procedure

UN Doc.CRC/C/5: General Guidelines regarding the content of Initial Reports to be submitted by States Parties under Article 44, paragraph 1 (a), of the Convention

UN Doc. CRC/C/10, 1992: Committee on the Rights of the Child: Report adopted by the Committee at its 46th Meeting, on 9 October 1992

UN Doc. CRC/C/15/Add.2, 1993: Concluding Observations of the Committee on the Rights of the Child: Sweden

UN Doc. CRC/C/15/Add.18 (Concluding Observations): Pakistan. 25/04/1994.

UN. Doc. CRC/C/15/Add.40 (Concluding Observations): Sri Lanka. 21/06/1995.

UN Doc: CRC/C/15/Add.88 (Concluding Observations): Democratic People's Republic of Korea. 5/06/1998.

UN.Doc. CRC/C/15/Add.126 (Concluding Observations): Norway. 28/06/2000.

UN.Doc: CRC/C/15/Add.130 (Concluding Observations): Suriname. 28/06/2000.

UN Doc, CRC/C/15/Add.137, 2000: Concluding Observations of the Committee on the Rights of the Child: Colombia

UN.Doc. CRC/C/15/Add.149 (Concluding Observations): Palau. 21/02/2001.

UN. Doc. CRC/C/15/Add.153 (Concluding Observations): Democratic Republic of Congo. 9/07/2001.

UN Doc. CRC/C/15/Add.168 (Concluding Observations): Cape Verde. 7/11/2001.

UN Doc. CRC/C/15/Add.190, 2002: Concluding Observations of the Committee on the Rights of the Child: Sudan

UN.Doc: CRC/C/15/Add.192 (Concluding Observations): Republic of Moldova. 31/10/2002.

UN.Doc: CRC/C/15/Add.214 (Concluding Observations): San Marino. 27/10/2003.

UN.Doc: CRC/C/15/Add.224 (Concluding Observations): Guyana. 26/02/2004.

UN.Doc. CRC/C/15/Add.233 (Concluding Observations): Panama. 30/06/2004.

UN. Doc. CRC/C/15/Add.234 (Concluding Observations): Rwanda. 01/07/2004.

UN. Doc. CRC/C/15/Add.237 (Concluding Observations): Myanmar. 30/06/2004.

UN. Doc. CRC/C/15/Add.244 (Concluding Observations): Kyrgyzstan. 03/11/2004.

UN. Doc. CRC/C/15/Add.250 (Concluding Observations): Luxembourg. 31/03/2005.

UN. Doc.CRC/C/15/Add.259 (Concluding Observations): Philippines. 21/09/2005.

UN. Doc. CRC/C/15/Add.261 (Concluding Observations): Nepal. 21/09/2005.

UN Doc. CRC/C/16 (Sessional/Annual Report of Committee): Report of the third session of the Committee on the Rights of the Child:.05/03/93.

UN Doc. CRC/C/33, 1994: Overview of the reporting procedures.

UN. Doc. CRC/C/38: Report adopted by the Committee at its 209th session on 27 January 1995. 20/02/1995.

UN. Doc. CRC/C/43: Report adopted by the Committee at its 233rd meeting, on 9 June 1995. 09/06/1995.

UN. Doc. CRC/C/49/2: Submission of Reports by States Parties: States Parties to the Convention on the Rights of the Child and its two Optional Protocols and related status of submission of reports. 10/07/2008.

UN Doc. CRC/C/58, 1996: General Guidelines regarding the form and contents of periodic reports to be submitted by states Parties under Article 44, paragraph 1 (b), of the Convention.

UN Doc. CRC/C/70/Add.15, 2003. Second Periodic Report of Jamaica to the Un Committee on the Rights of the Child.

UN Doc. CRC/C/70/Add.17, 2002: Second Periodic Report of Sri Lanka to the UN Committee on the Rights of the Child.

UN. Doc. CRC/C/97 (Report of the Twenty-Forth Session: Geneva, 15 May – 2 June 2000): Iran: 22-76.

UN. Doc. CRC/C/114 (Report on the Twenty-Ninth Session: Geneva, 14 January – 1 February 2002): Bahrain: 452-500.

UN. Doc. CRC/C/121: Report on the thirty-first session. 11/12/2002.

UN. Doc. CRC/C/132 (Report of the Thirty-Third Session: Geneva, 19 May – 6 June 2003): Cyprus: 89-151.

UN Doc. CRC/C.11/WP.6. (List of Issues): Finland. 27/11/95.

UN Doc. CRC/C/Q/ISR.1 (List of Issues): Israel. 14/06/2002.

UN Doc. CRC/C/Q/NET.1. (List of Issues): Netherlands. 30/06/99.

UN Doc. CRC/C/Q/NPL/2 (List of Issues): Nepal 04/02/2005.

UN Doc. CRC/C/Q/PHL/2 (List of Issues): Philippines. 04/02/2005.

UN Doc. CRC/C/Q/RWA/2 (List of Issues): Rwanda. 09/02/2004.

UN Doc. CRC/C/SLE/Q/2: (List of Issues): Sierra Leone. 4/07/2007.

UN.Doc. CRC/C/SLE/CO/2 (Concluding Observations): Sierra Leone. 20/06/2008.

UN Doc. CRC/OP/AC/1, 2001: Guidelines Regarding Initial Reports to be submitted by states parties under Article 8(1) of the Optional Protocol to the Convention on the Rights of the Child on the Involvement of Children in Armed Conflicts.

UN. Doc. CRC/C/OPAC/AUT/1 (Initial reports of States parties due in 2004): Austria. 08/07/2004.

UN. Doc. CRC/C/OPAC/BGD/Q/1 (List of Issues): Bangladesh. 02/11/2005.
UN. Doc. CRC/C/OPAC/BEL/1 (Initial reports of States parties due in 2004): Belgium. 15/08/2005.
UN. Doc. CRC/C/OPAC/BEL/Q/1 (List of Issues): Belgium. 15/02/2006.
UN. Doc. CRC/C/OPAC/BEL/Q/1/Add.1 (Written replies from the Government of Belgium): Belgium. 03/04/2006.
UN. Doc. CRC/C/OPAC/CAN/1 (Initial reports of States parties due in 2004): Canada. 29/07/2005.
UN. Doc. CRC/C/OPAC/CAN/Q/1 (List of Issues): Canada. 16/02/2006.
UN. Doc. CRC/C/OPAC/CAN/Q/1/Add.1 (Written replies by the Government of Canada): Canada. 28/04/2006.
UN. Doc. CRC/C/OPAC/CHE/1 (Initial reports of States parties due in 2004): Switzerland: 14/07/2005.
UN Doc. CRC/C/COL/Q/3 (List of Issues): Colombia. 15/02/2006.
UN. Doc. CRC/C/OPAC/CRI/1 (Initial reports of States parties due in 2005): Costa Rica. 22/12/2005.
UN. Doc. CRC/C/OPAC/CRI/Q/1 (List of Issues): Costa Rica. 16/10/2006.
UN. Doc. CRC/C/OPAC/BGD/1 (Initial reports of States parties due in 2005): Bangladesh. 23/12/2005.
UN. Doc. CRC/C/OPAC/BGD/Q/1/ Add.1 (Written replies from the Government of Bangladesh): Bangladesh.
UN. Doc. CRC/C/OPAC/CHE/Q/1 (List of Issues): Switzerland. 02/11/2005.
UN. Doc. CRC/C/OPAC/ESP/1 (Initial reports of States parties due in 2004): Spain. 16/10/2006.
UN. Doc. CRC/C/OPAC/ESP/CO/1 (Concluding Observations): Spain. 17/10/2007.
UN. Doc. CRC/C/OPAC/FIN/1 (Initial reports of States parties due in 2004): Finland. 10/03/2005.
UN. Doc. CRC/C/OPAC/FRA/1 (Initial reports of States parties due in 2005): France. 06/11/2006.
UN. Doc. CRC/C/OPAC/FRA/CO/1 (Concluding Observations): France. 05/10/2007.
UN. Doc. CRC/C/OPAC/GTM/CO/1 (Concluding Observations): Guatemala. 12/06/2007.
UN. Doc. CRC/C/OPAC/GTM/Q/1 (List of Issues): Guatemala. 19/02/2007.
CRC/C/OPAC/GTM/Q/1/Add.1 (Written replies by the Government of Guatemala): Guatemala. 23/04/2007.

UN. Doc. CRC/OPAC/ISL/1 (Initial reports of States parties due in 2004): Iceland. 17/07/2005:
UN. Doc. CRC/C/OPAC/ISL/Q/1 (List of Issues): Iceland. 16/02/2006.
UN. Doc. CRC/C/OPAC/KAZ/1 (Initial reports of States parties due in 2005): Kazakhstan. 21/11/2005.
UN. Doc. CRC/C/OPAC/KAZ/CO/1 (Concluding Observations): Kazakhstan. 17/10/2006.
UN. Doc. CRC/C/OPAC/KAZ/Q/1 (List of Issues): Kazakhstan. 23/06/2006.
UN. Doc. CRC/C/OPAC/KAZ/Q/1/Add.1 (Written replies by the Government of Kazakhstan): Kazakhstan. 23/08/2006.
UN. Doc. CRC/C/OPAC/KGZ/Q/1 (List of Issues): Kyrgyzstan. 16/10/2006.
UN. Doc. CRC/C/OPAC/KGZ/1(Initial reports of States parties due in 2004): Kyrgyzstan: 22/05/2006.
UN. Doc. CRC/C/OPAC/LTU/1 (Initial reports of States parties due in 2005): Lithuania. 29/06/2006.
UN. Doc. CRC/C/OPAC/LTU/Q/1 (List of Issues): Lithuania. 22/06/2007.
UN. Doc. CRC/C/OPAC/LTU/Q/1/ Add.1 (Written replies from the Government of Lithuania): Lithuania. 14/09/2007.
UN.Doc. CRC/C/OPAC/LUX/1 (Initial Reports of States parties due in 2006): Luxembourg. 06/11/2006.
UN. Doc. CRC/C/OPAC/LUX/Q/1 (List of Issues): Luxembourg. 29/06/2007.
UN. Doc. CRC/C/OPAC/LUX/Q/1/Add.1 (Written replies by the Government of Luxembourg): Luxembourg. 22/08/2007.
UN. Doc. CRC/C/OPAC/MLT/1 (Initial reports of States parties due in 2004): Malta. 10/11/2005.
UN. Doc. CRC/C/OPAC/MLT/Q/1 (List of Issues): Malta: 21/06/2006.
UN. Doc. CRC/C/OPAC/MLT/Q/1/ Add. 1 (Written replies by the Government of Malta): Malta. 10/08/2006.
UN. Doc. CRC/C/MUS/CO/2 (Concluding Observations): Mauritius. 17/03/2006.
UN. Doc. CRC/C/OPAC/NOR/CO/1 (Concluding Observations): Norway. 06/07/2007.
UN. Doc. CRC/C/OPAC/NOR/Q/1 (List of Issues): Norway. 08/03/2007.
UN. Doc. CRC/C/OPAC/NOR/Q/1/Add.1 (Written replies by the Government of Norway): Norway. 14/05/2007.
UN. Doc. CRC/C/OPAC/NZL/1 (Initial reports of States parties due in 2004): New Zealand. 30/07/2003.
UN. Doc. CRC/C/OPAC/QAT/Q/1 (List of Issues): Qatar. 22/06/2007.

UN. Doc. CRC/C/OPAC/QAT/Q/1/Add.1 (Written replies by the Government of Qatar): Qatar. 06/08/2007.
UN. Doc. CRC/C/OPAC/SLV/1 (Initial reports of States parties due in 2004): El Salvador. 15/08/2005.
UN. Doc. CRC/C/OPAC/SLV/Q/1 (List of Issues): El Salvador. 09/02/2006.
UN. Doc. CRC/C/OPAC/SLV/Q/1/ Add.1 (Written replies from the Government of El Salvador): El Salvador. 12/05/2006.
UN. Doc. CRC/C/OPAC/SWE/1 (Initial reports of States parties due in 2005): Sweden. 10/07/2006.
UN. Doc. CRC/C/OPAC/SWE/Q/1(List of Issues): Sweden. 08/03/2007.
UN. Doc. CRC/C/RUS/CO/3 (Concluding Observations): Russian Federation. 23/11/2005.
UN. Doc. CRC/C/OPAC/SYR/1 (Initial reports of States parties due in 2005): Syrian Arab Republic. 18/04/2007.
UN. Doc. CRC/C/OPAC/SYR/CO/1 (Concluding Observations): Syrian Arab Republic. 05/10/2007.
UN. Doc. CRC/C/OPAC/SYR/Q/1 (List of Issues): Syrian Arab Republic. 29/06/2007.
UN. Doc. CRC/C/UGA/CO/2 (Concluding Observations): Uganda. 23/11/2005.
UN. Doc. CRC/C/UZB/CO/2 (Concluding Observations): Uzbekistan. 02/06/2006.
UN.Doc. CRC/C/OPAC/VNM/Q/1 (List of Issues): Viet Nam. 20/06/2006.
UN. Doc. E/C.12/1/Add.35 (Concluding Observations of the Committee on Economic, Social and Cultural Rights): Ireland. 14/05/99.
UN. Doc. E/CN.4/1997/74, 1997: Commission on Human Rights: Effective Functioning of Bodies Established pursuant to United Nations Human Rights Instruments: Final Report on enhancing the long-term effectiveness of the United Nations Human Rights Treaty Systems.
UN Doc. E/CN.4/1994/91: Commission on Human Rights: Rights of the Child

Internet Sources

'About us', *CORE* (http://www.coremanipur.org/about_us.html, 2 July 2010).
Amnesty International, 'United Nations Proposals to Strengthen the Human Rights Treaty Bodies' *Amnesty International*

(http://asiapacific.amnesty.org/library/pdf/IOR400182003ENGLISH/$File/IOR4001803.pdf , 15 December 2008).

'Charter of the United Nations' *The United Nations* (http://www.hrweb.org/legal/unchartr.html , 19 August 2009).

'Child Recruitment continues in over one dozen countries, reports Ban Ki-moon' UN News Centre (http://www.un.org/apps/news/story.asp?NewsID=25440&Cr=child&Cr1=soldier , 2 March 2008).

'Child Soldiers Global Report 2004' *Coalition to Stop the Use of Child Soldiering* (http:www.child-soldiers.org/library/global-reports?root_id=159&category_id=165, 15 January 2007).

'Child Soldiers: Global report 2008 "Facts and Figures on Child Soldiers"' *Coalition to Stop the Use of Child Soldiers* (www.childsoldiersglobalreport.org/content/facts-and-figures-child-soldiers , 10Janury 2009).

'Child Soldiers and Small Weapons of Mass Destruction' (http://www.achart.ca/publications/child_soldiers.html , 15 June 2007).

Coalition to Stop the Use of Child Soldiers, 'Croatia', *CRIN* (http://www.crin.org/docs/resources/treaties/crc.37/Croatia_CSCS_ngo_report.pdf, 27 May 2010).

Coalition to Stop the Use of Child Soldiers, 'Child Soldiers: CRC Country Briefs: Pre-sessional Working Group for 34th session – Bangladesh', *CRIN* (http://www.crin.org/docs/resources/treaties/crc.34/Bangladesh_CSCS_ngo_report.pdf, 26 May 2010).

Coalition to Stop the Use of Child Soldiers, 'Child Soldiers: CRC Country Briefs: Pre-sessional Working Group for 34th session – Brunei Darussalam', *CRIN* (http://www.crin.org/docs/resources/treaties/crc.34/Brunei_CSCS_ngo_report.pdf , 20 May 2010).

Coalition to Stop the Use of Child Soldiers, 'Child Soldiers: CRC Country Briefs: Pre-sessional Working Group 36th session - Dominica' *CRIN* (http://www.crin.org/docs/resources/treaties/crc.36/Dominica_CSCS_ngo_report.pdf, 1 June 2010).

Coalition to Stop the Use of Child Soldiers, 'Child Soldiers: CRC Country Briefs: Pre-sessional Working Group for 36th Session – Liberia', *CRIN* (http://www.crin.org/docs/resources/treaties/crc.36/liberia_CSCS_ngo_report.pdf, 26 May 2010).

Coalition to Stop the Use of Child Soldiers, 'Kyrgyzstan' *CRIN* (http://www.crin.org/docs/resources/treaties/crc.37/Kyrgyzstan_CSCS_ngo_report.pdf, 27 May 2010).

Coalition to Stop the Use of Child Soldiers, 'CHILD SOLDIERS USE 2003: A Briefing for the 4th UN Security Council Open Debate on Children and Armed Conflict, Angola' (http://www.child-soldiers.org/document/get?id=690. , 16 January 2008).

Coalition to Stop the Use of Child Soldiers, 'Voices of Child Soldiers' (http://www.childsoldiersglobalreport.org/content/voices-child-soldiers , 15 April 2009).

'Code of Conduct on Arms Export' (http://ec.europa.eu/external_relations/cfsp/sanctions/codeofconduct.pdf, 10 April 2008).

'Committee on the Rights of the Child- Working Methods, "Overview of the Working Methods of the Committee on the Rights of the Child"' (http://www.ohchr.org/english/bodies/crc/workingmethods.htm, 19 December 2008).

'Common Article 3' *ICRC* (http://www.icrc.org/Web/eng/siteeng0.nsf/htmlall/genevaconventions #a1, 15 May 2009).

'Country Classifications' *World Bank* (http://web.worldbank.org, 8 May 2007).

'Declaration of the Rights of the Child (1959)' *The Circumcision Reference Library* (http://www.cirp.org/library/ethics/UN-declaration/ , 7 July 2009).

'Declaration on the Protection of Women and Children in Emergency and Armed Conflict (1974)' *Office of the United Nations High Commissioner for Human Rights* (http://www2.ohchr.org/english/law/protectionwomen.htm, 10 April 2009).

'Fact Sheet No.16 (Rev.1), The Committee on Economic, Social and Cultural Rights' (http://www.ohchr.org/Documents/Publications/FactSheet16rev.1en.pd f , 15 February 2008.

'Fact Sheet: A summary of the Rights under the Convention on the Rights of the Child' (http://www.unicef.org/crc/files/Rights_overview.pdf , 10 June 2009).

'FACT SHEET: THE Committee on the Rights of the Child' (http://www.unicef.org/crc/files/Committee_fact_sheet.pdf, 10 February 2009).

'Freedom in the World 2006' *Freedom House Organisation* (http://www.freedomhouse.org/uploads/press_release/fiw07_charts.pdf, 22 March 2007).

'Frequently Asked Questions' *Coalition to Stop the Use of Child Soldiers* (http://www.child-soldiers.org/childsoldiers/questions-and-answers , 11 January 2008).

'Frequently Asked Questions' *ICC* (http://www.icc-cpi.int/NetApp/App/MCMSTemplates/Index.aspx?NRMODE=Published&NRNODEGUID={D788E44D-E292-46A1-89CC-D03637A52766}&NRORIGINALURL=/Menus/ICC/About+the+Court/Frequently+asked+Questions/&NRCACHEHINT=Guest#id_1, 9 August 2009).

'Geneva Declaration of the Rights of the Child' *UN Document: Gathering a Body of Global Agreements* (http://www.un-documents.net/gdrc1924.htm, 8 September 2009).

'Human Rights Treaty Bodies: Monitoring the core international human rights treaties', *Office of the UN High Commissioner for Human Rights* (http://www2.ohchr.org/english/bodies/treaty/index.htm, 18 October 2008).

Human Rights Watch, Children's Rights Division 'BURMA (MYANMAR): Right to Education, Recruitment and Use of Child Soldiers', (http://www.crin.org/docs/resources/treaties/crc.36/Myanmar_HRW_ngo_report.pdf , 21 June 2010).

Human Rights Watch Children's Rights Division, 'Colombia: Children Affected by Armed Conflict', *CRIN* (http://www.crin.org/docs/resources/treaties/crc.25/colombiaNGOreport1.pdf, 19 June 2010).

Human Rights Watch. 'Stolen Children: Abduction and Recruitment in Northern Uganda March 2003 Vol 15, No 7A', *Human Rights Watch* (http://www.hrw.org/en/reports/2003/03/28/stolen-children, 20 May 2010).

I CC (http://www.icc-cpi.int/Menus/ICC/Home, 9 August 2009).

'Impact of Armed Conflict on Children: Children at both ends of the gun' *UNICEF* (http://www.unicef.org/graca/kidsoldi.htm , 15 December 2008).

"In-Depth: Guns out of Control: the continuing threat of small arms" May 2006 (http://www.irinnews.org/pdf/in-depth/Small-Arms-IRIN-In-Depth.pdf , 15 May 2008).

'International Council of Women' *Global Hand* (http://www.globalhand.org/data/organisation.2007-06-30.7154102560/ , 12 September 2009).

'International Court in first case' *BBC NEWS* (http://www.bbc.co.uk/2/hi/europe/6131198.stm, 16 May 2009).

'International Court of Justice: ICC hears of child soldiers hell in first case', 26/01/09 *Euronews* http://www.euronews.net/en/article/26/01/2009/icc-hears-of-child-soldier-hell-in-first-case/ (10 April 2009).

'International Humanitarian Law and International Human Rights Law: Similarities and Differences' *ICRC* (http://www.icrc.org/Web/Eng/siteeng0.nsf/htmlall/57JR8L/$File/IHL_and_IHRL.pdf, 15 June 2009).

'Introduction: A Human Rights Issue', *Global Initiative to End All Corporal Punishment of Children* (http://www.endcorporalpunishment.org/ , 10 July 2010).

'Ms Vuckovic CV' (http://www.see-educoop.net/experts/data/0147e.htm , 15 July 2007).

National Alliance of Child Rights Organisations (NACRO), 'CRC Alternative Report' *CRIN* (http://www.crin.org/docs/resources/treaties/crc.39/Nepal_Nacro_ngo_report.pdf, 19 May 2010).

Nationsonline, 'The Continents of the World' (http://www.nationsonline.org/oneworld/continents.htm, 2 June 2007).

'NGO Alternative Reports Submitted to the Committee on the Rights of the Child', *Child Rights Information Network (CRIN)* (http://www.crin.org/docs/resources/treaties/crc.25/annex-vi-crin.asp , 18 February 2010).

NGO Forum On the Rights of the Child, 'Supplementary Report to the Initial Report of the State Party of Sri Lanka on the Implementation of the Convention on the Rights of the Child', *CRIN* (http://www.crin.org/docs/resources/treaties/crc.9/Sri_Lanka_Forum_NGO_Report.pdf , 23 May 2010).

NGO Group for the Convention on the Rights of the Child, 'A Guide for Non-Governmental Organisations Reporting to the Committee on the Rights of the Child (1998 Edition)', *CRIN* (http://www.crin.org/docs/resources/publications/NGOCRC/NGOCRC-Guide-en.pdf, 6 May 2010).

NGO Group for the Convention on the Rights of the Child, 'A Guide for Non-Governmental Organizations Reporting to the Committee on the Rights of the Child (2006 Edition)' *CRIN* (http://www.crin.org/docs/Reporting%20Guide%202006%20English.pdf , 3 June 2010).

'Office of the Special Representative of the Secretary-General for Children and Armed Conflict' *UN* (http://www.un.org/children/conflict/english/theoffice.html , 10 March 2009).

'Past Membership of the Committee on the Rights of the Child (1991-2003) (http://www2.ohchr.org/english/bodies/crc/docs/MembersCVs/PastMEMBERSHIP.pdf , 12 February 2008).

'Reservations, Declarations, Observations and Derogations – CRC- Cook Islands' *Bayefky.com* (http://www.bayefsky.com/pdf/cookislands_t2_crc.pdf, 16 May 2009).

'Reservations, Declarations, Observations and Derogations – CRC- Oman' *Bayefky.com* (http://www.bayefsky.com/pdf/oman_t2_crc.pdf , 16 May 2009).

'Submission to the UN Committee on the Rights of the Child on Ireland's 2nd Periodic Report on the Rights of the Child', *CRIN* (http://www.crin.org/resources/infoDetail.asp?ID=10074&flag=legal, 8 July 2010).

'Structure of the Court' *ICC* (http://www.icc-cpi.int/Menus/ICC/Structure+of+the+Court/, 9 August 2009).

'The Coalition' *Coalition to Stop the Use of Child Soldiers* (http://www.child-soldiers.org/home, 28 May 2010).

'The International Convention on the Elimination of All Forms of Racial Discrimination' *Australian Human Rights Commission* (www.hreoc.gov.au/racial_discrimination/guide_law/icerd.html, 10/12/2010).

'The United Nations Human Rights System' *Human Rights Education Association* (http://www.hrea.org/index.php?doc_id=437 , 10 May 2008).

UNICEF, 'Action Plan for Children Affected By War, Progress Report January – June 2004' (http://www.unicef.org/videoaudio/PDFs/plan_progress_june04.pdf , 15 February 2008).

'UNICEF'S role in the monitoring progress', *UNICEF* (http://www.unicef.org/crc/index_30214.html , 13 May 2010).

'United Nations Entity for Gender Equality and the Empowerment of Women' *UN Women* (http://www.unwomen.org/ , 20/11/2010).

'United Nations Special Session on Children (8-10 May 2002)' (http://www.unicef.org/specialsession/rights/path.htm, 6 October 2009).

US – Child Soldiers (http://www.us-childsoldiers.org, 15 June 2010).

US Department of States, 'Background Note: Netherlands Antilles' (http://www.state.gov/r/pa/ei/22528.htm, 2 June 2007).

'US Military Assistance to Countries Using Child Soldiers: 1990-2007' *Centre for Defense Information* (http://www.cdi.org/PDFs/CSBillCharts.pdf , 15 February 2008).

'What is Child Soldier? *Plan* (https://www.planusa.org/contentmgr/showdetails.php/id/2147 , 15 October 2008).

'Who we are and why we exist', *ISPCC* (http://www.ispcc.ie/About-Us.aspx, 1 July 2010).